S⁻

20

1

3

.2

1

23

ESCAPE FROM BAGHDAD

JAMES ASHCROFT

with Clifford Thurlow

Published by Virgin Books 2009
2 4 6 8 10 9 7 5 3 1

First published in Great Britain in 2009 by
Virgin Books
Random House, 20 Vauxhall Bridge Road,
London SW1V 2SA

www.virginbooks.com
www.rbooks.co.uk

Addresses for companies within The Random House Group Limited can be found at:
www.randomhouse.co.uk/offices.htm

The Random House Group Limited Reg. No. 954009

A CIP catalogue record for this book
is available from the British Library

Hardback ISBN 9781905264889
Trade paperback ISBN 9780753519936

The Random House Group Limited supports The Forest Stewardship Council
(FSC), the leading international forest certification organisation. All our titles
that are printed on Greenpeace-approved FSC certified paper carry the FSC logo.
Our paper procurement policy can be found at www.rbooks.co.uk/environment

Mixed Sources
Product group from well-managed
forests and other controlled sources
www.fsc.org Cert no. TT-COC-2139
© 1996 Forest Stewardship Council

Typeset in Sabon by Palimpsest Book Production Limited,
Grangemouth, Stirlingshire

Printed and bound in the UK by
CPI Mackays, Chatham ME5 8TD

IN MEMORIAM

Philip

Jason

James

Hendriks

Johannes

Mohanned

Hayder

Riyadh

Ziadh

Khaled

Sean

Oleg

Vance

Susie

When unable to wear the lion's skin, clothe yourself in the fox's . . . either the highway of courage, or the byway of cunning . . . and the wise have won much oftener than the valorous.

Baltasar Gracian, *The Art of Worldly Wisdom*

Old age hath yet his honour and his toil;
Death closes all: but something ere the end,
Some work of noble note, may yet be done . . .

Alfred Lord Tennyson, 'Ulysses'

The shifts of Fortune test the reliability of friends.

Cicero, *On Friendship*

If therefore, there be any kindness I can show, or any good thing I can do to any fellow human being, let me do it now, and not defer or neglect it, as I shall not pass this way again.

William Penn

The Babylonians, in order to reduce the consumption of food, herded together and strangled all the women in the city – each man exempting only his mother and one other woman whom he chose out of his household to bake his bread for him.

Herodotus, *The Histories*

The sand of the desert is sodden red –
Red with the wreck of a square that broke;
The Gatling's jammed and the Colonel dead,
And the regiment blind with dust and smoke.
The river of death has brimmed his banks
And England's far, and Honour a name . . .

Sir Henry John Newbolt, 'Vitaï Lampada'

They've got us surrounded again, the poor bastards.

Creighton W. Abrams, Jr.

GLOSSARY

.50 cal   12.7mm-calibre anti-matériel round, also a term used to refer to the Browning machine-gun firing that calibre

5.56   5.56 x 45mm-calibre rounds, standard NATO calibre since 1979

7.62 NATO   7.62 x 51mm round used in the **GPMG** and rifles such as the G3 and FAL

7.62 short   7.62 x 39mm round used in the **AK47**, **RPD** and SKS

9-milly   British Army slang for 9mm pistol

AAFES   Welfare shopping organization establishing shops for US forces around the world on US bases. Commonly known as the **PX**

Abrams   US main battletank M1A2, probably the best in the world, 120mm main armament, **.50 cal** machine-gun and two 7.62mm **GPMGs**

ACOG   American 4x magnification optical rifle sight

Actions on   Term used to describe standard operating procedures for any given scenario

AK47   Soviet assault rifle firing **7.62 short**, available folding or fixed stock with 30- and 40-round magazines or 75-round drum. Later models also known as AKM.

AIF   Anti-Iraqi Forces, official nomenclature for insurgents.

AP Armour Piercing

Barrett M82/M107 .50 cal anti-matériel semi-automatic rifle

BIAP Baghdad International Airport

Blackhawk US utility helicopter, military designation UH-60, usually armed with two machine-guns, either 7.62mm **GPMGs** or mini-guns

Blackwater Blackwater Security Consulting, a strategic division of Blackwater USA, a PSC operating in Iraq

Bradley Bradley **M2** Infantry Fighting Vehicle, or M3 Cavalry variant tracked, armed with 25mm chain-gun and 7.62mm **GPMG**. Usually carries TOW missiles, although some variants carry anti-aircraft Javelin or Stinger missiles. Three crew and six passengers in the M2

Browning Browning Hi-Power pistol, or GP35, a 9mm automatic pistol with a 13- or 20-round magazine. Made by **FN**. Sometimes also used to refer to the Browning M2 **.50 cal** machine-gun

Casevac Casualty Evacuation

CF Coalition Forces

'Commando cord' Tightly woven, thin, green utility cord capable of taking a fully laden soldier's weight, used by Royal Marines. Apparently just like para cord, but 'just a little bit stronger'

CP Close Protection, bodyguarding activity

CPA Coalition Provisional Authority, the interim government installed by the US government after the invasion of Iraq. Also refers to the presidential-palace compound later known as the 'Green Zone', the 'International Zone'

DF Defensive Fire

Dragunov Soviet-bloc semi-automatic sniper rifle firing 7.62 long

DynCorp DynCorp International, a PSC operating in Iraq

Egyptian PT Sleeping

FN Fabrique Nationale. Belgian firearms manufacturer that has produced some of the best weapons in the world, used by armies the world over, including the **Browning** pistol, the **MAG**, the **Minimi** and many others

GPMG General-Purpose Machine-Gun. See also **MAG**

GPS Global Positioning System, satellite navigation system that can be handheld, the size of a cellphone, or vehicle-mounted and, for no good reason anyone could ever explain to me, anything up to the size of a dustbin lid on the roof

Green Zone Or 'GZ'. Compound surrounding the **CPA** and US Embassy palaces, approximately 4 sq km in the centre of Baghdad. Later known as the International Zone or IZ

Humvee Standard 4x4 utility vehicle of the US forces. Armed with anything from **SAW**s and 240s to **.50 cals** and **Mk19s**

ICDC Iraqi Civil Defence Corps, local troops recruited and trained by **CF** to carry out military security duties. They had a reputation for being corrupt, with a strong tendency to desert with all their kit

IDF Indirect Fire

IED Improvised Explosive Device. A bomb

ING Iraqi National Guard. Replaced the **ICDC**

IP Iraqi Police, also known as 'Iraqi 5-Oh' or 'Baghdad's Finest'

Jundhi Term given for local-nationality truck drivers

Jimpy See **MAG**

Katyusha Artillery rocket

KIA Killed In Action

Kiowa OH58D Kiowa Warrior, single-engine US attack/recce helicopter with two universal weapons pylons capable of accepting combinations of Hellfire missile, the Air-to-Air Stinger (ATAS) missile, 2.75" Folding Fin Aerial Rocket (FFAR) pods, and a **.50 cal** machine-gun. Tons of high-tech avionics make this an extremely versatile helicopter, but the extra weight of weapons and electronics systems has given this airframe a reputation for very difficult auto-rotations in the event of engine failure

LAV   Light Armoured Vehicle, usually wheeled 8x8. Used by many countries in multiple configurations, originally based on the MOWAG Piranha Chassis

LMG   Light Machine-Gun

Long   Slang for rifle, i.e. a long weapon as opposed to a **Short**

M1   See **Abrams** main battletank

M16   Standard battle rifle of US forces, firing 5.56mm rounds

M2   See **Bradley**

M203   40mm grenade launcher fitted under barrel of **M16** or **M4**, sometimes just referred to as the '203'

M240   See **MAG**

M249   See **Minimi**

M4   5.56mm carbine, compact version of **M16** rifle

MAG   General-purpose machine-gun manufactured by FN. An excellent and extremely reliable design used all over the world, firing 7.62mm NATO from a disintegrating belt left-hand feed, recently adopted by US forces as the **M240** or M240G (Marines), used by the British Army since 1964 and simply called the 'GPMG' or more affectionately the **'jimpy'**

Minimi   Light machine-gun manufactured by **FN** of Belgium, firing 5.56mm from a disintegrating belt left-hand feed, also capable of feeding from **M16** magazines if no belted ammunition is available. A compact and reliable weapon when in good condition. Used by US forces under the designation **M249 SAW**

Mk19   40mm automatic grenade launcher, vehicle- or tripod-mounted

MNF-I   Multi-National Forces Iraq, new politically correct term for Coalition Forces

MRE   Meals Ready to Eat, US ration packs

ODA   Operational Detachment Alpha

PKM   Soviet **GPMG** firing **7.62** long from a non-disintegrating belt fed in from the right-hand side. Also known as 'PKC' or 'BKC' by the Iraqis

PMC   Private Military Contractor

PSD   Personal Security Detail, used as a noun or a verb

PX   See **AAFES**

RPD   Soviet machine-gun from 1953, very light, fires **7.62 short** from a non-disintegrating belt fed in from the left-hand side. Manufactured and found in most former communist-bloc countries and especially SE Asia. Also known as 'Degtyarev' by the Iraqis

RPG . RPG-7 rocket-propelled grenade, a common Soviet weapon featuring a reusable launcher tube and a separate rocket with an 84mm high-explosive anti-tank warhead

SAW   Squad Automatic Weapon. See **Minimi**

Septic   Or Septic Tank, rhyming slang for Yank

Short   Slang for pistol or sidearm

Sig   Sig Sauer firearms manufacturers, who produce the quite excellent P226 and P228 pistols amongst other weapons

USP   A Heckler & Koch pistol

VBIED   Vehicle-borne **IED**

VCP   Vehicle checkpoint, a British term. US equivalent is TCP, Traffic Control Point

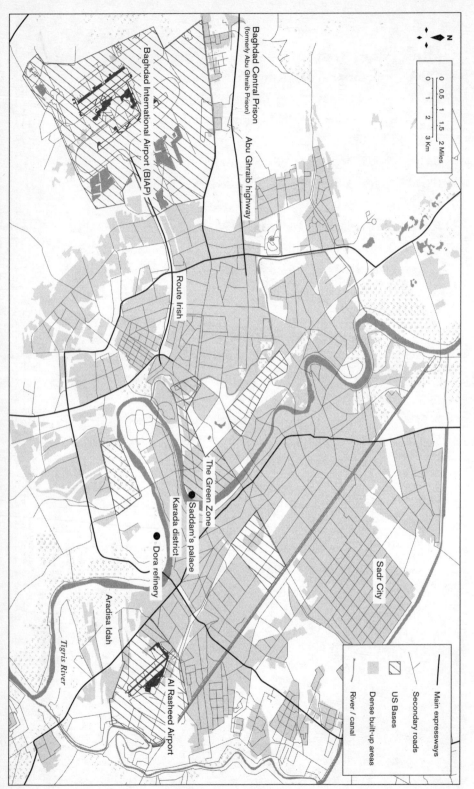

Baghdad

Baghdad Central Prison
(formerly Abu Ghraib Prison)

Baghdad International Airport (BIAP)

Abu Ghraib highway

Route Irish

The Green Zone

Saddam's palace

Karada district

Dora refinery

Aradisa Idah

Tigris River

Al Rasheed Airport

Sadr City

N

| 0 | 0.5 | 1 | 1.5 | 2 Miles |
| 0 | 1 | 2 | | 3 Km |

Main expressways

Secondary roads

US Bases

Dense built-up areas

River / canal

Escape route – Baghdad to Amman

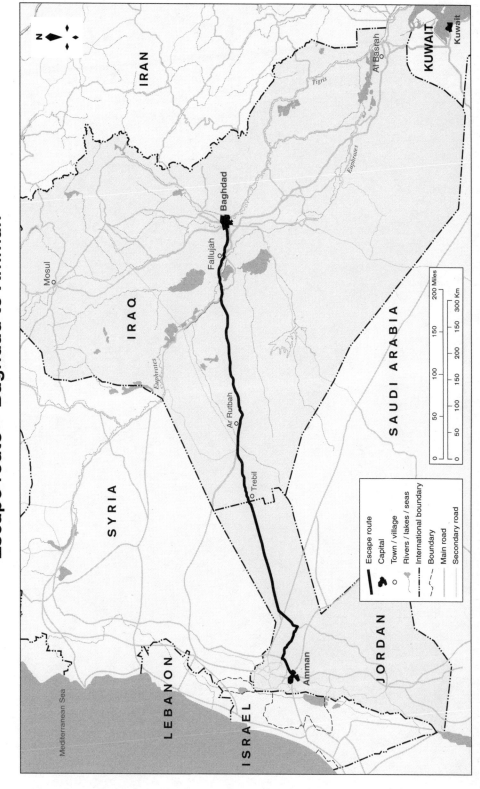

PROLOGUE

O N WEDNESDAY, 19 March 2003, my former regiment, the Duke of Wellington's, joined the Coalition Forces in the invasion of Iraq.

It happened to be my daughter Natalie's third birthday.

I was working in a law office in the City and watched the news in a wine bar at lunchtime. As I travelled home that night on the Tube with a pink box tied in ribbons, I had a taut feeling in my gut and it felt as if my tie was strangling me to death. I daydreamed of quitting my job and rejoining my old battalion, but in three weeks the famous statue of Saddam was toppled and the war was over.

But the seeds of dissatisfaction had been sown. Law and the London Underground were not for me. I was thirty-seven years old. I was drinking a bottle of wine with dinner every night and grey hair was beginning to thread through the bronze.

A month passed and I got a call from an old army buddy by the name of Angus McGrath, a former infantry officer like myself, a fellow Scot not known for wasting 50p on a friendly phone call. He was working in Baghdad for a private security group called Spartan. They needed more bodies – $500 a day to begin with, full insurance, an easy job you could do standing on your head, start immediately.

I didn't need to think twice. After Oxford, I had gone to Sandhurst and served as a captain for six years in hotspots like Northern Ireland and Bosnia. It wasn't a great life, but the company had been great, I had taken pride in my achievements and, most importantly, I was good at it.

Krista, the lady in my life, wasn't exactly thrilled, but she knew me well enough to know that I wasn't happy in my career and the money, at least, was going to pay off our credit-card bills. I went out and bought cargo pants, desert boots, some sand-coloured shirts, a couple of holsters, a pair of shades and a daysack to throw it all in. Before the week was out, I was at Heathrow, waiting for my flight to Amman.

From 2003 to 2005, I worked with a team of former British and South African soldiers as a private security contractor. Of the first $80 billion of reconstruction money granted to Iraq by the US Congress, 30 per cent was for security, and Spartan won the contract to train a guard force of 1,500 Iraqis to protect the nation's water supply.

We lived outside the protection of military compounds in a small house within the Baghdad community from which we recruited our men and which had become our home. For eighteen months during the peak of the insurgency we trained them and fought next to them, enduring both countless bombardments and small-arms fire. And when the infighting between Shia and Sunni became endemic, insinuating itself even into our close-knit units, they betrayed us and chased us out of the city, completely ignoring every tactic of urban warfare I'd taught them – the whole extraordinary escape recorded in my book *Making a Killing*.

I was lucky to survive and only did so thanks to our interpreter Sammy – Assam Mashooen, a former pilot in Saddam's air force. With about a hundred guards chasing me over the rooftops from the old bus depot where we'd built our HQ, Sammy appeared in his old Toyota. The back door flew open and he drove me to safety as I bled from a leg wound all over his seats.

Still, Iraq had been a great job. At the end of the day I had paid off all my debts, made good friends and done a job that I justifiably felt proud of.

I never went back to my law office in the City. Instead, I scored a cushy number doing various security jobs in sunny Africa. But just when I had finally forgotten Iraq and written it off as a colourful chapter relegated to history, I got a call from one of my old South African comrades.

I may have forgotten about Baghdad, but it seemed that Baghdad had not forgotten about me.

CHAPTER 1

THE SEA OFF Côte d'Ivoire is silver-blue with whitecaps that break around your feet like foam from a cappuccino. The sun bakes your brain and burns your skin. You're just dying to dive in and cool off, and can't help wondering whose idea of irony it was to fill the most beautiful stretch of water in the world with sharks.

It's not that I don't know the statistics. I do: you're more likely to die being kicked to death by a horse in your own bedroom than by shark attack. But facts don't cure phobia and fear. One time I was swimming quite happily and suddenly got the feeling that something was wrong. As I stopped to tread water I suddenly knew a shark was underneath me. In a flash of panicked spray I was out of the water and panting with adrenalin on the side, much to the alarm of the family sunbathing on their deckchairs who looked at me in bewilderment and then peered curiously into the water of what was the small and fairly shallow pool of our five-star hotel.

'Sorry.' I laughed at them nervously. 'Cramp,' I added, pointing to my leg before hobbling unconvincingly off to my lounger, where my wife Krista was leafing through a magazine.

She did not bother looking up from her reading, used to my strangeness, although I noticed she was pursing her lips thoughtfully again. It usually meant she was wondering why she hadn't just married that nice kid who used to sit at the back of the maths class and who was now a rich doctor back in Oslo.

'Another shark, was it?' she murmured, raising an unconcerned eyebrow, and turned another page.

'No, no,' I chortled, massaging my thigh dramatically, 'just a little cramp, but don't you worry, I'm sure I'll be fine. Hard as nails, me.'

She laid the magazine down on her lap and peeked over her shades at the pool.

'It seems to have gone now, James,' she said.

'That's because you terrified it,' I replied.

She was looking up at me, smiling now, eyes sparkling the same colour as an Arctic-blue sky, and so beautiful that she still took my breath away, just like the first time I saw her. After five years refusing point-blank to marry me – after her nasty divorce from a sergeant, Krista doesn't much like soldiers, or ex-soldiers for that matter – we'd finally tied the knot when I got back from being a private security contractor in Baghdad.

She had looked me in the eye and informed me that being officially married to me would make things much easier in terms of sorting out my estate in the likely event of me dying on the job. Especially since we had two children. Natalie was six now, the image of her mother, and had a baby sister, Veronica, just taking her first steps and getting territorial with her own bedroom and its menagerie of stuffed toys and finger paintings Blu-Tacked to the wall.

We'd been living the dream in Africa – a pool, nanny, two cars – but we were having trouble getting Natalie into a decent enough school and were worried about both the girls getting malaria, and at the end of 2006 we moved back to London so she could go to kindergarten. It was the heady days of rocketing property prices and we got back on the property ladder with a ground-floor four-bedroomed flat with a big garden and a bigger mortgage. Huge. A telephone number. No worries, the agent said, it'll double in value in five years.

We signed the agreement, the housing market promptly nose-dived, and I headed back to West Africa to sign on with the Proelio Security Group to tidy up whatever mess they could find in the region, which looked like an eternal fount of well-paid work for as long as I wanted it. Central Africa in particular, from Guinea on the west coast all the way through to the Congo and Uganda, is plagued with bands of tribal, often drugged-up, cannibalistic militias, some of whom the Libyans helped set up in the 1990s. There are innumerable vicious organizations, of which only a few have achieved notoriety in the West, such as the Janjaweed in the Sudan and the child soldiers of the Lord's Resistance Army in the Democratic Republic of Congo, a complete shit-hole of a country when the Belgians were there and which, as far as I could see, has only gone steadily downhill since they left in 1960.

After a three-week close protection task in the DRC with a Red Cross team assessing some of the most ravaged and pitiful small towns and villages I'd ever seen in my life, it was like a holiday when I landed the maritime security contract policing the shimmering, if shark-infested, seas off Côte d'Ivoire.

Although technically we had an anti-piracy role, 99 per cent of the work involved interdicting poachers, by which I mean fishing vessels either unlicensed or from neighbouring countries.

The work was pretty easy. Very easy, actually. We had paid inform-ants, or *gardiens*, up and down the coast, and whenever someone saw a boat they didn't recognize, they would call us up with their location and a rough description of the target vessel. We would hit the water with our converted trawler carrying two high-speed, semi-rigid inflatable boats, known as RIBs, and intercept the poachers before they had a chance to head for home.

Government commissions on each arrest were generous, and

the lifestyle was fantastic – lobster, squid, yellowfin tuna with plantains and *aloko*, fried bananas; white fish, swordfish, rainbow fish. They love fish in Côte d'Ivoire – they even put them on their postage stamps. We'd get the grill going at sunset and watch the sky turning pink with a beer or a glass of *bangui*, palm wine, the devil's own brew. Most nights I'd call Krista as she was putting the girls to bed in London, before sleeping the sleep of the just in a hammock left behind by the French contractor I'd replaced.

We spent the rest of the time hanging around the beach, playing frisbee and volleyball when it was cool in the morning, and wakeboarding up the mouth of the river. I never did any wakeboarding in the sea, partly due to the choppy surf, but more so because I was sure I'd seen black fins breaking the surface, bull sharks, makos, tigers, you name it, they were out there, waiting.

I went back to London once a month and I'd been home with the girls for Christmas. It was now the beginning of spring 2007, and back in Iraq the crisis was about to peak; the so-called 'surge' had taken some twenty thousand extra American troops into the trouble spots of Iraq, and they were going at it hammer and tongs in the streets of Baghdad. For my part I was exceedingly happy to be 6,000km away reading about it in the newspapers, lounging smugly on the beach with Antoine pouring fresh coffee into my mug.

That's when the call came in that a foreign trawler had been seen in our area.

The bad news was that one of our RIBs was out of the water with Philippe, an ex-legionnaire and my deputy, trying to sort out the engine. We always deployed with two boats for safety, but it was a still, sunny morning with clear weather reported by the local met office, and since the fishing boats rarely gave us any trouble, I returned the frisbee to Philippe with a curling back spin and told him I'd take out a single RIB for the intercept.

According to the phone list I had pinned to my planning board and map, the *gardien* who had called in the intruder was at one of the closest villages, only 3km away, and reported that the vessel was just a couple of miles offshore. This was unusual since they mostly hit the outer banks where the vast schools of fish were being legally plundered by trawlers from the European Union, but at the same time it was a bonus since there was no need to waste time loading up the RIB on to our mother ship, the converted trawler itself.

Instead of a day-long haul out to the banks, this would be a quick outing. I was interested as to why this particular ship was hugging close to the shore rather than hitting the rich fishing banks, and eager to relieve the boredom of an uneventful morning. Later on I would kick myself and remember how much I loved boredom.

I wandered back to the shed, dumped my coffee on to the sand, dunked the mug in a bucket of sea water before rinsing it straight from a bottle of Evian, and stuck the mug back on the shelf. I pulled on my low-silhouette flotation vest and on top of that my chest rig holding a SAPI bulletproof chest plate, the satphone, eight AK mags and my pistol already holstered. My sunhat, polarised Oakleys – a Christmas present from Krista and the coolest shades money can buy – and fingerless sailing gloves completed my stunning fashion ensemble.

Within two minutes of receiving the call my crew and I were casting off from the jetty. We were in an 8m, deep-V hull RIB with solid pontoons of air-filled honeycomb synthetics; with our twin 250hp Evinrude outboard engines we would be on top of the target boat within ten minutes of the call being made, easy.

I breathed deeply, filling my lungs with the salty sea air and let myself be thrust back into the seat as the helmsman in front of me pushed the throttles wide open. The Evinrudes roared and we surged forward across the clear blue water, the canvas of the sunroof snapping above our heads in the wind. On beautiful, sunny days like this, I loved my job.

I flipped on the RIB's VHF, and got a positive radio check back from the ops room at the beach. The GPS beeped cheerfully when I turned it on, and while that was booting up, I busied myself putting some extra sun block on my nose, cheeks and arms. With that important task over, I reached up and unstrapped my AK47 from the rack, pulled it out of its plastic bag and slung it across my chest.

There were three of us on the RIB, one on the helm, one gunner for the GPMG mounted just in front of the helmsman, and the third man to act as boarder for the target vessel if required.

My helmsman was Maxime, a tall, skinny, coffee-coloured half-caste; my gunner was Antoine, with skin as black as coal, nominally from a Muslim tribe up north, but not averse to sinking a few beers with the team at the end of a hot day. Both men were local Ivorians with murky histories, but during our training rehearsals and drills it was obvious that they were both trained professional soldiers and had clearly gained a great deal of experience in the country's recent civil war.

Antoine and I both sat astride the central bench behind the helmsman, but when we got to the target area we would get into our ready positions.

I shouted over the roar of the big motors. '*Ça va avec votre femme?*'

His wife was eight months pregnant and had been sick with hypertension and diabetes. She had been for a recent check-up and was resting at home. Antoine leaned forward and a smile broke on his lean face.

'She goes well. The baby will come any day.' He pointed at himself. 'I'll be there with her.'

It reminded me that I hadn't been there when Veronica was

born. Or Natalie, come to think of it. At least my school French was getting a workout.

'Good man,' I grinned, and we high-fived.

The RIB reared up against the swell. I threw my weight forward and the prow thumped down again into the surf. As we rose up again, what I assumed was the suspect vessel came into view over the horizon.

I gave the order to load.

Antoine moved forward and put a belt of 7.62mm on the GPMG, cocked it and applied the safety catch. I put a magazine on my AK, took off the safety but did not cock it. I then did the same for Max's rifle, which was in the rack at the side of the helmsman's position. He also had a pistol on his belt. Both of us racked and de-cocked our pistols before re-holstering them. In the unhappy event you ever need to draw your secondary weapon, it needs to be ready to go immediately.

The other vessel did not respond to my radio challenge on the standard frequency, but then again if it was not a commercial trawler it might not even have a radio. We started to move in closer to voice range.

Boats and the sea are a noisy environment, and I clanked and bonged as I scraped forward past the other two men before perching in the bow with a megaphone and a pair of binoculars. We flew the Ivorian flag high and in good view, so that other vessels would not mistake us for pirates ourselves. In addition Antoine was a deputised official of the Ivorian Ministry for Animal Production and Fisheries, so we had some official paperwork, laminated and stuck to the helm, that we would wave about when we boarded.

Max slowed right down, only keeping enough power on to maintain our station. Without the full acceleration of the engines, the RIB took on a dramatic, if slow, rhythm, as we settled into the rocking swell of the ocean. We stood off at about 100m to have a look at the target vessel.

It was a standard 12m fishing boat, about the same length and width as a long school bus and almost the same shape, with a primitive, unstreamlined look. It had been knocked together out of dark timbers, with only a tiny wheelhouse at the back.

I told Max to bring us in closer, and picked up the megaphone to call out our challenge. The vessel had not yet deployed its outrigger poles for nets, which I thought strange. But then again I supposed they were miles off the usual fishing areas. I also noted that only two men were in view, both at the wheel. They were black Africans, dressed simply, no tribal symbols, with nothing to indicate that they were anything but local fishermen. I was slightly annoyed that they had not cast nets yet since, if they had taken a large catch, we would have got a quantity of fresh fish added to our commission for the arrest.

The guys on board didn't seem to be alarmed and were also just idling their engines. They too rolled in the swell. I could hear the slap of the waves against their hull.

I tapped Max to stop us and brought the megaphone up to my lips. At that moment the man in their wheelhouse shouted an order and four men popped up on the side rail. I had just enough time to realize that they were armed, when the man at the bow fired his RPG with a colossal and blood-freezing bang.

Almost immediately the rocket hit the water between the two boats without exploding but drenching us in a wall of spray.

I flinched backwards, bouncing off the pontoon behind me in stupefied shock. Fortunately my hands knew what they were doing. By the time I finished blinking stupidly I had reflexively cocked my rifle and had it up in the ready position at my shoulder.

'*Feu! Feu! Tirez!*' Fire! Fire! I screamed at Antoine as I took aim and squeezed off a burst.

He was already ahead of me and had started firing even as my mouth opened. Unfortunately, with the RIB bobbing up and down, his first burst went all over the place, stitching up the water and the stern of the other boat.

I cursed as I realized that without thinking I had shot the RPG man. Having already fired his rocket he was out of action until he reloaded and was now the least dangerous of the enemy crew. If I had been a little more switched on, I would have aimed at the guy on the machine-gun. What can I say? Sometimes it's just not your day. I can only put it down to the fact that I had not finished my morning coffee.

I put down another three rounds to distract the others before looking up at Maxime to see what the hell he was playing at. He should have already rammed the throttles open to get us out of there. I also wondered who the hell these guys were – pirates, I assumed, although extremely rare in this area. The civil war was supposed to be over, and all the rebels were up in the northern half of the country, above Yamoussoukro, the capital.

My mind went into overdrive and seconds seemed to stretch into endless minutes, though scarcely a couple of heartbeats had passed. Maxime hit the throttles with one hand while the other hand held the VHF mike to his mouth as he sent a terse contact report. I heard the reply. Good. At least Philippe would know we were in trouble. The beached RIB only had one engine off-line. He could still use the other one to get out here with his crew.

We started to move. I was still looking back at the fishing boat. The two men by the wheelhouse had disappeared. I didn't know if they had been shot or were taking cover.

There were still two others left facing us at the rail, and to my horror one of them had an MG42. Although manufactured under various model names all around the world over the last sixty years, this was essentially still the same superb killing machine that the Wehrmacht had used to decimate Stalin's hordes on the Eastern Front. It has a ferociously high rate of fire, nearly twice that of most other automatic weapons, pumping out twenty bullets a second.

Places in Africa where there was no food or water, there was always plenty of high-class weaponry. I had no idea how so many MG42s had found their way to West Africa but the Yugoslav versions, the M53, were seen regularly in the hands of local militias, along with soviet PKMs and FN MAGs just like the one on our RIB.

Here she comes.

The beast burped once and a wall of bullets hit our RIB, shredding a huge section of pontoon and the hull at the waterline. Antoine and I fired back as fast as we could but we were at a disadvantage, firing from a moving and far less stable platform than the enemy.

None of our shots hit the two remaining pirates, and as the MG42 gunner hunched his shoulders, ready to fire again, Antoine's eyes met mine for a split second, then we both threw ourselves gracelessly backwards over the side of the RIB.

Just before I hit the water I saw Maxime launching himself over the back of the engines. That same moment, the helmsman's post disappeared in a spray of plastic. The GPS, the radio, the turbo and temperature gauges, the rev counter, the emergency flares, the whole lot sprayed into metal and plastic confetti as three hysterical bursts pounded into the centre of the RIB and exploded out the other side.

I now had more immediate problems, like sinking. My flotation vest was not a purpose-designed military version that could provide buoyancy for a soldier with fighting equipment, just a thin windsurfer's vest, and I was being pulled down by the weight of my chest rig. I was treading water frantically as I unclipped the satphone from the rig and stuffed it down the front of my vest. Next came my Sig Sauer pistol – hard to replace and even harder to fill in the police paperwork for, if I lost it – which I threw with a shout to Antoine, who had just surfaced next to me.

The pirate machine-gunner was still firing away at the RIB and I cringed, thinking about the cost of replacing the equipment, especially the engines, maybe even the whole boat. It was insured, sure, but getting replacements out here was going to be a nightmare. The engines alone could cost nearly $18,000 each. Philippe, an emotional Frenchie and our *de facto* engineer, looked after the Evinrudes as if they were his babies. He was going to go completely mental.

These thoughts were slipping inanely through my mind as I continued to struggle with the weight of the eight mags and the SAPI plate in my chest rig dragging me down. I took a deep breath and let myself sink as I unsnapped the quick-release buckles and wriggled it off.

The AK was slung around my neck and banged gently against my elbows and face as I took two full mags out of a pouch and then let the chest rig slip into the depths of the ocean. I shoved one mag down the front of my flotation vest and clutched the other as I kicked hard and swam back to the surface.

I blinked salt water out of my eyes. It seemed as if I'd been sinking for a long time, but only a few seconds had passed and nothing had changed. The MG42 was still busy turning the RIB into Swiss cheese as it moved off around the front of the fishing trawler. Both Antoine and Maxime appeared to be fine, treading water next to me. I wasn't sure if the pirates had realized that we had all baled out, but once they did it would be very easy for them to take their time and gun us down.

As often happens in a contact, my thoughts raced along at lightning speed. I knew we would only have one chance – or one good chance, anyway – and I instantly changed out my half-empty magazine for the full one in my hand. I let go of the half mag, pulled back the bolt slightly to check chamber to see that I had a round up the spout, and let the water, if any, trickle out of the barrel.

I was squinting in the bright sunlight and realized with dismay that I'd lost my new Oakleys. Shit. I'd need to buy a new pair exactly the same and not tell Krista I'd lost the ones she'd given me. I pushed the bolt firmly back into place.

At the same time for some reason I remembered on my close-quarter battle course the thickly accented Irish colour sergeant gravely showing us a film clip of Robert De Niro checking the chamber of his pistol. The colour sergeant then switched off the video and turned to us, solemn and threatening, to say, 'If Robert De Niro checks chamber . . . then YOU will check chamber!'

Since we were all just swimming with nothing but our shorts and sea water between us and an enemy machine-gun at point-blank range, I was also wondering how much water it took to slow down a bullet. I was sure I'd seen some documentary where someone had tested it out, but for the life of me I couldn't remember.

I vaguely recalled in my Arctic training the preparation of bunkers out of packed snow, which by the way is astonishingly bulletproof – not that I had ever had the chance to put this know-ledge to practical use in the deserts of Iraq or in the steaming jungles of Africa.

Then I snapped back into the present and very real danger. I focused on slowing my breathing. I kicked my legs, making the most of my vest's buoyancy, and turned the sights of my rifle on the machine-gunner.

Despite my frantic activity and daydreaming, less than twenty seconds had passed since we he'd hit the water. With the machine-gun hammering away in his shoulder, the pirate had remained fixed on keeping his shuddering sights on the moving RIB without noticing he was firing at an empty boat. He only realized as he came to the end of his belt, when he stood up straight to get a better look down into the shredded RIB.

Most helpful of him. Thank you.

I gently but firmly squeezed the trigger, concentrating on main-taining sight picture as I shot him in the head, and the pirate dropped bonelessly out of sight. His colleague leapt up in almost comical astonishment, looking around wildly, so I gave him the good news too. My shot clipped the rail and hit him low centre of mass and he clutched himself and shrieked in a gratifying manner as he fell backwards out of sight.

We stayed like that for a few moments while I kept my sights on the empty rail next to the abandoned MG42, just in case there was anyone left full of horrible pirate life on board. I could still hear the man that I'd wounded squawking plaintively, gibbering and generally carrying on, but there was no sound from anyone else.

I watched in disgust as our RIB chugged slowly over the swells, vanishing towards the horizon, then turned back to the enemy vessel.

'Antoine, Max,' I called. 'Get over there and see if you can climb on board. I'll cover you from here.'

That's when I remembered the sharks.

CHAPTER 2

I HADN'T HEARD from Cobus for a long time and his terse two-word text 'call ASAP' seemed ominous. He'd stayed on in Baghdad and was doing some kind of liaison job for Colonel Steve 'Mad Dog' McQueen. There are two sorts of US Army colonels. Mad Dog was the good sort; the moniker came from his college days playing football, and he had the scars that showed he'd almost gone pro.

I wandered away from the barbecue, punching in numbers, and stretched out on the sand. The colour was fading from the sky from yet another incredible sunset. Soon the night would be black.

Cobus didn't waste words with pleasantries. 'Ash, you have time to talk now?'

'Yeah, shoot.'

'It's Sammy. He's in deep *kak*, man.'

A tremor ran up my spine. Cobus was a ruddy-faced South African with blue eyes like an apostle and no time for bullshit. We'd worked together for Spartan Security for the best part of eighteen months in Baghdad, training a team of 1,500 Iraqi guards to protect the nation's water supply. When Cobus said someone was in the shit, they were in it up to their necks.

'Not another kidnap?' I said.

'Worse, Ash. He's on a Shia death list. They are actively hunting for him and his family.'

'Fuck . . .'

The line was silent for a moment. Then Cobus got into the details. The American troop surge was keeping the jihadis' heads down, but infighting between the religious factions had turned Baghdad into a bloodbath – rape, murder, thievery, revenge killings, female suicide bombers – you name it, they had some, and it had been going on for years, the violence and body count disguised by the ongoing insurgency against the CF.

The White House and Downing Street had accelerated the process of 'Iraqification' and handed over government adminis-tration and security to their Iraqi counterparts as fast as possible and irrespective of how unprepared or corrupt they might be.

George W. Bush would soon be on his way back to the ranch. There had never been enough troops on the ground to occupy the country effectively, and any US officer who had the spine to ask for reinforcements had ended his career by disagreeing with the 'yes' men in the Pentagon who only wanted to hear good news. The surge in my opinion was an indication that someone had finally gagged Rumsfeld and that the higher command had got some oxygen up to their collective brain after four years of farce and failure, not to mention thousands of unnecessary casualties.

Sammy, formerly Wing Commander Assam Mashooen of the Iraqi Air Force, was a veteran pilot who had trained in Southampton and flown hundreds of missions for Saddam Hussein in the Iran–Iraq War. He had been the chief interpreter for Task Force Fountain, the guard-force training programme my former employer Spartan had won from the first $87 billion reconstruction package awarded by the US Congress – of which, incidentally, $30 billion had been for security alone. Sammy was also a good friend.

Back in Iraq the new quasi-democratic republic was Shia-dominated. Shia hardliners were scrambling for positions in the army and security forces, while Shia militias were settling old scores, kidnapping and killing anyone who got in their way.

Death squads were roaming the streets and, although Coalition Forces were taking fewer hits, the death toll among Iraqi civilians was as high as it had been at any time since the iconic toppling of the Saddam statue in April 2003.

Sammy's crime? He was a Sunni, part of the old ruling class under Saddam – the tyrant had personally presented him with a gold-plated pistol for his bravery fighting the Iranians. He was loud, generous, extravagant and he had saved my life. More than once.

Even worse, the 'Iraqification' process had now handed over to the Iraqi ministries full records of all the reconstruction work carried out to date. This included all HR files and personnel records. As a typical example of how one bureaucratic oversight can have terrible consequences, Shia politicians, and therefore their related militias, now had the full details down to ID card number and the home address of every Iraqi 'collaborator' who had worked for the hated Americans. Overnight entire families were tortured, slaughtered and the bodies piled up in heaps.

For the first three years of the war, the average number of civilians killed in the violence had hovered between 11,000 and 14,000 each year. For 2006, the year after I left, and the first year after 'Iraqification', it had more than doubled to nearly 28,000. The press always reports on the horrific bombings claiming a daily toll, but they fail to mention that the number of civilians killed by gunfire and executions outnumbers by more than three times those killed by IED explosions. And of all those deaths throughout Iraq, over half took place in Baghdad, where Sammy and his family were now on the run. Thinking about it made me feel ill.

I had spent many evenings gossiping with Sammy's wife, Fara, in French, something we did to annoy Sammy because he didn't speak the language. I remembered Fara saying she was lucky to be married to a true hero, not that we ever let Sammy know that. 'It will make his head swell.'

He already had an oversized head on his short, stocky body.

He had full lips always ready to smile, a barrel chest and the predictable moustache with waxed tips sharp as the nose cone on a MiG jet. Sammy was fair-skinned, and his fine golden hair was always carefully lacquered over his bald spot. Sammy had used his savings from Spartan to buy a new house. When his brother was kidnapped, he sold it instantly to pay the ransom. When they demanded the cash, I know exactly what he would have replied.

I am ready.

Whatever the question, whatever the problem, Wing Commander Assam Mashooen was ready to deal with it.

Fuck.

I had tuned out for a moment. I stared out to sea. It was as smooth as glass, but I could sense the black fins like knife blades under the surface. It was at night when they came out to feed. Bastards.

I tuned back in again.

'Colonel Ibrahim?' I said.

Cobus hissed and said, 'He's now IP, one of the commanders.'

The IP was the Iraqi Police; in truth, the Shia police. I was too cynical about the amount of nepotism there even to bother about being surprised.

I let another 'Fuck' slip through my closed teeth. One of the things you have to do is trust your own instincts. I'd never trusted Colonel Ibrahim. I don't think any of us did. But he was there. He was efficient. He commanded the respect of the men, and he was a Shia. We were an equal-opportunities employer, Sunni, Shia, Kurd, Christian; in our own small way we were trying to show that, irrespective of old loyalties and grievances, they now had the chance to work together to build a better country for the 26 million Iraqis. It was naive on our part, and disappointing after eighteen months' training a multi-ethnic guard force that it had all fallen to pieces so quickly.

Back in the old days when we were operating from a converted bus station in Aradisa Idah, if we needed fresh belts for the RPD light machine-guns or a plasma-screen television, Colonel Ibrahim went to Sadr City and got them for us; chocolate bars, leather coats, Austrian Glocks for our Afrikaners, pirate DVDs – like Father Christmas, the colonel returned with his sack full of goodies. Did he take a commission? Of course he did. That's how it works.

From the moment he met Sammy with his sprayed hair and easy smile you could literally see the chemistry explode. It was like the reverse of love at first sight. The two men were opposites, Sunni and Shia, informal and rigid, a nominal Muslim and a man who professed unwavering faith. Sammy was round, soft-bodied, playful, like a dolphin. Ibrahim was tall, dark, lean and hairy, with small, dark darting eyes and quick movements. A shark.

That first impression only grew worse as Ibrahim discovered that the plump little Sunni had many natural leadership qualities. The men liked Sammy irrespective of their ethnicity or religion. The hired guns at Spartan liked Sammy. Colonel McQueen liked Sammy. Sammy liked his whisky and, good officer that he was, when others lost their heads, his stayed firmly on his big shoulders.

One time, when the guards were attacked by insurgents during training, they scarpered immediately. Sammy fought off the attack single-handed, then walked around, still under fire, collecting the AKs the boys had dropped in the fields along the way.

'How do you know all this, Cobus?' I asked, interrupting his flow.

'Colonel McQueen has intel,' he replied. 'The IP are actively looking for Sammy and he has been asking us for help.'

'So, drive him into the Green Zone,' I said, which seemed pretty obvious to me.

'Ash, it's his whole family, eleven people. The Americans won't take any Iraqis in.'

'Shit.'

I had of course been reading about it in the media. The issue of Iraqi interpreters and other workers being abandoned by the Coalition countries to the mercies of the insurgents was unfortunately not that well publicized yet. This despite repeated protests from enraged American and British ground commanders who had confirmed that these individuals had shown unswerving loyalty and had risked their lives accompanying troops on patrols and combat missions on a daily basis, sometimes for years. Instead of offering these people protection or asylum, they had been used and were now being discarded.

'If Mad Dog could, he would. You know that,' said Cobus.

'Yeah, I do.' I said. 'So what next?'

'Ash, Mad Dog has a convoy going to Mosul – Sammy has family there, and a house. It should be safe and, if it's not, they can cross the border easy enough to Turkey,' he said. 'Sammy can take two cars and tag along with the convoy.'

'That's a relief,' I said.

'There's one hitch,' Cobus added, and I thought there would be. There always is.

'Which is?'

'Sammy and his family can't drive out of the city on their own. They'll be gunned down. And they can't travel with the convoy without a CF or PSD Westerner nominally in charge,' he replied. 'McQueen can arrange up-to-date PSD passes, weapons permits. Everything you need . . .'

'I need? Aren't you guys going to take them?'

'There aren't enough of us. There's only me and Colonel McQueen left in the office now, with a couple of clerks. Mad Dog asked me to ask you, he asked for you personally.'

'Very flattering,' I said, thinking it's because he knows I am a soft touch, although I couldn't help wondering why he didn't call me himself.

'We will need at least six of us to man two escort wagons. So that means the two of us here, plus you and three others,' he continued. 'You should be in and out in a week, maximum.'

'Who are the other three?'

'That's not set up,' he said, and added, 'Can you call some guys? You know, the usual suspects.'

'Yeah, sure, I guess so,' I said. 'When's the party start?'

'You know what they say – yesterday. McQueen's organizing the convoy just to take Sammy up north,' he added. 'Soon as you're ready.'

I paused to think. There was no question that I wouldn't go back. Cobus must have known that. McQueen must have known that. If the boot had been on the other foot, what would Sammy have said?

I am ready.

We'd lost one RIB. The other was still out of commission. A week wouldn't make a lot of difference one way or another.

'What kind of money is Mad Dog talking?' I now asked.

The pause on the line extended.

'There's no budget, Ash . . .'

'You're kidding me!' Of course, there was no money. I hadn't been thinking it through.

'No, I tell you true, man. Papers, weapons, vehicles. Colonel McQueen can lay anything on in terms of kit, but there's no budget.'

'I don't have that many friends, I guess – can't afford to lose any more.'

We paused again.

'How long?' he now asked.

'I'll be there in two days.'

'That's great, Ash. I'll let Mad Dog know. Call me when you have your flight details.'

I touched the red button and the screen faded.

The first stars had come out. I watched the clouds of bats swooping amongst the tops of the palm trees. *Back to Baghdad for free, Jesus wept*. At least I knew why Mad Dog hadn't called me himself. He was too bloody embarrassed.

CHAPTER 3

THERE WAS AN upside to my swift departure.

I called Krista immediately after speaking to Cobus. 'Hi, honey, pleasant surprise for you, I'll be home tomorrow.'

I was using my *I'm sorry I'm late back from the office* voice, which was supposed to put Krista at her ease but always made her suspicious.

'What's happened, James?' she said.

'Just for the day.'

'You're all right?'

I wasn't sure what to tell her. What Krista didn't know she didn't have to worry about. Me going into danger for money she was happy about. Me going into danger for free – well, I was fairly confident that would not be well received. The silence stretched.

'Absolutely,' I told her. 'Tanned and gorgeous. Have a quick gig to do. I'll be away a week, darling, then back to see you in London.'

'What time do you get in?' she asked.

'Ill send you a text when I've got a ticket.'

'I'll be there,' she added.

'Kiss. Kiss.'

Mwaaah.

I called my boss on the office phone. Seeing that the team was going to be out of action while they replaced the RIB, my taking a week out worked out very nicely for Proelio – they weren't going to have to pay me. The boss didn't ask where I was going or what I had to do.

I sat back staring at the planning board and maps on the wall as I thought about what I'd agreed to do. No one on the Circuit was going to give up their time to PSD a convoy from Baghdad to Mosul for free. It would have to be someone who knew Sammy. That left only six men; three Brits, Seamus Hayes, who'd been our team commander at Spartan, Les Trevellick and Dai Jones; and the three South Africans, Wayne, Étienne and of course Hendriks, the best shot I'd met with anything that fires bullets.

We'd shared a house together in the heart of the Iraqi community, the so-called Red Zone. We'd shared beers together, we'd been shot at together, and we'd eaten so much roast lamb together that, since our unceremonious departure in 2005, I had not touched the stuff again.

I don't believe in looking back. The past has gone; like the inevitable, you can't change it or do anything about it. But it had been a good time, on reflection, and I had every reason to believe that if any of the guys weren't on a job, they would come on board. I sent them all an email outlining the situation and telling them that I would be back in London to give them a call the following day.

I served myself another burger from the grill and grabbed a beer from the fridge before telling the guys I'd be leaving for a week.

'You're in charge of something important while I'm away,' I said to Maxime, 'frisbee practice. You still don't have that back-hand spin.'

'*Comment?*'

How do you say spin in French?

'It doesn't matter.'

He offered to drive me to the airport and I said goodbye to

Antoine. With the contract on hold, there was an upside for Antoine. He was going to be able to spend more time with his wife in those crucial weeks before she gave birth. I liked Antoine, he would be a good father. I didn't bother saying goodbye to Philippe. He was still sulking about the lost RIB. I hoped that he would be over it by the time I got back.

I went back to the office with my beer and spent an hour on the phone organizing a ticket through the agent we used in Abidjan.

I hit the hammock early and next morning took a dawn run along the beach, stretching my legs out a bit before the ten-hour flight. The sea was smooth, not a fin in sight, and the whisper of wind warned that a storm was coming. Now I came to think about it, it didn't surprise me that Sammy was on a death list and Colonel Ibrahim was commanding the IP. It was the perfect metaphor for the chaos in Iraq. Good men were fleeing or being assassinated and the bad guys were taking over.

Back at our beach house I chowed down some scrambled eggs with grilled fish and some of the ubiquitous West African *fufu*, prepared as *foutou banane*, drained my coffee cup and wondered if I would have time to pick up anything from town as a present for the Krista and the girls; probably not, but I'd have a look in duty-free.

At the airport I went speedily through immigration. I didn't have any luggage, just a day pack and a novel in French I'd been working on for about a hundred years.

The airport was the classic Third World combination of cleanliness and filth, but at least they served amazing coffee from locally ground beans and those big buttery croissants as fine as any I had eaten in Paris. I took a seat on a high stool at the fly-blown counter in the departure lounge and, the moment my coffee was put in front of me, the phone hummed with the arrival of a text.

It was from Étienne asking if I was free to talk.

I called back straight away. 'Hi, Étienne! *Hoe gaan dit?*'

'Hey, Ash, *baie goed dankie, en jou?*'

'Working on my tan in Abidjan, mate. So what do you think, can you help out for a couple of days?'

'No can do, man, *dit spyt my werklik.* The same goes for Wayne. We are both currently on a job in Nigeria.'

'No problem, mate, understand.' Shit.

'It's *kak*, man. Bad timing.'

'Sex and comedy,' I quipped. 'It's all about the timing, mate.'

'*Ja*, I remember.'

'OK, I need to run now and get on a plane. Listen, say hi to Wayne for me. Étienne, you stay safe.'

'Ach, you too, man. Ash, you know that we're not going to be there to look after you this time. You have learned to shoot now, yes?'

For eighteen months all of us on the team in Baghdad had bet our hard-earned US dollars against each other in weekly shooting matches and for the first few weeks the Boers had cleaned us out. Even Dai Jones never got a look in and he was a trained sniper. It was only when we started to put in some fitness, stress and some more complex shoots that we Brits started to hold our own and win some money back.

'Yes, very funny,' I sneered back. 'You keep on with the English lessons, mate, you're getting much, much better – I nearly understood half of what you said just then.'

We both laughed and hung up. Fuck, I thought. Two out, four to go. Still, the first calls are bound to be negative, I reasoned. Étienne and Wayne didn't have anything to weigh up, they were already committed.

I'd been thinking about Dai. I knew he'd taken a job in Afghanistan, and was surprised when the phone vibrated on silent mode and that familiar army Cockney accent was blasting my ear drums.

'So what's up, then, you fucking fruit?'

'I was looking for a Welsh sheepshagger to come and suck my knob in Baghdad for a week. In and out. One task.'

'When's the off?'

'Day after tomorrow.'

'Pull the other one, mate. I'm on fucking R&R in Dubai.'

'Then it's just down the road.'

'Money?'

'Root of all evil apparently,' I said. 'Did you ever see *The Magnificent Seven*?'

'What you on about?'

'The situation is like a bad film script, mate. Sammy's on a death list and the new police chief's none other than Colonel Ibrahim.'

'That cunt.' What I had said must have sunk home. 'Shit, what is Sammy going to do? What can we do?'

'Mission of mercy, mate. Not a mercenary mission,' I added. 'Six men, our old crew, obviously, and it's a one-day job. Escort Sammy and his family up to Mosul with a convoy Mad Dog's laying on. We've done the same thing a hundred times before. You'll be back at the pool in Dubai before you can sing the Welsh national anthem.'

'Why can't the Septics take him?'

'Politics, they're not taking in any interpreters as asylum seekers at the minute, mate. Come on, you've read the papers, haven't you?'

'No, I mean why can't Mad Dog organize them a military escort?'

'Some regulations. I'm not sure exactly what, but what it boils down to is that the convoy won't take Sammy's packet in unless there are some white-eyes as PSDs with them.'

There was a long sigh and I could almost feel his hot breath in my ear.

'How many in so far?'

'You're it. I thought I would try the most gullible first.'

'Always the fucking first . . .'

'Let me know when you're arriving at BIAP. I'll send a limo.'

'Rupert, one more thing: how many of the seven were still standing at the end of the film?'

'Three.'

'Yeah, that's what I thought.'

The line went dead.

Two out, one in. That cheered me up.

After the usual African chaos boarding the Air France flight, I was greeted with the usual French disdain by the cabin crew. So, everything was normal. I cleaned every scrap of food from the plastic containers on the flight and dozed off with the sky streaked in reds and yellows. One of the tricks I had learned in the army is to eat what's put in front of you and sleep whenever possible.

CHAPTER 4

EVERY TIME I bowl into an airport and find Krista waiting for me it's just like the first time I laid eyes on her. I stop, my breath catches, and I marvel at my own good fortune.

You lucky bastard.

She rarely smiles. She looks into my eyes to see if I'm hiding something; at my movements, to see if I'm hurt. But then, when she does smile, the sun shines on me.

It was dead on eight o'clock. I was first off the aircraft and first through customs, in a dark blue polo shirt, chinos, my day sack with its multitude of pockets and pouches, and a fantastic tan from months of beach frisbee. She was waiting in a grey skirt, a red jacket nipped in at the waist, platinum-blonde hair drawn back in a pleat. I wondered if she was thinking how lucky she was.

Every man thinks his wife is a beauty, at least he should, and in my case I had no doubt – tall, leggy and elegant with blue eyes that were bright and piercing and held an alluring blend of candour and hidden depths. She had come from Norway to England to study international relations at the London School of Economics and would have returned to Oslo if I hadn't swept her off her feet.

Well, that's how I liked to remember it. Krista's circle in South Kensington had made friends with some young officers I knew and she'd decided quite rightly that the whole lot were a bunch of obnoxious Hooray Henries who drank too much and haw-hawed for no apparent reason. I explained to her the difference between the Guards & Cavalry and the rest of the army, the latter group, I assured her, being much nicer people.

A movie? Dinner? Coffee?

'I don't drink coffee, and I must tell you that I have been previously married to a British soldier. He was a pig and I despise you all.' *Ah, that would explain the attitude.* I mentally cursed whatever idiot had made my task so much more difficult.

'High tea at Claridge's? A lovely Pad Thai at Sri Siam? How about you let me buy you at least one, harmless glass of wine here at this bar.' I looked down at the bar where her hand was already gently cradling a glass of wine. 'Excellent, I see you already have a drink. Well, that saves me both time and money.'

She hesitated. I thought there was a smile hovering about her pink lips.

'You are very persistent,' she said.

'That's because I'm a Scot,' I replied. 'You must know the story of Robert the Bruce and the spider?'

'No, I don't think I do.'

So I told her. Robert the Bruce had fought six battles, trying to drive the English out of Scotland, and lost every one. Defeated, his army scattered, all hope gone, he found himself in a cave, watching a spider spinning a web. Six times the spider tried to leap from one wall to another across the cave and six times it fell and hung from a thread. On the seventh go the spider succeeded. Robert the Bruce marched out of the cave, called his men to arms and finally drove the English back across the border.

'But surely the Scottish were defeated in the end,' she said, and I just loved the way the little furrows ran across her brow.

'Actually the correct term is "the Scots", and we in fact conquered England, which now forms the southern province of Greater Scotland,

I think you'll find. As a beautiful foreigner I can forgive you that misunderstanding. Later, after these drinks, allow me to show you the rest of my kingdom,' I replied, and the smile finally blossomed.

I mentally filed away the fact that she had had a previous bad experience with the army. For the rest of the evening, I kept my left fist gripped tight under the table to remind myself to shut up and listen. I asked Krista about herself, her ambitions, her family and noted that she had achieved her amazing figure through a lifetime of cross-country skiing. When she asked about me, I shrugged modestly and murmured as little as possible whilst directing the conversation back to her. I would, in fact, be leaving the army soon in any event. I would be returning to civvy street and intended pursuing a career in law.

'Very sensible,' she said approvingly, and thawed even more.

She was a sensible woman, and I loved her all the more years later when we were living together and I eventually quit the deathly gloom of a law office in the City of London to begin a career in private security and she accepted my decision without a murmur.

Now we were married. Natalie, our eldest daughter, was just like her, Krista in miniature, and in Veronica I saw more of myself, running before she could walk, headstrong, little plump legs covered in scratches and bruises, baby teeth gripped to hold back the tears.

All these images swam into my mind as I strolled out of the arrivals gate at Heathrow. Krista was waiting. The girls were staying overnight with my mother and we set off in our ageing but comfortable Range Rover.

The phone rang while we were driving. I thought it was just as well to get it out in the open this way. It was Seamus. He sounded depressed and, like Cobus, didn't waste any words.

'What's up with Sammy?' he began.

'He's on a Shia death list. Colonel Ibrahim's out to slot him and Mad Dog and Cobus are trying to organize an escape out of Baghdad. They need our help.'

Despite the fact I hadn't seen him in months, his voice was as familiar to me as my own. I could picture his eyes closing in anger on the other end of the phone, and no doubt the tic was starting up in his neck.

'When do we have to be in country?'

'ASAP. I'll be leaving London first thing tomorrow,' I said. 'Dai's up for it. I'm waiting on Les and Hendriks. I'd like six men, but I need four.'

'Well, now you've got three.'

'One thing, mate, Mad Dog's arranging the logistics but there's no budget.'

Krista did not move a muscle, but the temperature in the car suddenly dropped.

'Fuck it, he'd do the same for us.' Seamus didn't even hesitate.

'Any news from Les and Hendriks?' I asked him.

'Hendriks has dropped out of sight. I've not been in touch with him for a while, if I'm honest. And Les has got some bird twenty years younger than him. They met running a marathon.'

'That'll do it,' I said.

'He'll be up for it, Ash.'

'Thanks, mate.'

'I'll be there the day after you. Just check your email and get us picked up at the BIAP.'

'Will do.'

I clicked off and sat there nursing the phone. We were on the motorway. The road was clear. Krista didn't say a word. It was always a dilemma knowing how much to tell her, how much to hold back. As they say back in the mob, you hope for the best but plan for the worst.

'I remember you talking about Sammy,' Krista said, breaking the silence.

'Yeah, he's a good guy.'

'He must be.' Her words hung in the air.

'He is, Krista. I survived every day out in Iraq and made it back home to you because of all of those guys – and Sammy was one of us.' There was no real need to belabour the point. I had told her the stories of our house being attacked and how Sammy had rescued me single-handed when I was cut off alone and on the run from a howling pack of armed Iraqis.

Right from the first day I had met him, Sammy had risked his life to look after me. And then, damn near every day after that, he and I had worked side by side, often in harm's way, with him facing the extra danger of the commute back and forth through a city at war, placing his own family at risk because he was working for the hated foreigners.

Krista knew all of the stories. Some of them had moved her to tears, and some of them she even told to her friends herself. She didn't say another word.

I had been away with the army many times, but Iraq had been more intense and more unpredictable. I'd kept the worst from her, but she knew that our company had lost men killed and wounded.

'It's an escort job,' I said. 'Piece of cake. Something we've done a hundred times before.'

She shook her head, as if she didn't want to hear, and stroked a wayward curl behind her ear. Krista followed the news. She knew what was happening in Baghdad. She knew that, if I'd returned from Africa and was flying out twelve hours later to Amman, I'd already made up my mind, so there was no point in arguing. I am sure Krista was weighing up the words I'd said to Seamus: *death list . . . out to slot him . . . no budget.* With Proelio, I had a life insurance worth £250,000 – not a lot for a woman alone with a mortgage and two young children, but £250,000 more than the fat nothing she'd get if anything happened to me on this unexpected mission.

There was a parking spot close to the house. She zipped in and killed the engine.

The flat smelled of flowers, talcum powder and the Jo Malone Tuberose I'd bought at Christmas – 'the perfume of sex', said the guy in the store. I stripped off my clothes and, except for my boots, stuck every stitch I was wearing in the wash-and-dry cycle.

When I came out of the shower, she was waiting in bed, bare arms over the sheet, the lamp on in the corner, her hair like a golden halo on the pillow.

We made love like it might be the last time.

CHAPTER 5

I T'S A 30KM drive from Jordan's Queen Alia Airport into Amman. I had forgotten how long the drive was and had the time to realize that I was back in the Middle East, with ragged palms lining the highway, the familiar reek of ancient dust, and a taxi driver who steered with one hand on the wheel, like a boatman gripping the tiller on a fishing boat. By the time we reached the hotel I had zoned out and had to shake myself awake.

I tipped the taxi driver and had a quick look around the street for anyone suspicious before walking into the lobby to check in. It was an empty gesture; everyone on the street looked suspicious to me, but at least no one seemed to be looking at the hotel. It was a cheap three-star hotel, nondescript and not far from the city centre. Apart from the fact that I would be paying for this myself, not on Spartan's expense account, I had deliberately chosen the hotel because of its low profile.

Just over a year ago three very nice hotels had been the target of a coordinated attack by suicide bombers. The Grand Hyatt, Days Inn and the Radisson SAS had all been used frequently by contractors and engineers transiting through Jordan into Iraq. It had always seemed a huge security risk to me and it was of little surprise to anyone in the industry when finally the enemy had acted and hit them. It made sense to me. Hotels in Jordan are a softer target than waiting until the Westerners passed into Iraq, protected by armed convoys or bases surrounded by barbed wire and concrete blast walls.

Around sixty people were killed, and over a hundred injured. Ironically, only four of the dead were American; 90 per cent of those affected were Arabs. Both the government and the Jordanian public were in uproar against this attack, and the al-Khalayleh family – whose infamous son Ahmed, perhaps better known as Abu Musab al-Zarqawi, was leader of al-Qaeda in Iraq – was forced to take out ads in all of the major Jordanian newspapers, condemning the attack and completely disowning young Ahmed. Small three-star hotels enjoyed an unprecedented surge in business from thousands of tanned, fit men looking to stay only one or two nights in Amman.

Talking of which, I had safely packed away my contractor clothing and was travelling dressed as a gauche tourist in a bright, floral Hawaiian shirt. I made sure everyone heard me asking the clerk how long it would take to get to the beautiful lost city of Petra and how long would it take to see the whole site. While he processed my passport and produced my card-keys, I also feigned interest in the hotel's own shuttle bus to the Dead Sea.

Finally I grabbed the key and strolled upstairs, clutching my tourist maps. I smiled pleasantly at the porter carrying my bags and tipped him a couple of JDs. He beamed back at me, ignorant of the fact that he had been hauling around my travel selection of holsters, helmet, body armour and telescopic sights.

After I showered, I threw caution out the window by getting a cab to the Marriott to have dinner at the Library. It may not have made sense from a security standpoint, but it was something of a good-luck ritual every time I went into Iraq, and I figured the risk worth taking. Not that I was superstitious, but not performing a good-luck ritual that had always worked before is just asking for trouble.

Going into Iraq, you're thinking, *This might be my last decent meal before I get slotted*. Coming out, it's a celebration that the bastards missed again. Besides which, I justified to myself, I might bump into someone I knew there and catch up on some useful gossip. I sat at a corner table, back to the wall, and chose a 2003 Château Puyanché to go with the chateaubriand, flown in no doubt from Europe.

The waiter returned with the bottle. He poured an inch of wine into the glass. I swirled it around like a connoisseur, waited a moment, swirled it around again, and took a sip.

'Mmm. Very nice.'

'Thank you, sir.'

He bowed and half-filled the glass. I pushed my Oakleys up into my hair, and shook my phone awake to make sure I had service before placing it on the table.

A few moments before my flight from London, I'd got a terse text reply from Hendriks.

Cannot help, man. 2 broken legs. Off road for 3 months.

That was a blow, I had counted him in already and realized that in my mind I had already felt, if not complacent, at least comfortable knowing that his reliable wiry frame was going to be watching my back. Biting down on my disappointment, I'd grinned to myself as I typed a reply:

Crap excuse, disappointed you couldn't make up something more believable. Cannot believe you have let me AND Sammy down.

I knew that it would enrage him, and the thought of him gritting his teeth in fury made me chortle happily as I hit 'Send'. Hendriks was an old hand in Africa, ex-32 Battalion, a mercenary from the old school, cropped grey hair, scars crisscrossing a face burned almost black by the sun, ice-blue eyes that missed nothing, cynical, sharp, cool as an iceberg and, of course, sadly out of action. I wondered how the fuck he had managed to break both his legs. I wondered what the other guy looked like.

Three out. Two in. One to go. I was surprised not to have heard from Les Trevellick yet and guessed the new lady in his life was keeping him busy.

The steak was medium-well, a touch of pink, green beans, potatoes cut in slices and pan-fried. I'd been drinking faster than I thought and poured the last of the wine into my glass. I'd intended drinking half the bottle and leaving the rest, but good liquor and good intentions don't go together. The 2003 was a fantastic year: hottest summer on record, the grapes turning into a potent elixir and – it's a funny old thing, but – the more you drink, the better it gets.

I gazed about the dining room. Four tables were occupied. Three with groups of men. Directly in my line of vision was a couple with two girls aged about ten and twelve; the woman calmly dignified in a blue headscarf and gold bangles, the girls in dark green kilts and white blouses, their father paying his three women equal attention. He was clean-shaven in a beige suit and white shirt, an oil executive, I imagined, one of the 90 per cent who saw no future in fundamentalism.

I took a sip of wine, rolled the liquid around my mouth thoughtfully and let it glide down slowly.

Three of us so far. One pending.

With Sammy's family and luggage, we'd have to make a three-car packet, with at least two of us in each vehicle. Even with Cobus we were still one short, although Sammy was familiar enough with our drills. Both he and his brother would be armed. I had no doubt that the canny pilot had managed to keep hold of his old weapons passes.

If we were still undermanned, maybe I could pick up one of

the Serb dealers-in-death who hung out at the Palestine Hotel and lived for the adrenalin rush of action?

There were a lot of maybes. Like maybe I should have asked Cobus more about the tasking. And maybe I should have considered Krista and the girls before racing back to a war zone that was just hotting up, with the Americans executing a surge of troops to inflict a decisive blow on the insurgents. So decisive that the media had already capitalised it as 'The Surge'.

On the face of it, the task looked painless: a three-rig packet in the midst of a US convoy armed to the teeth with .50 cals and Mark 19s. But Sod's Law – or Murphy's Law, as they say in the United States – has it that whatever can go wrong will go wrong, and at the worst possible time, in the worst possible way.

I downed the last of the wine in one gulp. Sod all that savouring the hues and flavours. I had a pain across my shoulders and an uneasy feeling in the pit of my stomach. Call it instinct. Call it a 2003 Bordeaux. Call it what you will, but going back always carries the ghosts of old anxieties. Going back to Baghdad was like putting your head over the parapet just to see if there were any sharpshooters out there waiting to take a pop shot.

All day the same cycle of thoughts had been spinning through my head. For his own reasons, Mad Dog had stuck the responsibility of getting Sammy's family to safety on my shoulders. I had to get them out of reach of the Shia death squads, and get the team out without any dramas.

Back when I had been a captain in the Duke of Wellington's, whenever you deployed on operations, you had the comfort of knowing that the full machinery of the British Army was behind you and you had the immediate support of your own battlegroup, battalion and company.

As a security contractor, the infrastructure is weaker, but at least there is some support, although your obligations are different. You look out for yourself and your comrades. If a job looks too dodgy for the money, you say no. I weighed every contract on a finely balanced scale: the money, love of family and my life on one side; on the other, the risk of violent and painful death, possibly grotesque maiming and spending the rest of my days in a bucket with feeding instructions on the side, possibly kidnap, torture and a lead role in an al-Qaeda beheading video.

My mind drifted back to our ambushed convoy of oil tankers, the deafening racket of machine-gun fire as we had assaulted the enemy firing line, and the thud of the American Mk19 grenade launcher hammering away under a sky black with smoke. That had been a bad day at the office, and the enemy had not even really been trying to hurt us, just cause a diversion while they stole some tankers. The loss of one tanker in a fireball the size of a football pitch had been a price they were willing to pay.

I tore my mind away from thinking too much about the last time I had been in Iraq. It was a dangerous thing to do and at any moment I might remember that I had left there after being betrayed by my own Iraqi guards in an incident that had me running alone and bleeding through people's back gardens, pursued by an armed mob of over a hundred men. No, not the kind of thing to dwell on before jumping on a plane back there.

I usually spent more time reminding myself about the money. A week's job like this would have been worth a nice five grand. Oh, I nearly forgot, we weren't getting paid on this one.

On this job there would be no pay cheque and no supporting infrastructure. We were totally reliant on Colonel McQueen to plug us into the CF convoy and even to get us safely back and forth from the BIAP to the Green Zone. He would be the key to this whole trip. Without him we were just a handful of lunatics jumping on a plane into hell.

The waiter shuffled up with the bill. I signed the chit and dropped five JDs between the covers of his little leather booklet. Hopefully the wine would help me sleep.

CHAPTER 6

I'D WATCHED THE news clips and listened to the reports coming out of Iraq and, despite the positive media spin, knew that things had not improved since I left in mid-2005. The opposite, in fact. A year and half had passed and I had a feeling of *déjà vu*, that Baghdad was in a time warp. That I'd never really been away.

The flight from Amman to Baghdad was the same as ever, with the usual bizarre mix of security contractors and other unidentifiable odds and sods, all of them eyeing up the South African stewardess, since she was likely the last attractive woman they would see for several months. In the meantime I was considering a slight problem as the flight pulled in to the terminal. How to get through passport control.

There was no problem booking flights to Baghdad, especially if a US military colonel could email the booking in for you; the only drama might come at Immigration when you disembarked. Previously, if you were stupid enough to get on a plane to Baghdad, people assumed you were supposed to be there, although I remembered that you could still run across the odd peace-loving hippie, independent journalist, armoured-car salesmen, even the occasional missionary, turning up on spec, smiling in a bewildered fashion and looking around for a ride into the city.

All you needed was to show the immigration officer a passport from one of the Coalition countries. Hell, when I first came into Iraq in 2003, there hadn't even been an immigration department. Once past the Jordanian border controls you could just walk, drive or fly in, and *abandon hope all ye who enter.*

Just before I left in 2005, the Iraqis had stopped the influx of lunatic tourists and you now also needed some form of ID to state that you were either working for one of the embassies or for the MNF, Multi-National Force. Unfortunately, although I still had a pocket full of MNF and Department of Defense identity cards, they were all out of date.

The catch-22 that most people faced was that new cards were issued *in Baghdad,* so if you were not bypassing immigration by coming in on a military flight, you needed a formidable letter to assure immigration that you were formally invited and would be picking up said ID card upon arrival at Camp Victory. Mad Dog had not managed to get me that letter yet, so I would just have to try and bluff my way through.

When I strolled up to the immigration desk I gave the official my biggest smile and happiest '*salaam alaikum*' as I slapped down my British passport. He smiled politely, looked through the passport and held out his hand.

'CAC card,' he pronounced it *kak*, Afrikaans for 'shit', but I knew he was asking for my DoD Common Access Card.

I dutifully pulled this out and presented it with another blinding smile and my finger helpfully covering the expiry date a year earlier.

The officer looked at me unamused and pulled it out of my hand to examine properly. The smile disappeared. A torrent of Arabic followed, which I presumed indicated that he was unhappy and that my card was out of date.

'They told me in Jordan', I murmured quietly, 'that I could buy my visa when I arrived here.' I pulled out fifty US dollars and tucked them into my passport in front of him and said, 'VISA?' more simply.

'*La, la, la!*' No, *no, no!* He looked around nervously.

I couldn't believe that I had come across the only honest Iraqi official in the country. I looked around with interest to see who might be watching him.

'*Ta'al*,' *Come*. He gestured for me to follow him as he held my passport in one hand and the expired CAC card in the other as if it were a snake.

Iraqi soldiers pointed guns at me and followed. The rest of the queue watched open-mouthed with interest. I felt even more conspicuous, bearing in mind I was wearing yet another colourful Hawaiian shirt.

The immigration officer led me into a small room with two older, fatter uniformed officials with impressive shoulder boards and even more impressive moustaches. Much jabbering in Arabic followed and I was relieved to see that there was no anger in their expressions, only curiosity.

'Letter?' The older one said, miming opening a letter at me and waving a piece of paper by way of illustration.

'No, no letter, it didn't arrive yet.' I shrugged. 'I have to pick up my new CAC card in Camp Victory.'

There was more discussion amongst the moustaches before they turned back to me. Apparently there was some confusion over my place of birth.

'*Inteh inglizia?*' *Are you English?*

'*La, la.*' I was properly horrified and it must have shown on my face. 'I am Scottish, from Scotland.' I waved my hands in a Scots manner. 'You know Scotland?'

The moustaches looked at me blankly.

'*Al Haw-rus-tralia?*' one of them ventured.

'*La.*'

'*Al Sa-houth Hafrica?*' The most senior one smiled at me triumphantly.

'*La.*'

The smile faded. I racked my brains but had no idea how Scotland had been translated into Arabic. I tried to remember the conversations I had had with Sammy about the Scots. Suddenly I was struck with inspiration.

'You know Mel Gibson?' I looked from one face to another. 'Mel Gibson?'

They all looked at each other and muttered. One of them said *'Dirty Harry'* and there was a flurry of *'la*'s as the rest shouted him down and I heard one say *'Lethal Weapon'*.

'Na'am! Lethal Weapon – Mel Gibson!' I jumped in. God bless Hollywood. 'Do you know *Braveheart*? *Braveheart*, anyone?'

I acted out wearing a kilt and painting my face blue, finishing by riding a horse and booming out, 'FREEDOOOM!'

'Na'am! Al Braveheart,' cried one of them. 'Freedom, yes, freedom very good, mister. Freedom from Saddam!'

Finally I used my hands to indicate England with Scotland on top and tapped my chest to say 'Scotland. Braveheart. Freedom'. They loved it and all laughed and clapped. Yup, that was us, all the best of friends.

'You, mister,' wheezed out the most senior man, 'you are Scotland man, yes? You come,' he motioned with his hands carrying something, 'freedom to Al Iraq, yes?'

'Yes, I bring freedom to Iraq.' I knew that by now nearly every Iraqi hated the foreign jihadis with a passion. 'I come kill Al-Qaeda,' I said, drawing an imaginary sword and hacking off heads. They all liked that.

Guns were pointed at the floor, moustaches beamed and within seconds my passport was stamped, hands shaken all around, and after a cup of sickly sweet *chai* I was escorted through immigration by the chief himself, plus entourage all chanting 'Freedom' and pretending to wear skirts. They even gave me my fifty bucks back in the passport.

Finally.

I walked out into the sunlight, *namastay*ed the heavily armed ex-Ghurkhas employed by Global, who grinned back happily as I crossed the concourse.

No running kids and crowds of tourists here. Just men in uniform, a couple of VIPs in suits being picked up by their PSD teams, and men like me in combat pants and desert boots. I watched a couple of USAID staffers packing their bags into the armoured bus taking them to the Green Zone.

Cobus was waiting by a couple of Humvees in his dusty body armour, covered in guns and knives and carrying enough ammunition for ten men. He looked exactly as I had seen him two years before, although his bronze hair was touched by new flashes of grey. At least that was a change. We shook hands and hugged fiercely. I felt a couple of bones crack. His blue eyes were piercing, and alive with laughter.

'Very colourful, you fokken *doos*,' he said, smiling and fingering my Hawaiian shirt.

'I'm on leave, remember? Not working.'

He leaned forward and his voice deepened. 'Good to see you, man.' He demonstrated a plane taking off with his hand. 'You'll be back in London for the weekend.'

'Good. It'll be nice to spend some more time at home with the mortgage.'

His eyes narrowed. 'You bought that new place for Krista?' he asked.

'The day before prices started falling.'

'Ach, yissss,' he hissed, grimacing in sympathy.

Cobus had bought a piece of land when he left the army and planned to settle down as a farmer as soon as he'd paid off his loan – bonds, they called them. Most of the South African contractors were ex-military and ex-police who'd begun their careers in the old apartheid days and had found there was no place for them in modern South Africa. After twenty years fighting bush wars in Namibia, Mozambique, Angola and who knew where else,

Cobus had taken to life as a hired gun, but never forgot to say grace before slicing into his roast lamb. He saw no contradiction in being a committed Christian and being paid to fight. He always believed that he was on the right side.

Self-justification? Self-delusion? We all have these thoughts rattling around inside our heads and we all have to look at ourselves in the mirror at the end of the day and be proud of what we do and who we are.

There are on the Circuit some trigger-happy adventurers who shoot and scoot with little provocation, Rambo lookalikes in headbands with bandoliers of cartridges. Sometimes you come across some cold-blooded killers. But these men are in the minority. As PSDs, we don't get paid to kill people. We get paid to protect people, protect the water supply, bodyguard journalists and aid workers, keep our heads down and keep our clients out of trouble.

'Do you know what happened to Hendriks?' I asked.

'An accident clearing some land on his farm,' he said, and lowered his voice again. 'He's spending three months in bed, with his wife looking after him.'

Hendriks was hard as steel, the most accomplished piece of military machinery any of us had ever known, but rumour had it he was terrified of the little lady at home.

'Time to get your boots and spurs on, Ash.' Cobus opened the door of the Humvee and started pulling out weapons and ammunition.

I nodded up at the 240 gunner in his turret, who nodded back. I noted the factory-produced shield, armour and ballistic glass panels that surrounded him. It was a far cry from the old days when all of us, contractors and CF both, were welding on home-made armour plates.

There was a nip in the air, but the sun was breaking through the city smog. Useful, seeing as I'd packed my fleece away in my day sack. I glanced back at the lintel above the exit. They had taken down the letters spelling out Saddam Hussein the moment the war ended, but the faded outline on the concrete below the letters was legible last time I was at the airport and Saddam Hussein's name was present still, a ghostly reminder that among the Sunnis there were some now calling those the good old days.

The machine-gunner gazed at me through protective goggles – admiring my shades, I guess – and watched with interest as I opened up my Bergen to extract my gear. I put on my body armour and helmet, my tactical vest and filled pouches with AK magazines as Cobus handed them to me. I stuffed the Beretta M9 pistol he gave me into a chest pouch. I didn't want the hassle of looking through my luggage for an appropriate holster. Time enough for that later.

Finally Cobus passed me a Russian-made AKM and reminded me to keep it unloaded until we exited the BIAP. I filled a couple of other pouches with field dressings, put my map and compass into another pocket and did a quick radio check with the little Motorola walkie-talkie Cobus provided. I checked myself one last time, slung my Bergen into the rear Humvee and jogged forward to join Cobus in the back of the front vehicle. He was holding the all-important ID and weapons passes, which I slotted into the passholder around my neck.

The US soldiers with us got themselves comfortable and eventually we moved off down the road. I looked past the booted feet of the turret gunner sitting above us to the other side of the Humvee, at Cobus. He saw my questioning look and I swirled my hand in a wave that encompassed the vehicle and its crew.

'I wasn't expecting the limo and chauffeur service?'

'Someone owed Mad Dog a favour after we checked out something for them in Aradisa Idah,' he said, reminding me of our old home, 'and they run us around once in a while if they have no missions on.'

As we approached the final roadblock everyone loaded up – magazines and belts of ammunition on to their weapons. Cobus and

I magged up, cocked our rifles and put safety catches on. I rested my AK barrel on the window sill while I loaded and made ready my pistol, before holstering it in a spare mag pouch. Then I picked up my rifle again and got into character as we rolled left and right through the chicane and out of the BIAP on to Route Irish. The engine roared and the convoy raced off like a pack of wolves, the traffic parting like antelope as we hit the highway at a steady 100 klicks.

What I could see through the armoured windows was the usual stock-car race along the BIAP highway, six lanes of cars and trucks squeezing into every space, kamikaze drivers speeding the wrong way, donkey carts, abandoned vehicles stripped of tyres, seats, engine parts; anything removable was removed. There were blown up, burned-out and bullet-riddled wrecks, piles of garbage, plastic bags like kites drifting on the wind, women with children standing on the side of the road, and you weren't sure if they wanted to cross or were lookouts warning bombers hidden on bridges and flyovers that the Great Satan was passing in his mobile fortress.

IEDs were getting more elaborate as the insurgents learned how to utilize pressure plates and explosively formed penetrators (EFPs). I had been keeping up to date on the counter-measures as well, which ranged from jammers operating at different frequencies to metal poles extending from the front of vehicles, sometimes with heated elements at the tip, to pre-detonate wire- or infra-red-triggered devices before the vehicle was in the target area.

It was a constantly changing game, and as soon as one set of counter-measures came in, the enemy was developing another technique to try to get around them. Rumour and intelligence both claimed that the more sophisticated explosives were being supplied over the border from Iran, the other main oil producer, which I could well believe.

Oil and war were the opposite of oil and water. They went together. This was the oil war, the juice offensive, the gas campaign. One day, Iraq would be as rich as Saudi Arabia, and the big oil companies were already positioning themselves to get a piece of the action. A day spent Googling combinations of war-oil-iraq-bush will give you nightmares and enough conspiracy theories to fill a library.

According to the Pentagon, EFPs were crossing the border from Iran and had been responsible for killing 170 US servicemen in Iraq since 2004. No one appeared to have told Bush, Cheney and Rumsfeld that 'democracy' in Iraq with its 60 per cent Shia population would deliver the country into an alliance with Iran, virtually 100 per cent Shia, and America's ideological enemy since Ayatollah Khomeini overthrew the US-backed Shah in 1979.

The dynamics of the region had not been considered, and it had been clear to me the first time I was in Iraq that no post-war reconstruction and nation-building strategy had been developed before the invasion in March 2003. Defense Secretary Donald Rumsfeld and his inner circle at the Pentagon didn't even seem to be bothered to pretend that they were not making it up as they went along.

There were many errors in the early months, allowing the sacking of the museum containing some of the world's most ancient and important Mesopotamian artefacts for one; allowing the local population to loot and burn themselves back into the Stone Age was another; and thirdly the lack of any immediate and effective reconstruction effort to win over the local population and keep them busy. I mean this was Occupation 1.01, basic stuff. In addition, there were two dire, stand-out decisions that made the situation worse, if anyone could believe that possible, and, like the aftershocks of a volcano, would continue to carry a human and social cost for years to come.

The first of those ill-judged decisions was the sacking of everyone who had been a member of Saddam's Ba'ath Party, which meant the entire stratum of management that administered the ministries, local-government councils, universities, hospitals, the post office, public transport, registration of births, deaths and marriages, all the minutiae of civil life, including the management of every bank and corporation in Iraq. In one stroke, Paul Bremer, under orders from his boss Donald Rumsfeld, removed what little organization remained in an already chaotic nightmare.

Secondly, Bremer disbanded the police force and the armed forces, resulting in the consequent rise in crime across the board: revenge killings, kidnap, burglary – you name it, it increased. Slightly puzzling as well, since any prior thoughts of what the Coalition was going to do after dethroning Saddam and his regime had vaguely mentioned handing the responsibility for security straight to the Iraqi Police and Army. From a military standpoint, it was madness disbanding the army and sending one and a half million armed men home with no prospects of income to support their families except for crime or the insurgency.

Opening up the economy to market forces and genuine foreign exchange rates had already had a catastrophic effect on unemployment and recruitment into the insurgency. This was throwing petrol on to a fire.

Before the war, al-Qaeda did not operate in Iraq. Saddam had banned any entity that might compete with his own autocratic rule, and he and Osama bin Laden had been fierce enemies since bin Laden had offered to fight the Iraqis in the first Gulf War. However, within months of the war ending in 2003, foreign fighters were slipping over the completely porous border from impoverished Yemen, Algeria, Afghanistan, Pakistan, Syria, Chechnya and God knows where else, lured by the incentive of a $1,000 reward for shooting an American soldier, the cash funnelled through militant groups reportedly bankrolled in Saudi Arabia and the Gulf.

It had been assumed by the architects of war that, when it was all over, the 26 million Iraqis would rush from their homes, those not flattened in the blitzkrieg, and cast flowers before the marching boots and rolling tank tracks. Old men would weep. Girls would cast off their veils and dance. After thirty years of Saddam despotism they would gratefully accept an imposed democracy and vote for the US-friendly exiles flocking home in their Western-style suits with entourages of men in dark glasses.

It didn't happen and no one in the White House, or in Whitehall for that matter, seemed to have spared a moment to consider how many Coalition troops were going to be needed to hold this three-ring circus together after victory. The generals had estimated half a million. Rumsfeld had reckoned thirty thousand, and allegedly fired anyone who didn't agree. No plan or orders had been disseminated to those on the ground to guide them after Saddam's government fell. Coalition combat units reached their military objectives, dug in, and then watched while the local population pillaged and burned their own cities, out of control for weeks.

War. A moment of neo-con madness. After the annihilation of the Twin Towers in New York President Bush had seemed weak and at a loss. He had to make a show of strength to punish al-Qaeda. Afghanistan fitted the bill. Fair enough, it was and still is a haven for the al-Qaeda leadership, their cells and training camps.

But as for Iraq, no one outside of the White House or the Pentagon really knew why they had invaded the place. We had spent many evenings debating all the most likely rumours and conspiracy theories – many of them quite believable – but at the end of the day none of us really knew.

Oil seemed the most likely answer, but even I was swinging around to the belief that even that may have been just another red herring. The fact that Bush and most of his team in the White House were oil men and Iraq was sitting on the world's second-largest deposits of oil after Saudi Arabia, may have played a part in their decision to punish Iraq for 9/11. But just as Iraq's armed forces weren't fit to stand up to a First World army for more than a couple of weeks, the basic infrastructure of the Iraqi oil industry had been in a steady state of collapse since the British had built it nearly fifty years previously. Billions of dollars would have to be spent over at least a decade to uncap even a fraction of its potential.

The justification for war was Saddam Hussein's build-up of weapons of mass destruction. It was discussed at the UN. Many times. The UK produced a study later found to be some student's PhD thesis taken off the Internet; and in the US, General Colin Powell, the Secretary of State, provided the UN Security Council with a montage of aerial images showing what looked like mobile homes modelled by five-year-olds. The anti-war alliance laughed, and even the general didn't look as if he believed what he was saying. It didn't matter. Bush, Rumsfeld, the neo-cons and thus America were going to war. You're either with us or against us.

Just before Christmas, I had read in the press that a British diplomat in the UN who had spent four and half years reading through the US and UK intelligence every day confirmed that the British government knew full well that Iraq's WMD capability did not pose any threat to the UK. It was effectively agreed between the US and UK that any threat had been contained already.

This information had been suppressed at the time of the invasion, under threat of breaking the Official Secrets Act. The diplomat also confirmed that a constant topic of discussion between US and UK officials was that Iraq would dissolve into chaos if invaded and regime change occurred. Interestingly, he also pointed out that the argument for UN sanctions against Iraq at the time was not because they believed Iraq had an effective WMD capability, but because they were failing to show properly documented proof of their destruction.

The elusive WMDs were never found and were no longer mentioned. There were no dirty bombs filled with anthrax and plague, no nuclear programme, no long-range missiles capable of being launched and reaching 'British interests' *within 45 minutes*, as Prime Minister Tony Blair had told the House of Commons.

Iraq was, and remains, a Third World country where, outside the cities, most people live in mud-brick houses without water or electricity and scratch out a living from the small arable areas around the great rivers that pass through the unforgiving desert, using the same tools as their ancestors used in biblical times.

It was shocking to me arriving in Iraq in the autumn of 2003, six months after victory, that most CF soldiers didn't know why they were there. Many thought Saddam was responsible for 9/11. They were there in this desert hell to subdue an imaginary al-Qaeda that was in fact unwelcome in Iraq and outlawed by Saddam.

I never pretended to know the answer myself, although it was a frequent topic of conversation amongst Westerners and Iraqis both. It seemed to me that the announcement of the 'War on Terror' was the very flame that had ignited Islamists on a global scale, and now even the War on Terror was being re-branded. The PR managers had tried calling it the 'Global Struggle Against Violent Extremism', but that had the same suspect resonance as *illegal combatant* or *extraordinary rendition*. In the Pentagon they had settled on 'The Long War' – four years so far at a cost in the spring of 2007 already rising above half a trillion dollars.

In the meantime that was half a trillion dollars of free advertising budget to every Islamist terror group in the world. From Pakistan to Indonesia, from Chechnya to Iran, from Syria to the Gaza Strip and literally dozens of other countries from Asia to Africa, it was clear to every Muslim that a Christian coalition had invaded a Muslim country and that the Muslim population was suffering as a result of it. The word 'crusade' carries extremely negative associations in the Muslim historical memory, and it was unfortunate that George W. Bush used it to describe his war on terror, and specifically the terror being espoused by Islamist militants. Small details such as the fact that the vast majority of the Iraqis were being killed by other Iraqis were beside the point. Thanks to the wars in Iraq and Afghanistan, global jihad had never enjoyed more support.

It is also shocking to me that few of those eager to rush to war in 2003 had ever seen war – Blair, Bush and many of the neo-cons, for example.

CHAPTER 7

I T WAS HOT and stuffy inside the body of the Humvee, noisy too. I wanted to hear more about Sammy, his family, Colonel McQueen's plans, but I wasn't going to shout over the noise and Cobus seemed content to gaze into space while he stroked his moustache.

It took us twenty minutes to drive down Route Irish. There were no dramas. The convoy slowed as we rolled through the chicanes approaching the West Gate. Civilian vehicles were lined up, waiting to be checked. We shot past them. The guards nodded to our gunners, and I was back in the Green Zone, the 'bubble', the International Zone, twenty square blocks of relative safety in a land still ripping itself apart.

Saddam must have been creating his own version of heaven among the marble monuments and numerous palaces, the effect lessened these days by the earth berms and T-walls made of blast-proof concrete slabs hung with chain-link fences and coils of razor wire, the zone watched over from checkpoints guarded by M1 tanks and Bradley fighting vehicles. It was, as Colonel McQueen once said, the ultimate gated community.

The route to McQueen's office in an annexe of the US Embassy took us past some sights I remembered – the Tomb of the Unknown Warrior and the enormous crossed sabres at the old parade ground, the backdrop for countless group photos of soldiers and contractors like me. I looked at it thoughtfully, remembering the 'last photo' we had taken there as a team before I had left Iraq, never expecting to come back.

As we rolled into the embassy car park, a medevac Blackhawk clattered in overhead, no doubt carrying some poor sod whose war had come to a painful end on a lonely desert highway. I could also see a couple of Marine Corps choppers out in the distance, a CH-46 and an escorting Cobra – a busy day in the sky, although the ubiquitous Blackwater 'Little Birds' were nowhere to be seen.

On the corner leading down to the river and the 'CSH' or 'cash', Combat Support Hospital, I could just about make out the shell of the Ba'ath Party HQ where Saddam had built his underground bunker, the dictator knowing in his subconscious that one day he'd be blasted out of office.

The old HQ was now overshadowed by a new recreation centre. The US was good at exporting Americana for its troops abroad. In every theatre I had been in, US bases were popular destinations for iconic brands of burgers and pizza. You could find most things in the PX/AAFES, but this was the first time I had seen a shopping mall built in a war zone. I looked forward to a quick tour through the shops before I left.

The new 100-acre US Embassy rising above the Tigris had the appearance of a prison, the construction cranes on the roof like giant vultures gazing out at the earth-walled houses of the city below. The complex is a fortress within the fortress, like Saddam's bunker, but so much larger, the largest embassy in the world – in fact, as big as the Vatican City.

I could already imagine the air-conditioned comfort within, the cinemas, restaurants, pools, gyms, hairdressers, parks and schools that would be 500m and an infinity away from the apocalyptic death zone outside, where my friend Sammy and his family were in hiding.

Why the United States needed to build its largest embassy in the world in Baghdad was the subject of endless rumour and argument, although all that untapped oil buried below the desert may have had something to do with it. The cost of construction was getting up to a $1 billion, the money allocated from the emergency Iraq budget agreed in Congress.

I don't want to seem cynical, but when I got to speak to the Iraqis in the coming days, they saw this architectural monstrosity as the symbol of who actually runs their country and, more important, an indication of how long they intended to stay. Americans have two eyes, an Iraqi friend told me, one on the natural resources and the other on their strategic position.

Iraq is encircled by Iran, Syria, Turkey and Jordan, and is just a short hop to Saudi Arabia and Israel.

On Iraq's eastern border lies Iran and, beyond Iran, Afghanistan. With its nuclear aspirations, support for Hezbollah in Lebanon and elsewhere globally, and a more cloudy but nonetheless cordial relationship with Hamas (Islamic Resistance Movement) militants in Gaza and Syria, Iran had been a pain in the dark places of US foreign policy for decades. Maintaining a secure presence in Iraq and Afghanistan wasn't merely logical, it almost looked planned.

There was talk of standing down the troops. But standing down in this instance simply meant getting the soldiers off the streets. No one in Baghdad, from the US officers to the gossips in the market place, believed for a moment that those 100 acres of fortified US facilities was anything but a state-of-the-art platform for the US presence in the area.

Most observers consider the post-war phase of Operation Iraqi Freedom a costly, catastrophic disaster. But a lot of Iraqis I have spoken to don't see it that way at all. They could not believe the most powerful country on earth was governed by a bunch of bungling, disorganized idiots (their words, not mine). On the contrary, they view the chaos as a punishment, a carefully conceived strategy devised by Donald Rumsfeld, his deputy Paul Wolfowitz and the Pentagon hawks.

I was amused to hear that the rationale behind this theory was that they believed the 'punishment' was in revenge for the 'massive defeat' inflicted on the US by Saddam in the first Gulf War, a victory they honestly believed in. After all, this 'Mother of All Battles' had lost the elder President Bush and his Republican Party a second term in office. To a nation used to nepotism and the corruption of power, it was no surprise that George Bush Junior was (a) the present President of the United States and (b) determined to wipe the stain of defeat from his family name.

For Iraqis, the war wasn't a war at all. The combined-arms blitzkrieg with which in only three weeks Coalition Forces inflicted military defeat on a country that had fought the numerically superior Iranians for eight years was, to Iraqis, literally incredible. The subsequent looting was a passionate and hysterical release of euphoria in their newfound 'freedom', a barbaric orgy while GIs stood by in their sunglasses watching thieves walk out of ruined hospitals with MRI scanning machines and from the museum with precious 6,000-year-old sculptures.

American and British bombing had taken out infrastructure as required in order to achieve military victory in the field. The mobs were allowed to strip the buildings down even to the doors, windows and wiring, taking Baghdad, and many other cities, back into the Middle Ages. As far as the locals were concerned, that had been the US plan from the beginning.

'This is no accident. I know,' I remember Sammy saying. 'They destroy Baghdad as a warning to the world. Mr Rumsfeld, he clever man.'

Sammy liked to play the fool, but I had learned that words of wisdom often came from his lips.

When asked why US troops didn't stop the lawlessness in Baghdad, Rumsfeld famously replied: 'Stuff happens . . . and it's untidy and freedom's untidy, and free people are free to make mistakes and commit crimes and do bad things.'

It sounded like quirky, good ol' boy honesty on Fox News, but it didn't play the same way to viewers in the Arab world watching Al Jazeera.

'We know,' said Sammy.

People in London – Washington too, I assume – were still obsessing about the legality of the war. Me included. But now I was back, I could see that this was irrelevant to the Iraqis.

What they wanted from the Coalition was fresh water, electricity and security. After that, they wanted the rule of law – even Saddam had managed that – and jobs so that they could support their families. Three years after Saddam fell they were still waiting, and it was a comfort to me that there were American officers like Mad Dog inside the Green Zone who saw that, beyond the politics, beyond their own promotions, was a community that had suffered thirty years of Saddam dictatorship and were suffering still after three years of calculated chaos or unprecedented incompetence, depending on which side of the T-walls you happened to be sitting.

Colonel Steve 'Mad Dog' McQueen, hair thinner, face more ravaged, eyes as keen as ever, was waiting for us at the bus stop as the Humvees rolled in.

'Go say hi,' said Cobus. 'I'll get your bag out of the other wagon.'

I grabbed Mad Dog's hand and we both grinned wildly at each other. It was fantastic to see him again. This was a man who had stood at my shoulder under fire when our house had been attacked three nights in a row, had been in more tight spots with me than I cared to remember, and more importantly had a sense of humour, which I had found rare in US officers above the rank of major.

'Nice shirt,' he said, eyeing my floral ensemble with amusement. He waved his hand around. 'Welcome home. Baghdad missed you.'

I smiled crookedly because, the funny thing was, he was right. With so many familiar sights, just in the last hour or so, it actually did feel like coming home.

From my day sack, I fished out some sports magazines and a bottle of whisky each for Mad Dog and Cobus, which seemed to please them. I noticed the sergeant standing off to one side. Mad Dog beckoned her over. She was stunning and walked towards us with a swing of her hips that turned every male head within a hundred metres. My mouth went dry.

'James Ashcroft,' McQueen said. I'd already seen the name flash CARILLO stitched on to the front of her body armour. Now I got the rest. 'Please let me introduce Sergeant Tanya Carillo, my right hand.'

She stretched out her own right hand and met my most charming smile with a glacial scowl.

'Call me James,' I said.

'I'll call you Asshat,' she replied grimly. 'Nice shirt, you asshat. Does this look like Hawaii to you?'

'Ah . . .' I gaped blankly at her open hostility.

Then she cracked up, laughing at the expression on my face – perfect American teeth, a spark in her wide-set brown eyes, her hair a long, dark ponytail that hung over one shoulder in a distinctly un-military fashion that I approved of.

'Colonel McQueen told me to bust your balls,' she added, her generous mouth in a wide grin, 'but I can't keep a straight face.'

'I was hoping you'd last longer than five goddamn seconds,' Mad Dog muttered in the background.

As we shook hands, I was sure she held on a fraction longer than was needed, and she held my gaze until I looked away.

I had already noticed that McQueen and Carillo were wearing helmets and body armour. In fact so was everyone else around me. I had dismissed it as a new regulation dress code that had been introduced during my absence. Previously everyone had wandered around the Green Zone in shirts and jackets.

'Has there been an increase in the threat level recently?' I knocked Mad Dog on his chest plate as we started walking towards the embassy entrance.

'Yeah, we just started receiving a load of IDF every evening. They normally start around 18:30 so we probably best get you inside.'

I glanced down at my Kobold – it was 5.30pm. I looked up to make a joke and saw Cobus freeze, his head cocked up, looking to the south. He seemed to be straining to hear something, but with the idling engines of the Humvees we could hardly hear ourselves talk.

I flinched as a colossal explosion rocked the traffic circle up at the junction of the 14 July Bridge 200m away. A huge cloud of smoke and dust rose up and shrapnel clattered over the concrete of the ceremonial archway and pinged off the metal statues of Iraqi soldiers in the centre of the circle.

Everyone's head whipped around, each looking for the explosion and asking themselves the same question, VBIED or mortar? If the insurgents had managed to get a VBIED through the front checkpoint that was very bad news. It was bad enough that they were landing mortars and rockets inside the Green Zone.

I remembered an attack the year before when a Katyusha rocket punched straight into the main-office hall in the embassy, bounced off the floor and back out through the roof without exploding. Three people were injured and one poor woman killed, a contracting officer, who was physically hit by the rocket and virtually torn apart as she was picked up and hurled across the hall by the impact.

I had been looking directly at the traffic circle and was aware that it was a mortar. It was huge, too, at least an 81mm. Cars veered crazily off the road and the few pedestrians hit the deck or ran for cover. Only one lone LAV hummed along obliviously. Within its armoured shell the crew was unconcerned about shrapnel.

We all ran for cover. It was chaos, bodies everywhere, like the start of the London marathon. The Humvees were the heavy armoured versions; they just slammed the doors shut and the gunners dropped down inside. The rest of us piled into ditches and under the concrete

'U's that had been conveniently spaced out around the car park for just such an eventuality. I moved quickly. I remembered clearly the last time I had been there a mortar had come down next to our house and blown some poor bastard driver's legs off as he stood next to his car.

As I dropped into a ditch, I turned and was knocked flat on my back by Tanya coming in after me; who, to be fair, had been thrown in bodily by Cobus. She lay full length on top of me, our faces inches apart, both of us open-mouthed in surprise, and I was just thinking it's a shame we were both wearing body armour when, a split second later, Cobus landed on top of Tanya like a pile-driver and pancaked us both with a sickening crunch.

Six foot three of heavy Afrikaner wearing his armour and full combat load must have weighed 300 pounds, and the shock drove all the air from my lungs. Nose to nose with me, Tanya's eyes bulged until they nearly popped out and her face was suffused with blood. She gurgled something incoherently. I couldn't feel my legs. I tried to explain that I needed to breathe but only a weak hiss came out.

'Yisss! That was a big one,' Cobus said. He slid off and wedged in next to me, waving a bottle in my face. 'Don't worry, man, I saved the whisky.'

I glared at him silently and suppressed the overpowering urge to vomit my lungs out.

Then he looked at the two of us. Tanya's head had flopped down on my shoulder in what would have otherwise been a gesture of fond affection.

'Fark, you two seem to be getting on together. You don't waste any time, hey Ash?'

'Unnh,' grunted Tanya.

I couldn't even manage that.

There was one more explosion further away, then two more in the distance. Silence fell, other than the idling engines of the Humvees.

'Urgh.' Tanya pushed herself off my chest to sit on my legs. She scowled at Cobus. 'What did you eat for breakfast, cement?'

I heard Mad Dog talking to someone and guessed he was at the other end of the trench. After a couple of minutes of silence people were looking out of their holes and from around vehicles.

'Guess that's it for the moment. Let's move it before the queue at the checkpoint builds up again.' Mad Dog's head appeared, blocking my view of the clouds. He leaned down and helped me up.

Cobus had my Bergen with him so we jogged over straight away to the Marine and Gurkha checkpoint to unload our weapons into the drum and get our passes checked. Everyone else started emerging from cover.

'Kept my whisky safe!' Mad Dog grinned like a schoolboy and passed his bottle to Cobus to carry through, since US military have a strict no-alcohol policy.

We walked around the side of the palace building to the accommodation cabins at the back. Row after row of container housing units, or 'CHU's, stretched out behind Saddam's swimming pool, each one surrounded by a wall of sandbags. Many of the sandbags had frayed and degraded because of the sunlight and leaked sand copiously, so that the walls lost their shape and sagged pathetically. Four years into the war and labour gangs of Iraqis were still being escorted in and out by US soldiers to perform sandbag-filling details. I am sure that each night they went home with their day's pay in US dollars to be debriefed by the insurgent commanders as to the exact location of military and sensitive emplacements within the Green Zone.

'You are staying in here with me just for tonight, Ash,' said Cobus as he unlocked a doorway and dumped my Bergen just inside. He pulled out a couple of folding deckchairs. 'I normally share with a Dutch officer. He finished his tour last week and his bunk is free until tomorrow or the day after when they allocate someone else.'

'Then where? And where are all of us going to sleep? Remember there are Seamus, Dai and probably Les as well.' I knew that Cobus would have sorted something out.

'The old American Special Forces villa by the river, you remember?'

Of course I remembered. We had known these guys for over a year, two different teams of Green Berets, one after the other, and when our house had been stormed by our own mutinous guards, it had been the SF villa that we had used as our emergency rendezvous.

'I am still in touch with the guys there,' continued Cobus, 'doing them favours and such like. It's a different team now from when you were here last, but all good guys. They are expecting you.'

Cobus unfolded the chairs between two faded sandbag walls and indicated that Tanya and I should sit down. He and McQueen perched on the corner of a stack of sandbags and both lit a cigarette.

'Welcome to my office,' Mad Dog said distractedly, and waved away the smoke. 'I've got to stop these things before I get home.'

It reminded me of Hendriks, these giants of men afraid of nothing but their wives. Maybe we all need something to be afraid so we don't forget we're not bulletproof.

'Cobus must have filled you in,' McQueen said.

'Not yet,' I said.

The two men exchanged glances.

'I'm making a courtesy call in Basra day after tomorrow for a couple of days,' Mad Dog continued. 'That'll give you time to see Sammy. You've got your team?'

'I've got confirmation from Dai and Seamus. I'm waiting on Les.'

'That's great. That's four of you, plus Sammy and Cobus, and I can lend you two of my sergeants. You'll meet them later. That makes at least eight of you, plus Sammy's brother if he is any good. More than enough. Cobus and Sergeant Carillo will handle the logistics,' he added. 'Anything you need, just tell them.'

Tanya smiled in acknowledgement. Our eyes met for a moment. I liked the arched lift of her eyebrows, as if she were studying a view.

'We already have three SUVs, and I have three sets of maps, plus all the waypoints plotted into my GPS. When you come up to the office you can plug into my laptop and download them on to yours.'

McQueen sighed. 'Monday already,' he said. 'We're set for your trip to Mosul Friday. Four days.'

'Plenty of time,' I responded.

He puffed away on his cigarette. For a fifty-six-year-old colonel, McQueen looked fit still, but there were bags under his eyes. He seemed listless.

A silence hung over our little group.

I broke it just to keep the conversation going. 'How are things out there?'

'Worse,' he replied. 'It has to get worse before it can get better.'

'We read in the papers the surge is working.'

'It is working. We were getting our asses kicked before, and now our guys aren't being harassed as much. But the Shi'ites are seizing power and crushing anyone who gets in their way.'

'Is Sammy in their way?' I asked him.

'He's a reminder of the past,' McQueen answered. 'You remember what Machiavelli said. The prince has to kill all his enemies if he's going to become king.'

'And who's the prince?'

'The man in black, our old friend Muqtata al-Sadr,' he replied.

'You think the order comes from al-Sadr?'

'No. No. No.' McQueen shook his head. 'While it's going crazy out there every man and his dog is settling old scores.'

'And Colonel Ibrahim's writing the death warrants?'

'That's the intel,' McQueen replied, glancing again at Cobus. 'Sammy's in a safe house with the family. Cobus will take you out there tomorrow.'

Cobus stood and the look he exchanged with Mad Dog suddenly made him look tired too. Cobus had been in Iraq for over three years and the liaison role he performed for McQueen must have put him out on the streets of Baghdad nearly every day. He was McQueen's eyes and ears in the city, a mission fraught with any number of dangers and too important to be compromised.

While most senior brass came to Iraq to oil their way up the greasy pole, Mad Dog was covertly looking out for the interpreters and informers who had laid their lives on the line supporting Coalition Forces and were now being abandoned by the Americans and British alike.

It was an issue that would disgust every soldier from Coalition nations who had served in Iraq. After the fall of Saddam and the liberation of the country from the Ba'athist regime, dozens, then hundreds of English-speaking Iraqis had signed up to act as interpreters, a resource desperately needed by every unit down to company and platoon level across the entire country.

Almost universally men, these unarmed Iraqis risked their lives every day on patrol with Coalition Forces, facing the same danger from gunfire and IEDs as did the Coalition troops. They then faced the additional danger of finishing their working day and having to go home unprotected, often to places where the local community might take revenge on them for aiding the invader. If identified as collaborators their entire family was at risk as well.

I had lost count of the number of horror stories I had heard of the chilling retribution carried out on interpreters and their relatives by the militias. Entire families, down to the children, would have their throats cut, women raped, the men tortured bestially before execution. I had read one report of a man having his face cut off with piano wire before he and his family were executed. It was anyone's guess as to whether they had made the family watch his torture and death first; more likely the other way around, they would have made him watch the deaths of his wife and children before killing him. There were even instances where the death squads had turned up to butcher the interpreter and, finding that he had escaped, had slaughtered the neighbours, just to set an example.

After three years many Iraqis who had worked for the CF, or even the new Iraqi government, were having to quit their jobs and move to different cities to save their lives and the lives of their loved ones. They had been betrayed in the cruellest of bureaucratic ironies. Due to the 'Iraqification' process – the daunting and illogical step of handing over all reconstruction efforts and entities to the control of the Iraqi government – the US government had overlooked several small matters.

The least of these was handing over control and management of any hospital or infrastructure project, government ministry or other entity. Everything handed over took on the same pattern – all current management were sacked so that relatives of the head man could take their jobs, regardless of whether they could perform those roles, or even read or write. The grudges resulting from this, both real and imagined, inspired rival militias to ever more frenzied fratricidal killings of their fellow Iraqis.

Another key issue is that when those entities were handed over, so were the administrative functions and paperwork, including material from the human-resources department. The Americans and British naïvely assumed that the new management would want to keep using the same workforce and focus on keeping the entities running, as opposed to concentrating on wiping out any opposition and enriching themselves.

The lack of thought put into the handover of the human-resources data was an inexcusable failure of operational security. It meant, for example, that if you were a Shia minister in charge of a new department, you now had all these neat and comprehensive files of the personal details of all of your enemies, the Sunni employees who had been 'collaborating' all these years with the American occupiers.

After the bulk of 'Iraqification' had been achieved in 2005, many military, State Department and DoD mandarins had slapped themselves on the backs for achieving the handover by the dates set by the Pentagon and White House. The majority knew that it was going to turn into a circus, but had no choice but to follow orders – whether they wanted to or not, the running of Iraq had to be handed over to its own people. The country, and Baghdad in particular, had then exploded.

Requests to the US and UK for asylum or refugee status from men who had faced the dangers of years of combat on behalf of the CF, who had been ostracized by their communities and who feared for their family's safety, were *all* declined. Bitter and abandoned, interpreters fled their homes. Untold numbers were caught by militias, they and their families killed. Letters of support and furious requests from high-ranking Coalition military officers were ignored by the US and UK governments back home in a shameful breach of trust and a total abrogation of responsibility.

Even according to conservative estimates, between 2004 and 2005 the average number of civilians killed per day had risen from twenty-three to thirty-six. Ask any liberal anti-war Westerner and they will assume these deaths are attributable to Coalition Forces. Ask anyone who has actually been to Iraq and they know that the vast majority are due to Iraqis fighting or murdering other Iraqis.

In 2006 this figure would double to an incredible average of seventy-two civilian deaths *every day of the year* with nearly 80 per cent due to executions and with over half these deaths in Baghdad itself.

Where my friend Sammy and his family were in hiding.

Mad Dog came to his feet. The briefing was over.

'Thanks for the ride in from the airport, by the way,' I said. 'I enjoyed the VIP treatment.' I knew that it was extremely unusual for the very busy CF to spare a patrol to pick up some random civilian contractor and I wondered what strings Mad Dog had pulled.

Colonel McQueen and Cobus exchanged looks, then the Colonel threw up his big shoulders in a shrug. 'I don't want to let the air out of your ego, Ash, but Cobus was dropping someone off.'

'You have good timing,' added Cobus with a rare smile.

'Speaking of which, it's a good time to get some food,' said McQueen. 'Anyone hungry?'

We trooped off in file. I followed Tanya Carillo along the corridor. The walls were temporary and swayed as we marched along.

I kept chatting, laying on the charm, and managed to draw out of her that she had three older brothers who were all anti-army. Tanya had enlisted to pay her way through college and couldn't get out until she'd cleared the debt; thousands of soldiers were in the same position.

She leaned back and whispered to me huskily. 'Back out there in the ditch? That was the closest I've been to a man for a long time,' she said.

I found that very hard to believe. I remembered Dai Jones's famous calculation that there were 100m of cock for every available woman in the Green Zone – and in Iraq 10,000 guys for every pretty girl. Being close to death gets the libido going, and it was astonishing on my first day back in Iraq that one of the most attractive women I'd ever seen in my life was coming on to me at that moment.

CHAPTER 8

I T WAS MIDNIGHT, the dull thud of mortars distant, hammering a different part of the city. I was in bed, in my section of the container, unable to sleep. I was thinking about the tasks and days that lay ahead, and also pondering the intriguing conundrum that was Tanya Carillo. Bearing in mind that I had only just left Krista, I felt guilty fancying the hell out of another woman, vaguely cross that that I'd let her slip through my fingers, and comforted that I hadn't been unfaithful, except in my head.

Before Cobus had organized the accommodation, Tanya had planned to book me into the Al-Hamra, a hotel that had the kudos of being outside the safety zone. The hotel was a feature-less, shell-peppered, ten-storey block of cement 200m from a fortified watchtower in a street guarded by a fleet of Humvees, but it appealed to aid-agency workers who wanted to remain independent of the Coalition, and journalists digging out the *real* story of Iraq. It was at the Al-Hamra, or the Palestine, another flophouse near by, where I had thought I might find a PSD who could spare two days to go along for the ride if Les was out of reach.

My first tasking with the Spartan team had been to bring Associated Press reporter Lori Wyatt from BIAP to the Green Zone. We'd come under contact from a ragged band of insurgents as we were entering the CPA gate and Lori had spent the entire gunfight spreadeagled below Les Trevellick, her dedicated bodyguard. They exchanged numbers, and Les for the following four weeks spent free afternoons in her room, exploring the deeper aspects of the British-American special relationship.

Although I had met Tanya in the same way, shortly before a contact, I had played a less heroic role than Les, who had protected his glamorous journalist with his own body whilst coolly returning fire and killing hordes of insurgents. I, on the other hand, had only lain at the bottom of a ditch for Tanya, and that fat bastard Cobus, to use as a crash mat.

Tanya Carillo must have assumed that the Al-Hamra was the kind of place where gun-slinging contractors preferred to hang out. My own memories of the Al-Hamra were more mundane, swimming in the pool at the regular Thursday-night parties and the much-photographed sign at reception: 'Please check your weapons at the desk.'

It made me wonder just what horror stories Cobus and Mad Dog had been telling her about me. They were both straight guys, I reasoned, and had probably done their best to contain their evil sense of humour. It occurred to me that I would only have a day or two with Tanya to stitch up Seamus and Les before they arrived and their charm offensive began.

It was disorientating to be back in Baghdad, and I lay on my thin mattress, thinking back over the events of the day. We'd survived unscathed from the bombardment outside the US Embassy car park. From the reactions of the others, I could tell it had been a daily event, a reminder that insurgents were out there, and could reach in at will. They didn't have to defeat the Americans, they just had to make them pay an unacceptable price for their presence, continue the dripping-tap torture of killings, maiming, suicide bombs, IEDs, sapping the morale of the occupiers and their collaborators and undermining their will to continue.

We had piled into the chow hall on the ground floor after dropping our weapons and my bag off at Cobus's container. It's a funny thing, but when you're still covered in debris from nearly being blown up, your food tastes amazing. I ate a chilli burger with 'Freedom fries', same as Mad Dog. Tanya, sexy as hell with dust stripes on her cheeks, had cod fillets flown in from the Eastern Seaboard and Cobus – I could scarcely believe this – had taken a plate of roast lamb.

Before eating, Cobus closed his eyes briefly and mumbled a prayer. Mad Dog lowered his head, and Tanya gazed at me across the table, eyebrows raised in two precise arcs. There was a look of wildness about her, a look that told me this girl didn't want to sleep on her own, not tonight, not after our close encounter in the ditch. In my easily adaptable memory I was already editing my role in the matter to a far more macho one.

McQueen and Cobus were chomping away.

'Do you like fish, Ash?' she asked. 'You must try it.'

She put a small piece of cod on my plate. I rolled my eyes and made sounds of sheer delight.

'Mmm, tasty,' I said.

We smiled. There was a frisson, a definite chemistry. Without her helmet and body armour on she was more feminine – stunning, in fact – and the guys at the tables around us could barely keep their eyes off her.

We talked openly around the table. Colonel McQueen was one of those American officers who discussed politics without calling you a commie bastard if you disagreed with US foreign policy. He knew a lot of things had gone wrong in post-war Iraq, an obscene amount of taxpayers' money had vanished into corrupt hands – American as well as Iraqi. But he genuinely believed in the underlying value of change in the Middle East and wanted to do his part in trying to make things better.

My arrival inspired him to recount several anecdotes from the old days when he and a couple of guys in his team would dress in civilian clothes, get tooled up with AKs and spend their time with us around Baghdad, and Aradisa Idah in particular, our old neighbourhood in the south-east corner of the city. He had a selective memory regarding certain incidents – I certainly didn't remember them being as humorous as he did. Still, we didn't call him Mad Dog for nothing. I also didn't remember myself playing such a courageous role in some of the adventures. Even Cobus choked on his lamb at a couple of the more outrageous ones. Tanya lapped up the stories and my embarrassment with obvious relish.

'Really, Ash,' she breathed huskily and fluttered her eyelashes in a parody of admiration, 'you carried two hundred nuns to safety single-handed? That's *amaaaazing.*'

'Well, Mad Dog carried a couple, and ah, it was probably nearer just the hundred, um, possibly even down in the double digits . . .'

'That's so interesting.' Tanya paused thoughtfully. 'And I never even knew there were any nuns in Baghdad,' she said innocently. 'And I hear you even rescued the puppies as well?'

'Well, maybe they were orphans, not nuns, I can't remember clearly now, stress of combat you see. Of course we rescued the puppies. In a situation like that, one doesn't think of one's own safety. The training simply takes over, you know.'

'Yes, and then *back home in time for tea and medals.* I know the rest of the story. God, you guys are such bullshitters.' She laughed delightedly. 'You must think I was born yesterday.'

Actually much of that story had been true. I looked forward to showing her the photos of the puppies on my laptop and watching her eat her words.

One thing Tanya did take note of was the fact that, despite being a full colonel, Mad Dog had been taking unusual risks, spending time nearly every day for two years 'outside the wire', often driving around with only a couple of sergeants for self-defence. Although charmed at the thought of sharing such experiences, Tanya had too much common sense to want to risk her life for the sake of adventure.

When she remarked on it, Mad Dog leaned across the table to her. 'We haven't lost a colonel in this war yet, and I ain't gonna be the first,' he said, and I remember a chill running down my spine. Every soldier is superstitious and knows that it's never wise to tempt fate.

We continued talking for the best part of an hour and Tanya seemed as if she couldn't tear her eyes off me. Maybe there was something stuck in my teeth? We swigged from cans of ice-cold Coke, and I could hardly believe it when suddenly she placed her cutlery American-style slantwise across the plate and got to her feet.

'It's been a pleasure. Good night, guys,' she said, and was gone.

We stood briefly, and if Mad Dog and Cobus knew I'd been harbouring great expectations, they didn't show it. We finished our meal and I sat there wondering if it had been a come-on set up by Cobus and McQueen.

Cobus got a plate of Twinkies, which he ate distractedly one after the other as the conversation switched to the surge. McQueen believed it would have the desired effect in the long run, even if right then the streets were more precarious than ever.

In January President Bush had ordered the deployment of twenty thousand additional soldiers in five brigades to Baghdad, and the tour of four thousand marines in Anbar province had been extended. The role of these troops was to assist the newly trained Iraqi forces in securing hostile neighbourhoods, to protect the local population and leave Iraqi forces behind to maintain peace.

The plan had been opposed by both houses of Congress. Opponents argued that Iraq had become an unwinnable sectarian civil war, and that the cost and duration of the deployment was unclear and diverted resources from the battle against a resurgent Taliban in Afghanistan. Like the insurgents in Iraq, the Taliban had learned that they did not actually have to win the war, they just had to fight on and survive in their holes until the enemy was exhausted and went home.

As commander-in-chief, Bush held sway and the surge reinforcements sailed in February. Donald Rumsfeld had been axed in December 2006 and Robert Gates was now Secretary of Defense. Bush had also appointed a new commander of Coalition Forces, General David Petraeus, a straight-talking PhD graduate in international relations from Princeton whom McQueen had marked down as a potential future president.

The number of troops serving repeat tours was rising, and extending tours of troops already in country had serious if predictable effects on morale. By the time an American infantryman had been in Afghanistan and was on his third tour of Iraq, he knew the statistics were weighing against him and was focused on staying alive. These troops were serving out their time, keeping their heads down, and they weren't signing on again once their time was up. But with a new general and the will to bring in surge troops to destroy the insurgents decisively, everyone was feeling the new sense of commitment in the air.

That isn't to say that the situation had not improved by spring 2007. It had. In Anbar, the most volatile province a year earlier, the marines were holding the ring and a fragile peace had settled on Ramadi, the capital, after Sunni sheikhs finally decided to reject the al-Qaeda-led insurgency in what had become known as the Awakening – *Sahwa* in Arabic.

As the former masters under Saddam Hussein, the Sunni had put up the fiercest opposition to the invasion. While they continued to live in biblical poverty, they were aware that in those other parts of the country where the Iraqi people had reached an understanding with the Americans, Shias and Kurds were now enjoying the benefits of reconstruction.

The followers of *Sahwa,* later dubbed the Sons of Iraq by

Coalition Forces, would in time be counted as allies in the struggle against al-Qaeda and Shia militants, and be paid and armed by the Americans. The Americans had followed the same strategy during the resistance war against the Russians in Afghanistan and armed the *mujahideen*, those swashbuckling freedom fighters reborn as the Taliban once they were in power.

The Sunni had boycotted regional elections and referenda in 2005. After *Sahwa*, they began to engage in the political process and largely accepted the results of the 2006 general election that saw the Shia political leader Nouri al-Maliki sworn in as prime minister. Hundreds of small parties had competed in the election, which turned out to be as democratic as one could hope for in a country with no tradition of democracy and where women do as they're told or get a backhander.

Al-Maliki was a modest, quietly spoken man who seemed reasonable and governed as a lion tamer governs a ring of lions in the circus – cautiously and knowing that he may get eaten at any moment.

Mad Dog believed the real power behind the Shia wasn't al-Maliki, and it wasn't the Iranian-born cleric Ayatollah Ali al-Sistani. It was Muqtada al-Sadr.

'The Iraqi Scarlet Pimpernel,' he said. 'They seek him here, they seek him there . . .'

Al-Sadr had gone to ground as the surge got under way in mid-February. Coalition chiefs wanted to believe he had fled to Iran, or Najaf, his clan base 16km south of Baghdad. Mad Dog believed he had remained in Sadr City all the time and was proved right on 25 February when a suicide bomb killed forty people in a student college and al-Sadr went public to announce that he was 'withdrawing his support' from the security crackdown.

Al-Sadr wasn't just some charismatic young punk with a scruffy beard and a black turban. He was believed by his Shia followers to be a direct descendant of the Twelfth Imam of Shia tradition, a living saint to the one-and-a-half million people crushed into

Sadr City, the Shia slum in the north-east of Baghdad once called Saddam City and renamed in honour of Muqtada's uncle, the martyred anti-Saddam cleric Muhammad Bakir al-Sadr.

Apart from being a saint with a bloodline going back to the Prophet, al-Sadr was the head of the Mahdi Army, a force of ten thousand well-armed followers that had grown from the body of students who had been with al-Sadr at seminary college before the invasion. After the fall of Baghdad, the Mahdi Army, uniformed in black with green headbands, filled the security vacuum in a string of southern Iraqi cities; they prevented looting in Sadr City and provided assistance to Shias who had suffered in the bombardment. By 2007, in Shia areas throughout the country the Mahdi Army was operating what was in effect a shadow government.

It was – by design or coincidence – in Sadr City that General Petraeus launched the surge, as I'd read in *The Times* online in Africa. Al-Sadr had not disappeared, 'fled to Iran', but was quietly watching and had tacitly supported the surge in order to prevent all-out civil war.

As far as I could see, he was continuing to play the long game. Once there is a pacified Iraq, once every cent of aid and reconstruction money has been sucked out of the US Treasury, in five years, or ten years, Iraq will drop all pretences of democracy – it does not exist except as a façade in *any* Arab country, with the possible exception of Lebanon – and become an Islamic republic like Iran, with Muqtada al-Sadr as president. The war, the deaths, the oil, the largest US Embassy in the world, all will have been in vain.

In the Pentagon, in the State Department, in Whitehall, no one before the invasion in April 2003 could see the big picture – myself and everyone on the ground in Iraq included. Iraq is too complex, too labyrinthine, too Byzantine. Its divisions are tribal, multi-faith, multi-ethnic; they go back to Mohammed and beyond to Mesopotamia and the beginning of human history.

I had already forgotten the myriad tribal details of Iraq and most of my Arabic during my last year in a semi-deliberate effort to fill up my memory with new details of African tribes and African wars.

But what that all meant to me was that lifting Sammy and his family from a safe house and joining the convoy going up to Mosul was going to be that much harder with the spike of violence between the US surge and the insurgents, and with the Sunni militias fighting al-Sadr's Mahdi Army, each jockeying for position in the aftermath of the surge.

Secretly, and I would want to check with Sammy first, I worried that with Anbar province turning hostile to the al-Qaeda foreign fighters, would they retreat to the north, and would Mosul be a worse place for Sammy to move to?

If that were not enough, the suicide bomb on 25 February revealed that the city was a powder keg and, more disturbing, it was a young woman who had strapped on a vest packed with explosives and detonated herself in the corridor at the Baghdad Economy and Administration College. Most of the forty dead and sixty injured were students studying economy and administration in a land desperate for economists and administrators.

There was nothing new about female suicide bombers in Iraq. The first came in April 2003 when two women, one of them pregnant, blew up their car at a Coalition checkpoint, killing themselves and three US soldiers. What was more alarming was that, since then, attacks by women had increased to about twenty a year, and the number was still growing.

At first we had attributed the phenomenon of female suicide bombers to one of the bizarre aberrations found in war zones. The aberration was largely forgotten when insurgents started using children as human bombs. The trend died out, thank God, but the number of female martyrs continued to increase at a bewildering tempo.

A large number of women who had been widowed during the

war, or had been both widowed and lost their children, had a burning desire for revenge. But what puzzled many observers was the frequency of teenage girls who had died as suicide bombers. Among these twisted sisters were the young and educated, girls devoted to the war against the Zionist crusaders who saw their sacrifice as a mark of jihadi chic. In a society based on institutionalized inequality and backwardness, for some it was a kind of female empowerment. I'd heard girls who like to go topless say the same thing.

Cobus had learned from the Iraqi Police, and informed the rest of us years before the story broke in the Western media, that the most horrific reason why some young women were strapping on explosive vests was because insurgent commanders – mostly foreign al-Qaeda fighters, it has to be said – were marrying rural teenagers, taking them back to their bases and leaving them alone to be gang-raped by their men.

There is no greater sin for a Muslim woman than having sex, even forced sex, with a man other than her husband. She is not an innocent; on the contrary, she has disgraced her father, mother and Islam. Upon his return the girl's 'husband' would feign anger and threaten to return her to her village under the shameful stigma of adultery and there she would be killed by her own relatives for dishonouring the family.

Traumatized, brutalized and immature, it was then very easy for someone to persuade the girl that the only way to redeem herself was through the ultimate act of jihad – a martyr mission. Often the recruiters were religious leaders and elder women committed to the insurgency.

I remember Seamus and Les and the others being sickened when Cobus told us what was going on. I was more depressed that in the name of religion such evil could surface.

After the Iran–Iraq War there were huge numbers of Iraqi women forced into prostitution simply through poverty. In a patriarchal society where many wives had never worked or developed sellable skills, if there was no extended family to look after you, a newly widowed woman had few options to support her children.

In this current war, with thousands upon thousands killed, I could imagine the rage and anguish that came to these widows of dead husbands and mothers of dead children. In the midst of that despair, with only a lifetime of prostitution to look forward to, then perhaps being a suicide bomber against those responsible did not seem such a bad option.

I only wondered that we had not seen more of them.

CHAPTER 9

BACK IN THE old days when I was working for Spartan we usually moved about Baghdad covertly in a packet of at least two discreetly armoured cars, blending in with the local traffic and staying within a couple of cars' distance of each other – not too close to be recognized as travelling together, yet close enough to give covering fire, ram other vehicles, whatever was needed if we found trouble, or if trouble found us.

Each man was armed with a rifle and pistol, and each car had a spare AK for guests and a machine-gun, either an RPD or PKM, and later a Minimi. In addition to the spare ammunition in our packs and in the cars, our body armour was covered in pouches stuffed with ammo, minimum twelve magazines per man and six hundred rounds in belts per gun.

Hopefully any gunfight would not need to be that long. Many PSD after-action reports I had seen had detailed contacts and rolling firefights that had often lasted for hours. Our main objective would be to break contact, extract as fast as possible and call in help. We had four types of comms for this purpose: personal VHF radios, mobile phones, satellite phones and vehicle-mounted VHF. When we went more high-profile in the countryside, we would also have vehicle-mounted HF with big giveaway antennas mounted on welded brackets.

Our most powerful defence, however, was our morning intelligence brief over maps and aerial photos from our local Iraqi staff, who would collate all the morning local gossip and potential enemy sightings and give us real-time warnings about what areas and roads to avoid for the day. In addition we would send out half a dozen random cars of Iraqis armed with radios, who would report routes clear for us as they drove around the city. There was little chance of betrayal, since even they did not know which car we would be following, if any.

Travelling in convoy, the front passenger of the lead vehicle would be on the radio giving a running commentary of what lay ahead to the guys in the second wagon – kamikazes, lunatics weaving a path down the wrong side of the road; potential IEDs concealed in rubble, dead animals, plastic bags; bearded men in *shemaghs* with tubes over one shoulder – either insurgents with an RPG or plumbers on their way to work. However, plumbers and carpet salesmen both had stopped walking around like that after a series of unfortunate reactions from the CF to these false alarms.

Today, though, as we set off to visit Sammy in his safe house, there were just the two of us in an unarmoured car and no back-up. Cobus was at the wheel of a Nissan Patrol and I sat at his side with the muzzle of my AK resting on the dash, the safety selector set to automatic. He drove with demonic concentration, his ice-blue eyes reading the road and the surroundings as if it was an abstract painting he was trying to fathom.

We were partially concealed from the side view by the smoky windows, but through the windscreen we must have appeared like a PMC recruiting poster with our suntans and fancy shades. The shades weren't just for looking good. There was no point taking the risk of being blinded by glass fragments if an IED or bullets blew the windows in. If there's one thing worse than being blind at the wheel of a fast car, it's being blind in the middle of a gunfight.

Cobus used the side mirrors and had angled the rear-view mirror to the passenger side so that I could use it to watch for any bad guys approaching from behind. Many PSD vehicles had two rear-view mirrors, one each for the driver and passenger.

Traffic clogged three lanes, cars sitting on your rear bumper honking and edging into every space. The air was thick with fumes and I was surprised to see so many people on the streets. The Iraqis are a hardy lot. They had carried on under Saddam Hussein and they carried on now as if life was normal, and I suppose the abnormal after four years of conflict had become normal: food shortages, electricity cuts, the omnipresent thud of gunfire, Humvee patrols on the ground and Blackhawks hammering through the sky above.

Despite the chilly weather, street traders with goods on makeshift tables had set up shop and were conducting brisk business under the overhanging arcades below blocks of flats and offices. Men in rags sold knotty vegetables, bright-coloured herbs and spices that spilled from the mouths of open sacks, electrical gear, seditious T-shirts, doll sets and plastic guns from China, chickens flapping in small cages, the meat being hacked from bloody carcasses like scenes from hell in medieval paintings. Sheep were held down and butchered on the street in full view of the rest of the flock, munching stolidly and unimaginatively on the rubbish and scrub next to the highway.

There was a steady trade in satellite dishes and DVDs. Iraqi men don't work, not more than a few hours a day if they can help it. They grow moustaches and soft bellies. They sit about in *chai* shops, smoking and drinking sweet tea and, when they're not thumping tables in heated debate, they are garrulous chatterboxes. The rumour mills never stop, the result of three decades of media censorship under Saddam. Gossip is the national sport and had been the fastest, sometimes only, way to get news. If Hajj pilgrims are slaughtered in Karbala or children are shot by a patrol in

Fallujah, people in the Baghdad coffee shops are discussing it ten minutes later.

It was mainly men out shopping, in groups for mutual protection. The danger of kidnapping was high and had become the number-one revenue stream for the militias and criminal gangs. With the Shia and Sunni at each other's throats, militant Islamists on both sides were using the chaos to push their own agendas, and every woman I did see that morning was wearing a headscarf, totally the opposite to the relatively religiously relaxed Iraqi capital I had known only a year before.

From the moment people got up in the morning until they went to bed at night, and even then, they were in danger. Every minute of every day and all through the dark hours of curfew you could hear gunfire, mortar, exploding grenades, wailing sirens, the thump and drone of Humvees and US armour clanking through the streets. Every day the people would ask themselves if there was something new to be afraid of – disease, drought, hunger, kidnap, the random death of their child.

Should they sell the house, bribe officials and flee to Jordan or Syria or Turkey? Or was it best to stay put, go to work, take the children to school, trade something for something else, speak to that neighbour who'd heard about a fresh supply of fuel or cooking oil or rice? Of course, don't forget that for single women there was always the option of prostitution; and for men, the militias, insurgents and criminal gangs all paid, if not well, then enough.

Only the desperate joined the Iraqi Army. After all, if you survived all the laborious push-ups, jogging, marching and numerous deranged exercises that kept a man from his God-given right to sit around all day smoking and drinking tea, the *Amerikeeyeh* might ask you to do something truly crazy, like go out and fight the insurgents.

If you were a Shi'ite, the civil service or Iraqi Police was a great career for anyone with the right connections, a relaxed moral stance towards corruption and an aggressive appetite for bribes. As a big plus, much of the job could be done sitting down.

From my experience in war zones around the world, even with hundreds dying every day, until it comes to visit death remains abstract. The people become numb to it. They tell themselves it's not going to happen to them, to their family. It's human nature to be positive, sanguine, to carry on, or simply to remain in denial.

Here in Iraq it was different. In this war, fear was an almost physical presence lying over the city. Nearly every family had some tale of personal tragedy to tell. Every community, every neighbourhood, every village had lost someone. Virtually any household would be able to name one or more relatives who had been killed. And they were sick of it, sick of living in fear, wondering if simply going out to buy bread for the family meal would get them kidnapped and killed. In this city of 7 million souls, there were 6.99 million who just wanted to get on with their lives, marry their daughters to a man with a job, buy a flat-screen telly and find current running through the wires when they flick the light switch.

'*Amerikaners*,' Cobus said, his first words since we'd left the Green Zone.

He changed lanes, cutting up the car behind, and the driver sat on his horn so long I was in half a mind to get out and give him a battering.

'Wanker.' I lowered my AK well out of sight.

Four Humvees hurtled by like a train with machine-gunners in armoured turrets scanning the crowds, the crossroads, the windows in the anonymous buildings lining the route, perfect for a pop shot. Machine-guns pointed front, left, right and back, and each man also had his M4 carbine ready for snap-shooting.

No one even noticed them, apart from the other drivers peeling out of their way.

'They're in a hurry to get home,' I said.

'*Ja*,' Cobus replied. He turned for a fraction and his cold blue eyes came to life.

His expression didn't change. It was as if his face was carved from stone. The grey creeping over his temples was the outward sign of deeper changes. Cobus had that weary look, the same as Mad Dog, the look that comes to men when they are trying to hold back the tide and the tide just keeps rising. Personally, I thought Mad Dog had been there too long, particularly as he regarded it as 'excellent news' that the Green Zone had been hit by only four mortars the previous day.

The phase following any conflict or coup is the most dangerous. It's the time when the more ambitious, ruthless men amongst the local movers and shakers are climbing over the dead to reach their goals. The Americans in Baghdad and the British in Basra had delayed this progression until the 'surge', an oddly fitting description for Bush's last throw of the dice.

The surge was designed to suppress Sunni al-Qaeda, the Shia Mahdi Army and the numerous insurgent groups that had been loosely unified confronting the invaders. Now the invaders were training Iraqi forces to take over policing the streets, the diverse groups were jockeying for power and far more innocent civilians than Coalition soldiers were getting slotted in the crossfire as the militants turned their guns on each other.

That period between 2003 and 2005 when we'd been building Task Force Fountain now seemed like a golden age. There had been an end in sight – the improvement of the water supply, and a new multi-ethnic Iraqi guard force in place to look after it. We'd taken raw recruits and turned them into soldiers – well, not soldiers in the sense that any Western army would recognize, but they had learned which end of a rifle was up, they worked as a team, and when the time had come, many of them had fought and died.

I was proud to have been one of the water boys. With generous funding from the US Treasury, Spartan had paid well, but I had never had any sense that we were exploiting the Iraqis. The bombing had destroyed large sections of the water network and we were making sure the insurgents didn't blow up the new mains as they were being laid.

That for me was the weakness of the insurgent ideology. They didn't care if they harmed their fellow Muslims and countrymen, denying them access to clean water, electricity, schools, women's rights, stability, security, jobs, food – all the basic building blocks of life. They wanted to show that the Great Satan's plan for democracy was against the ways of Islam and, to be honest, they were after power, pure unadulterated power.

Most of our Shia guards were now IP and their replacements would not have received the same training, a sorry situation for the water authority, as well as an additional risk to my team once we began the process of escorting Sammy and his family out of the city. The guards who had joined the police were loyal to Colonel Ibrahim. If we were spotted, it would be reported back up the line on the new American-funded comms in an instant. Ibrahim was a smart guy. If he had Sammy on a death list, he'd know exactly why we were back in Baghdad. Even worse, most of those guards could identify Sammy on sight.

Politics was infinitely nuanced and layered. The Pentagon neo-cons, when they were planning and executing the war, didn't for a moment consider that the Iraqis – Arabs in general – have a different social structure and a different way of approaching the most simple, everyday situations. Similarly neither did many of the reconstruction project managers. Even our own guards were out selling their uniforms, ammunition and vehicles. If petrol hadn't been so cheap they would have stolen that as well, and when there were shortages, we had had to place armed guards on our supply.

We weren't stupid. We had placed rival groups on the same shifts, to keep an eye on each other.

At least we lived and worked together with our employees. Most of the project managers in the Green Zone did not have that luxury, and I cannot even think how many millions of dollars were defrauded and embezzled in the multitude of scams that popped up amongst all the Iraqi projects. 'Ghost' employees who never existed but whose supervisors collected their salaries; real employees who never had to turn up in return for kicking back the supervisor 50 per cent; employees who sold their jobs in return for keeping 25 per cent of the pay; and even those sub-employees sub-contracting their jobs out to sub-sub-employees. And that's without including the money lost in procurement of materials and supplies.

The traffic thinned as we moved away from the centre. I could see the Dora oil refinery in the south of the city, a useful landmark with the tower topped by an eternal flame.

'Remember when we first got here and were always worried about getting lost in the city?' I turned to Cobus, who kept his eyes on the road.

'*Ja, ja*, you were a total *kak* driver, man, why do you think I am driving today?' Cobus answered.

Cobus hadn't left Iraq for more than a few weeks in the last four years and I guess was in no mood to reminisce about the good old days yet.

The apartment blocks had given way to three-storey concrete buildings, each one a small fortress with thick walls, ramparts surrounding flat roofs and narrow windows just right for a hidden sniper. The office buildings were concrete-grey, or sandy, and the residential houses were the same shade of pale sand as the desert beyond the city, the monotony broken by touches of colour from the tiled domes of mosques and the white minarets lancing the skyline. The palm trees that had survived the bombing had a surreal look about them, especially at night when the fronds danced in the wind and the city appeared to be populated by the spirits of the dead.

The road followed a long sweeping loop in the Tigris out to the peninsula. We turned into Karada, an area I knew, and it didn't surprise me that it was here that Cobus would have the best cover for covert operations. It was an area that both the MNF and Iraqis kept as secure as possible, and more importantly the only place where he could probably still nip in and out to buy booze and supplies.

Karada straddles both sides of the river and is one of the most affluent and best-integrated parts of Baghdad, with a mixed Shia, Sunni and – in small part – Christian population. The streets are laid out on a grid, many of the houses containing an inner court-yard and an extra floor that in a traditional Muslim house would be for the use of the women. It was in Karada that we used to buy overpriced goodies at the supermarket, paying with great bricks of Iraqi notes the shopkeeper fed into his electric counting machine.

'It was safe here last year,' Cobus said. 'The girls were going out without covering their hair.'

'What happened, the surge?'

'That as well. The Shi'ites are in the majority. They want to drive out their neighbours and take their houses.'

'I've seen the same all over.' I thought of the opportunistic civilians on the winning side in every war zone who flooded into abandoned towns and villages after the fighting to pick the best houses for themselves.

In Croatia and Bosnia it had been a regular weekend outing for families. They would pull up in front of nice-looking houses that hadn't been claimed yet, throw food through the doorways and then send dogs in first, in case those tricky Serbs had left any booby traps behind.

'Always the same,' Cobus said. 'We learn to love our fellow man but we love his property even more. You think there's going to be a settlement in Israel?'

'Not in my lifetime.'

'Not in anyone's lifetime.' He pulled in behind a truck loaded down with odd shapes, which I suddenly recognized as satellite dishes. The traffic stopped for a while and we were hemmed in by honking cars. I eyeballed a hostile young man in the car next to me until he eventually looked away.

We pulled away again. Cobus slowed as we passed the university – a Walter Gropius building mixing straight lines with traditional arches. It was completed in 1958, a date I recalled from school history because that was when twenty-three-year-old King Faisal II was overthrown by a group of Iraqi army officers, the coup paving the way twenty years later for Saddam Hussein.

There were students on the campus, running between classes, clutching files, their faces etched with that same desire for normality I'd seen in the city centre. In the end, it's the politicians who make war, the military executes it and the people suffer the consequences. An odd observation for a soldier? It's a simple truth. In the forces we aren't always dealt a good hand. We play with the cards we've got and do the best that we can. In Kosovo, Macedonia, Bosnia and a dozen African countries, NATO and the UN were often just trying to stop neighbours slaughtering each other. In Iraq now the war was winding down, Coalition Forces were doing the same. Maybe Cobus was right: we love our neighbour's property more than we love our neighbour.

In complete contrast to my grim train of thought, a wedding convoy streamed past, six or seven cars with windows open and Arab music blaring. The cars were absolutely stuffed with men, young and old, and kids and a couple of women, all laughing and singing, bombed on Sprite and Pepsi, waving at people as they passed. Two young men sat perched right up on the sills of the open windows filming over the tops of the cars, filming each other, the procession and the streets. Everyone smiled and waved at them.

Except me and Cobus.

Cobus pulled out his phone, pressed two keys. I heard it ring only twice before it was answered at the other end, with a tinny 'Hello?'

'*Salaam alaikum, ja,* it's me . . . *wahed dakaik, ziyen?*' One minute, OK?

I couldn't hear the reply, I was too busy looking out of the windows, covering my arcs, and checking the rear-view mirror to see if we were being tailed. This close to our destination I didn't want anyone following us in.

'*Goed,* see you soon. Hello.' He hung up.

I grinned, having forgotten how amusing I had found the Iraqi habit of saying 'hello' for goodbye on the phone. Cobus had obviously gone native.

We turned off into a side street and in two more turns we were deep in a residential area. Almost immediately, Cobus was pulling into a hurriedly opened gate and we parked up on the driveway inside the walled compound of a neat, two-storey house, out of sight of the road. The Nissan's engine shut off and in moments it was silent except for the birdsong. I glanced at my watch. It was coming up to ten. The smog was lighter by the river, the sky pale blue with ribbons of white cloud. Someone closed the gates behind us and we got out.

I'd been feeling on edge since I'd arrived back in Iraq. From the warm seas of Côte d'Ivoire to the crush of Baghdad, via a night with Krista in London, was a leap between extremes. Tanya Carillo had unsettled my equilibrium, and Cobus and Mad Dog had been so spare with their info I'd begun to feel as if I were in the wrong place at the wrong time. That if they were lifting Sammy out of Iraq, there should have been a way to do so without my involvement.

The moment I heard the birdsong in Karada, the muscles knotted across my back untied and the tightness in my gut disappeared.

I got out and was immediately engulfed in a huge embrace from Sammy.

'Hey, Sammy, you're fatter than ever. *Shlonek, ziyen?*'

'*Khullish ziyen, hamdillah!* Oh Mister James, it is very good to see you.' Sammy shook my hand manically and kissed me firmly on both cheeks in the Iraqi fashion.

We studied each other as we walked into the house together. Sammy looked a lot older, or maybe I hadn't remembered all the lines on his face, but his eyes had the same merry intelligent sparkle. I wondered what he was thinking about me. He was beaming away and wiping tears from his eyes.

'Welcome, welcome, please come in.' He gestured for me to enter the front room. 'You came.'

'I didn't have anything else to do.'

'You English . . .'

'Scots,' I reminded him.

He grinned, then became serious and waved a warning finger at me. 'I hear from Cobus, there are two childrens now, two girls,' he said. 'You have many responsible now.'

He looked at me pityingly, and I knew he was thinking how sad I must be not to have a son to leave in charge of the household when I was away.

'What's a life without responsibilities?' I said.

'Very good, Mister James. You are becoming an Arab.'

'Just James will do, Sammy,'

'*Na'am*, Mister James.'

We looked at each other and both broke out in enormous grins. Sammy was the same old Sammy, animated, gold hair sprayed in place, his white shirt neatly ironed.

We were in an old-fashioned kitchen with an iron stove and a motionless fan suspended from the ceiling. Brilliant light fell through the shutters on the small window and made stripes on the far wall.

On the table the delicacies in earthenware dishes made me feel guilty for those fleeting qualms about the task ahead. The food hadn't been prepared for the family. It had been prepared for me. Iraqis can be lazy, exasperating, and they may slit your throat without a second thought. On the other hand, they can be enterprising, adaptable and were often the most generous people I had met in the world.

We passed through the kitchen and climbed a flight of stairs into a living room where a row of Japanese prints was lit by the sun coming from an open window. I could smell incense – jasmine, I thought – and the dull odour of old dust in the Persian carpets. The room had ochre walls, low tables and big embroidered cushions with red and gold tassels. To one side, there was a carved chest with two sets of candelabra and a row of brass vases that sparkled in a band of bright light.

The family was lined up as if for a photograph, my gaze going from one to the next. They looked relieved but ground down.

'Captain Ashcroft,' Sammy said, and came to attention, playing the clown as always. 'British officer . . .' He beamed again. 'You remember my wife, Fara?'

Fara smiled as she offered me her hand. It was like a cold flower as it passed quickly across my palm. She was wearing a fitted maroon dress with a row of small buttons and a brightly coloured scarf that was tossed casually over one shoulder, perfectly modest but chic at the same time. She had studied French literature at the university and spent a year as an exchange student in Paris. She was the only woman I'd met in Iraq who spoke openly about the war and had her own point of view unfiltered through the opinions of her husband.

Now in her late thirties, as striking as ever, Fara had aged prematurely, the last few months of strain written in lines around her kohl-rimmed eyes. She was not the relaxed, friendly woman I remembered. Although obviously pleased to see me, she seemed distracted as we made our greetings. I leaned forward, pretending I was going to kiss her on the cheeks, and she shrieked and jumped away laughing.

I asked how she was, in French, and she replied, smiling, in the same language, relaxing a little as she remembered our ritual.

I presented my gift to the family to her, a little tea set in fancy porcelain with eight small cups. It was the colourful type of thing that people in the UK would have turned up their noses at, but the family was delighted. I wondered how many of their possessions they had lost, moving from safe house to safe house.

Then I shook hands with Sammy's brother, Abdul. He was a younger, plumper version of Sammy, his pot belly making him look pregnant in a long white dishdasha. Abdul had been the one that had been kidnapped and the family had been lucky to get him back alive. Many of those abducted were killed, even after the ransom was paid. After losing everything the family had moved into one small flat with minimal rent to pay. I had no idea whose house it was where they were now staying.

'*Shukran, shukran,* Mister,' he said. *Thank you, thank you.*

Abdul's wife, Ayesha, was thin and nervous. She lowered her eyes and did not offer me her hand. Even inside the house she was wearing a headscarf. I nodded and grinned at the six children: they were aged five to fifteen, the girls in kilts and long white socks, the boys in jeans and European shirts. They were the future. They were the people Iraq was going to need and was going to lose.

Sharif Mashooen, Sammy's father, stepped forward, spine rigid as if this were a parade and I was the inspecting officer.

'Thank you for coming, sir,' he said, bowing his head in a short, swift motion.

It was embarrassing. He had been a general.

The women and children left and the men sat in a circle on cushions. Sharif studied me, obviously wondering if he was right to put the safety of his entire family into my hands.

'How is Sandhurst these days, Captain Ashcroft?' he asked. His English was excellent.

'Just as tough as in your day, sir,' I replied.

'That's how it should be,' he remarked happily.

Sharif had gone through the academy in the 1950s or '60s and, as Sammy had once told me, served on the general staff under King Faisal II, grandson of the first king.

When the Ottoman Empire fragmented after the First World War, Iraq came under British rule. To quell the subsequent unrest, the British resolved to establish a monarchy. Knowing from experience that the natives would revolt if a sovereign were chosen from a rival community within the country, the net was cast beyond the borders. The long-term aim of the British was to unite the Shia, Sunni and Kurds, and keep Iraq stable for the cheap labour and oil British companies would extract from the desert – funny how some things never change.

The British settled on a scion of the old Hashemite dynasty from al-Hejaz, a town in present-day Saudi Arabia close to the Islamic holy cities of Mecca and Medina. He was crowned King Faisal in 1921 and was largely accepted by the troublesome Iraqis.

General Mashooen was one of the last survivors from the royal court. He must have been well into his eighties but remained every inch a British-trained officer with a clipped moustache, silver hair Brylcreemed with an immaculate parting and a suit with razor-sharp creases. He was from an old merchant family that had traded in the flowers cultivated for rose oil, big business when the first merchant ships from Europe ventured up the Persian Gulf.

The general was a devoted supporter of Mr Bush and continued to believe that the campaign to topple Saddam was the right thing to have done and would be beneficial in the long term. He didn't care if the war had been illegal or that Saddam didn't have WMDs. As almost every other Iraqi, he was unconcerned with such ridiculous trivia, which seemed to interest only a small community of people far away and unconnected to the real Iraq. An old soldier, he thought in terms of patriotism and practicality.

'Iraq has always survived the invader. It will survive this time,' he told me.

'You're not sad leaving everything behind?'

'Sad? No. It is the realities of change,' he said. 'You either bend like the willow or break like an oak. We Sunnis held the power. Now it passes to our brothers the Shia. Our turn will come again, mark my words. The best thing for us all was the end of Saddam.'

Three months earlier, on 30 December 2006, the first day of the Festival of Eid, when Muslims give presents, the gift to the nation was the execution of Saddam Hussein by hanging at an Iraqi army base aptly called Camp Justice. The tyrant's last wish was to be shot by firing squad. The request was denied and the execution was filmed by a guard on his mobile phone, the footage finding its way on to the Internet within hours. Another guard claimed the body of Saddam had been stabbed six times – true or false, it was a safe bet that General Mashooen was right, the Sunnis would rise again and one day the tomb of Saddam would be a place of pilgrimage. After the fratricidal inter-Iraqi carnage of the last few years, many of the Iraqis I had been friends with, Sunni and Shia both, were so sick of the criminal gangs, they had confided in me that if Saddam had come back they would have welcomed him.

The women and older children reappeared carrying trays with the food I'd seen in the kitchen, the earthenware dishes with hummus, falafel, rice wrapped in olive leaves, chicken, fish and warm pita. There was mint tea in a silver pot, served in tall glasses with little cakes sprinkled with sesame seeds. Ayesha and the children left again, but Fara tucked her legs under her and squatted on a cushion in the corner. Cobus sat down next to her and the two of them squabbled in a friendly manner, each trying to serve the other.

It was a special celebration, humbling me with their welcome, and a tray of precious cans of American sodas was produced for my selection.

Sammy piled a plate for me.

'Eat. Eat,' he said. 'You are thin.'

'I'm not thin, you're fat,' I replied.

Sammy slapped his belly with the palms of both hands. 'I am a camel,' he said. 'I fill up when there's food and I am ready to walk across the desert for a week without problem.'

Members of a family all play a different role. Sammy was the joker. Abdul was the quiet one. In the traditional way of well-heeled Iraqis, after the first son had gone into the military, Abdul had studied accountancy and, a Sunni, performed some minor role in Saddam's government – a job he would only have got as a member of the Ba'ath Party, an establishment figure in pre-war Iraq, a traitor in the eyes of the Shia extremists today.

The old general was the patriarch, but it was Sammy who had earned good money with Spartan and kept the family afloat. After we had left, Sammy had been unemployed and only gained a few dollars here and there, fixing cars and selling a few cans of black-market petrol. He poured tea and loaded my plate with sesame cakes.

'Eat. Eat. Tomorrow you may be dead.'

'And, if I'm not, I'll be fat.'

He liked that and laughed, then had to explain the joke to his brother.

Sammy spoke a quaint, old-fashioned English but he was quick-witted and I recalled the first time we had met. He had acted as our guide on a job to escort a French journalist to an interview near Fallujah. When we ran into an ambush, he drove off into the desert, leaving us bogged down and under fire. Les and I both swore to kill him if we ever saw him again.

Two minutes later, we were still trying to extract ourselves under heavy fire when Sammy reappeared, zooming in from the left in his ridiculous little car, he and his two cousins firing AKs out of the window into the flanks of a completely unprepared enemy. Their accuracy was shocking but, surprised, and now under fire from two sides, the enemy had quickly broken contact and withdrawn.

When they were out of sight, Sammy drove down the hill to join us. He was grinning from ear to ear, very pleased with himself.

'What took you so long?' I said.

'Traffic,' he replied without missing a beat.

We had all laughed, and I knew that this man would be a good friend.

We left one maimed vehicle stripped of equipment and headed for home with the gibbering reporter. More importantly, I poached Sammy for Spartan and offered him twice what he'd been earning working for the French.

We now had a depressing conversation about how the interpreters in Iraq had been abandoned by the British as well as the Americans. I didn't blame the family for being angry. Sammy mentioned that in October, just a few months back, seventeen young interpreters working for the British in Basra had been grabbed by jihadis while travelling on a bus. All had been beaten and executed, their bodies dropped around the city as a warning to other 'traitors'.

The mood was sombre after that and nobody said anything. Sammy refilled my glass. I ate another sesame cake. Fara caught my eye and we exchanged smiles.

'*Délicieux*,' I said.

We had gathered to discuss our plans for the escape, but the Iraqi way is to come at such things slowly. You can be on the point of defusing a bomb, but an Iraqi will insist on asking after your health before you start easing the detonator from the det cord. First you eat, you drink tea, exchange gossip.

Yes, Krista was well. Natalie was at school now. Baby Veronica was always getting up to mischief.

'A chip off the old block,' said Sammy.

Many Americans had grasped the value of social exchange so important to the Iraqis, the daily pleasantries that started every meeting, that you shared with colleagues and associates every morning, no matter that you might have seen them only a few hours previously.

Unfortunately others were often blunt, which they saw as efficient, but left Iraqis feeling offended. The combination led to some extraordinary consequences. The Iraqi minister in charge of environmental issues refused to hold meetings with Colonel Hind, the officer in charge of water management, until Mad Dog had replaced him at the CPA. Colonel Hind had not just slighted Iraqis, but upset just about everyone who met him. He was what Tanya Carillo would have called an 'asshat' and you don't want to know what we Brits called him.

The result was that Hind had been forced to send *us*, his contractor bodyguards, to meet with the minister. We drank tea, talked about Manchester United, and ex-Para Seamus Hayes and I made decisions on laying new water mains on behalf of the United States tax payer worth a hundred million dollars.

As I placed the empty glass on the zinc-topped table at my side it made a decisive ring, and there was silence as I outlined the plan – such as it was. I began by saying I expected Seamus, Dai and Les to be arriving by tomorrow. Sammy's eyes lit up.

'What a pleasure, to see Mister Les again,' he remarked, grinning widely.

Sammy had spent twelve months trying to kiss Les on both cheeks in the traditional matter and Les had spent those twelve months fighting him off, swearing it would happen over his dead body. The closest they'd got to being touchy-feely was arm wrestling, at which Les Trevellick – a former commando instructor – was unbeaten. I didn't mention that Les had yet to confirm. I still refused to believe he'd miss the party.

'When will leave, exactly?' Sammy asked, and intuitively I decided to hedge.

'That's not fixed,' I said. 'Colonel McQueen's going with a convoy up to Mosul. He'll escort us to the US base. We'll peel off and go straight to your house.'

'You must stay with us, Mister James, it is beautiful. It is where I am grow up as a boy. Lovely mountains, just like in the Scotland, home of the whisky.' As my 'brother', Sammy fondly imagined that Scotland was the same as the mountains in Iraqi Kurdistan, but with fewer Kurds and more golf.

'Let's not get too far ahead,' I said.

It occurred to me that Mad Dog had arranged the convoy to usher Sammy to safety, but he was a practical man who wanted to see as much of Iraq as he could before being reassigned. He was into ancient sites and I recalled him once saying he wanted to check out the sixth-century Monastery of St Elijah, one of the oldest places of Christian worship in the country. It happened to be just south of Mosul, within the perimeter of the US Forward Operating Base there.

I glanced around the room. 'You won't be able to take much,' I said. 'Just a few personal possessions.'

'That's all we have,' said the general. 'This is not our house.'

'It is the third safe house in three weeks,' added Sammy.

'Cobus is being cautious.'

'He is cautious man, no?'

The South African followed the conversation as if we were talking about someone else.

'When did you first know Ibrahim was gunning for you?' I asked.

'Mister James, I know immediately. There are no secrets in Baghdad.'

'We are being Talibanized, James,' Fara added from the corner.

I wasn't sure what she meant.

'Fara, she go to work, in the school,' Sammy explained. 'After Abdul was taken, we had nothing. Without Fara, we wouldn't eat. Then the Shia came, they want to have Sharia law – like the Taliban.'

'They want to make Iraq like the Afghanistan, or the Iran,' Fara added. 'The Shia are working with the Americans but they hate the Americans. They hate everything.'

Fara was naturally serene, an intellectual. I had never seen her so angry. Sammy was wringing his plump hands.

'They make her cover it the hair,' Sammy continued. 'Then they stop it, the women teachers. They stop it, the girls going to school. They do not want progress, they want more power, and in charge they put the criminals.'

General Mashooen had tears in the corners of his eyes. 'For the first time in my life I am afraid to go out,' he said, 'in my own city, where I have walked these streets for seventy years. I am afraid if I see these religious police I might kill them.' His frail, papery hands closed into outraged fists. He couldn't have killed a squirrel.

It flickered through my mind that as one of Saddam's generals it was unsurprising he had been strolling around without fear of being mugged.

Fara had come to her feet. I did the same.

'I am sorry, James, you understand,' she said. 'It has been hard. We are so happy that you come to help us. In Mosul, we can start again.'

The men stood. I glanced at my watch. We'd been in the house almost an hour. I had eaten enough to be polite and show my appreciation for their hospitality, but as little as possible. I knew that the children were waiting in the kitchen for whatever left-overs remained from the meal. I noticed all the adults had eaten sparingly as well.

'I have to go,' I said.

I went around the room and shook everyone's hand. Fara cupped my hand between her palms.

'Thank you for the lovely meal,' I said. 'Iraqi food is very good, I always tell my wife.'

They were all very happy at that. I had forgotten not to chew all the way down and nearly broken a tooth on the tiny stones you sometimes find in Iraqi rice.

'You are always welcome in my home,' she replied, and she shrugged, smiling, a little of the tension gone.

Sammy followed us out to the car while Abdul waited.

'I will let you know as soon as things are organized,' I said.

'Mister James, I am ready.'

I smiled. How many times had he said those exact words to me? No matter whether I was asking him to find decaffeinated coffee, or to go into a gunfight, he would answer the same way.

'This is in case . . .' I stopped myself from saying that I might not come back, for some unforeseen reason – no point tempting fate. 'This is in case of emergencies.' I slipped him 500 dollars without letting his family see. He didn't bother trying to protest. His family had been on the run for months now, and he was tired.

'And not a word about Mosul, not to anyone.'

'Of course.'

CHAPTER 10

Dai Jones got in at midday. I had dropped Cobus off back at the embassy to sort something out with Mad Dog and then went straight out to the airport in a single SUV with the two other members of Mad Dog's admin team, two sergeants named Shaun and Scott, who looked similar enough that they could have been brothers. They were both clearly happy to defer to me in terms of driving tactics and what our actions on drills were to be should we have a contact *en route*.

God alone knows what stories Mad Dog had been telling them about us. And I was the mellow one. Wait until the rest of the gang turned up.

Still, I watched Shaun and Scott as we drove up and they both seemed alert and comfortable with their weapons. They paid attention to the right combat indicators and choke points on the road, and I guessed that Mad Dog and Cobus had been taking them out around the city on a regular basis. I was pleased. They would be forming part of our escort team, and there was no room for passengers.

At 12.30pm on the dot, Dai walked out of the terminal, lighting a fag as the door opened, and we greeted each other wreathed in clouds of tobacco smoke. We went through the necessary pleasantries. He asked after Krista and the kids, and I discovered he was two girlfriends on from the one he'd had last time I'd seen him. I coughed through his smoke.

'Filthy habit,' I spluttered.

'Have a heart, Jim, I'm gasping after that flight. Bring back the good old days when you could smoke at the back of the plane.'

He looked around curiously, much as I must have done, I realized, to see if anything had changed, whether it still matched his memories of the place.

Dai had brought his kit and, as I handed over his ammo and ID cards, he filled his vest pouches and tut-tutted as he realised that the spare weapons McQueen had scavenged up for us were all AKs.

After our initial greetings we made the journey back down Route Irish in silence and I couldn't recall ever having gone so long without the soundtrack of Dai's voice and its constant swearing. Shaun and Scott kept their eyes on their arcs around the vehicle, but as soon as we got back into the embassy car park they goggled surreptitiously at Dai as he got out and stretched.

He lit another cigarette, took the smoke deep into his lungs and continued staring into the distance. The sun had found a gap in the smog and the chain-link fence around the T-walls glistened like strings of fairy lights. Soldiers and embassy staff walked around us. In the background a small convoy of MPs rolled past in their 'up-armoured' Humvees. Dai stared at it all, noting every detail. Reflective. We'd given a chunk of our lives to Baghdad and now that chapter was over it felt weird being back.

'This place is doing my fucking head in,' Dai said through a cloud of smoke.

'Nothing's changed, then?' I said.

He sniffed, had a good spit, and did a mock shadow box, weaving about me, feigning and throwing the odd slap.

'Where'd you get that suntan, you bastard?'

'Just under five grand a week, tax-free, playing frisbee on the beach.'

'Shit, nice work if you can get it. Ain't it about time you got a proper job telling us poor sods what to do?'

'That's what I've been thinking.'

He managed to get a good slap in and I got one back.

'Looking good, son,' he said, and stamped out his fag. 'Let's go and take the piss out of Mad Dog, shall we?'

We fell into step as we wound our way through the rubble left by last night's mortar attack. We passed four Iraqis in maintenance uniforms sitting on the kerb, drinking *chai* and smoking with grim determination, shovels and brooms neatly stacked next to them.

'You missed a bit there, sunshine,' said Dai, pointing at a pile of rubble.

'Hallo, mister,' one of them replied.

'Lazy fuckers.'

Dai was lumbering along like a gunslinger on his way to the OK Corral. He was as big as a house and had a similarity to his namesake, the footballer-turned-actor Vinnie Jones. Defenders went weak at the knees when they approached him on the edge of the penalty box. I'd seen militia guards and USAID staffers do the same when they came face to face with Dai. When the Welshman scowled he carried a palpable aura of imminent physical violence that rolled off him like a cold wave.

Despite the chill in the air, his sleeves were rolled up over biceps proudly displaying the Welsh red dragon tattooed on his right forearm. He'd grown up on army camps all over the world, then followed his father into the forces. Dai was in his early forties, and in twenty years' service to his country he'd seen and done it all.

'What's the package they're offering you out in Afghan? Making good money?' I asked.

It's what you always ask. You go into our line of work for the life and for the professionalism, but it's also about the money, and it's as rare as rocking-horse shit to find men who will give up their time and risk their lives for anything but the money. In three terse sentences, with only three 'fucks', he let me know the monthly wage, the leave package and what the insurance deal was.

'It's all right, but it's fucked out there. Afghan's not Iraq. We've been lifting al-Qaeda chiefs out of their holes – but what's the point?' he said. 'You take out one of the cunts and two more pop up like that monster who keeps growing new heads when you cut 'em off.'

'Hydra?'

'Yeah, that's the one, smartarse.'

'Benefits of a classical education,' I said.

He grinned. 'When are the others in?'

'I got a text from Seamus. He'll be here first thing tomorrow.'

'That it?'

'For now. I'm waiting on Les.'

We unloaded, re-holstered and slung weapons, *namastay*ed the Gurkhas guarding the gates and entered the building. As we made our way through the narrow corridors, the stomp of Dai's size-twelves made the walls tremble.

The door was open. We entered the office and Tanya Carillo's dark eyes almost popped out on stalks as she watched Dai leap at Mad Dog and make the same mock attack as he'd made on me. Shaun and Scott actually lurched forward ready to defend him.

'All right, my son?'

'Ducking and diving.' Mad Dog ducked and dived. 'What about you, old buddy?'

'Knackered, mate. Haven't slept for two days.'

'We haven't slept here for two months,' said McQueen.

'Tsk, tsk, you should stay off the Internet porn, Steve, it'll rot your mind.'

Colonel McQueen got serious. 'Did you have any problems getting through Iraqi immigration without a CAC card?'

'Never have any problems, me mate. I've got a valid CAC card from Afghan, innit?'

They settled down. McQueen glanced at Tanya.

'The one and only Dai Jones,' he said by way of introduction, and glanced back. 'Sergeant Tanya Carillo, my most valued assistant.'

'Better-looking than the last one,' said Dai. 'All right, treacle?'

'Doing fine, asshat.'

Dai raised an eyebrow, slumped down in a chair and lit a cigarette. Tanya had those perfect Cupid lips that turned into a bow as she smiled. She looked at me and we exchanged shrugs.

'Good to see you, mate,' he said.

'And you,' said McQueen. 'How's things in Afghanistan? We doing OK?' he asked, and I thought: here goes.

Dai didn't answer for several seconds.

'How's things in Afghanistan?' he repeated. 'I'll tell you how things are in Afghanistan. It's the arsehole of the world. Graveyard of empires, that's what they call it. Fucking British, we never even got in there, not with the whole of India under our belts. Alexander wasn't so great when he got to the Khyber Pass. How many Greek temples do you see in Afghanistan? I'll tell you: fuck all. Russians gambled the shop and lost it. You Septics made a pretty good go of it there after 9/11, doing very well actually . . .'

'Thank you . . .'

'. . . until you invaded Iraq, and then pulled all your assets out of Afghan to hunt down Saddam and his mates. Fucking waste of time if you ask me, and lost all the good ground you'd made getting into the tribes. As for us Brits, well . . . as usual Tommy Atkins is underappreciated, doing a fucking amazing job on half rations, undermanned, without the right kit and being let down about twice a day by those cunts in Whitehall. Bunch of tossers.'

Dai blew smoke towards the No Smoking sign and stabbed the air with an index finger the size of a pork sausage.

'Fucked,' he said. 'We need a shitload more troops, a surge just like this one here. And we need someone in the Pentagon to get some oxygen up to the collective brain cell you all share and realize that the Taliban isn't some super-evil global organization. In Afghan you need to deal with each tribe, each village and damn near each individual fucking farm to win them over one by one. That's how you'll do it, mate, one valley at a time. And don't get me started on the CIA, what a bunch of tossers.'

'Some of my best friends are CIA,' said Mad Dog,

'Then you want to get yourself some new mates, mate.'

I imagined Tanya Carillo had been warned. She sat coolly behind her laptop as Dai Jones spent the next few minutes ripping US foreign policy to pieces. I zoned out, feeling tired after two days travelling, and thought about Sammy and his family, whether they were doing any last-minute packing. Eventually Mad Dog took up his position straddling the corner of the desk.

Dai drew breath and continued. 'Your Congress is all about looking after number one and they don't give a monkey's about foreign affairs.'

'An interesting theory. But it's only a theory. There are people in Congress who do *give a monkey's.*'

'Colonel, you fink everyone's like you. They're not. They're wankers. What politicians worry about once they're in government is staying in government. You think those cunts care if there's fresh water in Baghdad or schools in Kandahar? Don't make me laugh. I've been in Lashkar Gah and I'll tell you what happens there, as soon as they build a new school, the Taliban come along and blow it up again.'

'So we build another school, and another,' said McQueen. 'That's why we're there. That's why you're there. We've got to show the people who do want schools that we're there to help them, we're there in the long term – there's no oil in Afghanistan.'

'There's nothing, mate, 'cept poppies. If rocks and ignorance ever become valuable they're sat on a fucking goldmine.'

'We've got to show that we will endure. That we've got more patience than the Taliban. That we've got right on our side.'

'But have we, though?'

'Why are you there?'

'For the money.'

'I don't believe you, Dai.'

'You'd better fucking believe it, 'cos it's the God's honest.' Dai stubbed out his fag just as Cobus walked in, carrying a cup of coffee from the chow hall.

'*Bliksem*, has someone been fokken smoking in my office?' Then he turned and saw Dai sitting at his desk. '*Ach nie!* I should have known it, it's the Welshman.' He turned to Tanya, 'It's going to take days to get the smell out of that chair. And I'm not talking about the smoke.'

'Jim!' Dai grabbed my arm in mock amazement. 'Fuck me it's a South African walking on its hind legs! Have you got a camera?'

'No smoking in the building you *doos*, can't you read yet? Do you want me to draw you pictures a fokken three-year-old can understand? We'll have every bugger down the hall complaining to the contracting officer about us!'

'Jim,' Dai whispered to me in disbelief, 'that noise coming out of its mouth . . . It's almost as if . . . it's trying to *speak* to us.'

The two men laughed and shook hands. Dai grabbed his day sack and pulled out two bottles of whisky, one for Cobus and one for McQueen. They both looked delighted, and Cobus's bag clanked as he put it away with the one I'd already given him. The three sergeants Shaun, Scott and Tanya all looked interested in the growing stash of booze.

'So, what we supposed to be doing, or is that top-secret?' Dai asked.

McQueen stretched a crick out of his back. 'Easy ride up to Mosul Friday. We'll take our two SUVs and escort Sammy's folks in three civilian cars. I've arranged for us to accompany a military convoy so there'll be decent comms and fire support for the journey. Sergeant Carillo is staying here to mind the shop. Me, these two,' he indicated Shaun and Scott, 'and Cobus, plus four of you. A piece of cake for you guys.'

'Why couldn't you just send 'em along with the convoy?'

'Against the rules. The US Army doesn't chauffeur Iraqi civilians.'

'Ill tell you something, Mad Dog, you must be the only bastard in Iraq who's not bending the rules.'

'Thing is, Dai, once you bend rules you end up with them broken. Then there aren't any rules.' McQueen threw up his wide quarterback shoulders. 'I'm looking forward to the ride.'

'We could check out St Elijah on the way back,' I said.

Mad Dog folded his arms and the way he nodded thoughtfully it was like he was considering the idea for the first time.

'That's a damned good idea, Ash,' he said. 'I'll have to take my camera.'

We filed out and made our way to the mess hall. It was packed with soldiers and civilians, trays clattering, food slopping on plates, cans hissing open. I took my usual cheeseburger and Freedom fries, left the tray on a table and went to the fridge to grab some drinks. Tanya followed and I picked out a Diet Coke and gave it to her while I grabbed myself two cartons of milk. She pursed her lips in thoughtful approval, realizing I had noted what she was drinking the previous evening.

'James, I wanted to say, I wasn't, you know, leading you on last night. I hope I wasn't giving out the wrong signals?'

'Signals? No, of course not. It never crossed my mind,' I said.

Lines furrowed her brow. 'Is that a fact? Hmm. I guess I must be losing my touch.' She smiled and the eyebrow went up. 'Look, when I said it was the closest I'd been to a guy for a long time, it was true. It is true.'

Tanya looked me straight in the eye and my pulse quickened.

I remembered studying her across the table the previous night, how her eyes had looked wild and full of strange energy.

'After the mortar attack and all,' she said, 'there was, like, a buzz going.'

I patted my heart. 'I felt it,' I said.

'Let's just, you know, see what happens?'

'Best offer I've had all day,' I told her, and the vague smile bowed her pink lips. She glanced across the hall towards Dai.

'He's something else,' she said.

'Not your type,' I replied and she flushed.

'I didn't mean . . .'

I grinned at her.

'You *doos*,' she said. 'I have no idea what that means, but you totally are one.' And her eyes had that wild look again.

Along with about a hundred other guys I kept my vision zeroed on Tanya Carillo's hips as we made our way back to the table. I plastered my cheeseburger in ketchup and watched Dai stabbing the air with his fork between mouthfuls of meat loaf. He was rattling out policy failures in Afghanistan while Mad Dog passively took it like a breakwater shrugging off the incoming waves.

Dai was now rambling on about Israel and conspiracies and God knows what, with loudly spoken words like *extraordinary rendition*, *Bagram* and *Guantánamo* starting to draw some attention from neighbouring tables.

During the invasion of Afghanistan, Dai was saying, the CIA was paying thousands of dollars in blood money for al-Qaeda suspects. He had seen a handbill spread among the Afghanis that promised 'wealth beyond your wildest dreams' for each terrorist handed in. And who did the tribal warlords hand over: goatherds, Pakistani teenagers, bin Laden's illiterate driver and as many of their own enemies and rivals as they could persuade the Americans to pay for.

'In December, a couple of months back, your lot let over three hundred prisoners out of Guantánamo, cleared of all charges after five fucking years,' Dai said, wiping his lips with the back of his hand. 'What does that say about the CIA and US intelligence?'

'It says, Keep your voice down a tad, there are guys in this room who are doing a good job – and there are guys who have lost their buddies.'

Tanya passed around some coffees and settled back in her seat.

'What about you, Dai, what do you think the war's all about?' she asked. 'Or is it classified?'

'Nothing I do is classified, darling. Open book, that's me.'

He leaned forward, folding his arms, and the red dragon seemed to be breathing as he held her gaze. He told her the same thing we always told newcomers to our debates. That basically we had no idea, none at all, because if we did, we wouldn't be debating it.

'Jim and me,' he indicated me with a shrug, 'we don't know, but then again, we're not supposed to. We're just the hired help. We just always find it surprising that whenever we have these chats where we put the world to rights and discuss slanderous rumour and hearsay, that none of you lot ever seem to ask yourself any of these questions.'

'Hey, at my pay-grade I just do as I'm told,' Tanya replied. She grinned at McQueen. 'What's your excuse, sir?'

'What, you think it's different when you're an officer? Hell, I'm just another soldier obeying orders, whether or not I know why. "Ours is not to reason why", remember?'

'Mate, been there and got the T-shirt,' Dai snorted.

They all laughed. At least there was something they agreed on.

'There is one more thing,' said Dai.

'Let's have it,' said McQueen.

'Globalization,' he said. 'Before we invaded Afghanistan, it provided about 20 per cent of the world's opium. Now it's 80 per cent. While we're kicking in doors and shooting up villages, the bandits are taking the raw product over the mountains to Iran and Turkey, where they turn it into heroin and flood the streets

Above: On the way into the Green Zone from BIAP. Note the factory armoured turret and M16 ready for snap shooting.

Above: Back in Baghdad!

Above: Cobus talking to Mad Dog and Scott in the Green Zone car park. Note Cobus and Mad Dog are wearing their pistols on their chests as they will be driving.
© Colonel Steve McQueen.

Above: Dai and Cobus waiting for some spit-roast lamb at the Green Beret villa.

Above: With two Iraqi guards at the villa. They are loyal allies of the CF.

Above: Les, Dai and Seamus on the range with AKs. Note the 40rd magazines.

Above: Bradleys on the 14th of July Bridge.

Above: On the 50 cal the morning after shooting up the AIF boat.

Above: Cobus and four of the youngest Mashooen children.

Ali, the loyal armourer and winner of Iraqi champion moustache three years running, with a PKM.

Above: A black marketeer trying to sell HK weapons – G3s, HK33s, 53s, MP5s, MP5ks. Unfortunately only one magazine each.

Above: Remnants of an 'excellent day'. Only four mortars hit the compound.

Above: An Iraqi interpreter translates for CF troops as they arrest a suspected insurgent. In the background there are detonators, maps and sacks of explosive being removed from his house. This is a good example of the high-risk, yet invaluable work done by thousands of interpreters every day to allow Multi-National Forces to carry out their missions.

Above: Foreign fighters from Yemen, Saudi Arabia and Syria captured by the Sunni Awakening Council and awaiting interrogation. They will most likely face summary justice and an unmarked grave, as would Sammy's family if captured by the Shia militias.

of London and Washington. I can't think of a better example of the free market – our junkies are funding the Taliban.'

'You're such a goddamn cynic,' said Mad Dog.

'Don't mean I'm wrong, does it?' he replied and leaned close to McQueen. 'Look, mate, in the War on Terror what are the goals exactly? What's the timeframe? The enemy is cunning and adaptable, and – instead of building hospitals, infrastructure and all that hearts-and-minds shit to draw local civpop support away from the radical cunts – we've only gone and poked the whole Muslim world into a right fucking frenzy, haven't we? It doesn't take the brains of an archbishop to see that invading Afghan and Iraq has given every Islamist nutter around the world a common cause, does it?'

Dai paused to swig some Coke, and I chipped in, reminding Mad Dog of a conversation we'd had a year previously.

'The thing is, Steve, the attack on the Twin Towers was the classic tactic of the underdog, to provoke the larger and more powerful party to overreact and push the undecided moderate population into the underdog's camp. The US reacted predictably and played right into their hands.'

'So what should we have done? Nothing?' demanded Shaun.

He was looking hot under the collar. Even Tanya had lost her smile. I realized that we were once again treading the edge of what was acceptable conversation.

'No, of course not,' I replied. 'Don't get me wrong. It's nothing personal. But consider this, after 9/11 the whole world was outraged, and that includes many moderate Muslims. 9/11 wasn't just a great opportunity for al-Qaeda to push the US into overreacting, it was a great opportunity for the US to pull away popular support for Islamist terrorism on a global scale.'

I paused. I held their gaze and they nodded grudgingly.

'So what are you saying?' said Shaun.

'You guys had the moral high ground. You had the choice to

do almost anything and the world would have supported you. And you chose War on Terror. Now, six years later, with US troops fighting in two Muslim countries and thousands dead on both sides, you've used up your credit in terms of public sympathy.'

They started to look stubborn again.

'So what was the right choice?' asked Tanya with a little steel behind her voice.

'War on Terror but with more thought put into it? Honestly I don't know,' I told her. I tried to be conciliatory and her frown turned into a thoughtful look. 'Who knows, maybe I would have chosen the same thing, because vengeance is all about emotional satisfaction for the public. But I'm not President of the United States. And his job isn't about satisfying emotional cravings, he has a responsibility to make decisions in the interests of the public good, even if those decisions are unpopular. I mean, can any of you look me in the eye and honestly say you believe that the wars in Iraq and Afghanistan have NOT increased terrorist recruiting and activity?'

'I guess not,' answered Tanya after a pause.

'And can any of you honestly say that it was a total surprise, that nobody thought that us invading Iraq was going to piss off Muslims around the world? Of course not. Everyone knew that that was not just likely, but almost a certain consequence of the invasion.'

The others all nodded, understanding.

'So,' I continued. 'I don't know what the right choice was, but I would hate to think that George Bush made this decision thinking about political survival and public opinion, rather than giving a bit more weight to the almost certain consequences. And the fact that I can even wonder about that is bad news in itself.'

'I promise you this,' continued Cobus, joining in unexpectedly. 'The war has made the world more unsafe, more terrified, and billions of dollars that would have been better spent on almost anything else have been transferred to private corporations supplying services for the war. Believe me, I'm in the security industry and we've never seen it so good. Profits are through the roof and, from a free-market point of view, as a contractor, this is a bottomless well of lucrative contracts with no incentive for it ever to end.'

There was a moment's silence following this unexpected announcement.

'Jeez, I forgot how depressing you guys are,' said Mad Dog.

'The truth hurts, mate,' said Dai.

CHAPTER 11

M AD DOG AND team were busy arranging his convoy to Basra.
He was taking Tanya with him, on her first trip 'outside the
wire' on a fairly straightforward run down Route Tampa. They
would depart at three o'clock the next morning. The two sergeants,
Shaun and Scott, were staying behind to mind the shop. Dai and
I had our packs on our backs, having packed up from Cobus's
container, and I felt at peace with the world as we took a stroll
along the blast wall-lined boulevards down to the river to meet
Cobus and pick up the vehicles scrounged up for Sammy's family.
After dropping them off Dai and I would be heading off to spend
the night in Aradisa Idah at the SF house.

Dai clicked, flicked and rolled his thumb over his Zippo in one
motion, and lit up. He smoked quickly, as if he was in a hurry
and wanted to get it over with. I told him about my meeting with
Sammy and his family. There wasn't much to report. They were
hanging on, keeping their heads down.

'I should have shot that cunt Ibrahim when I had the chance.'

'Make sure you take it next time.'

'You know what they say, Jim. Opportunity only knocks once.'

'Does it, though?'

He drew down on the cigarette and nodded as he thought about
that.

'We'll see,' he added, and ground out the fag beneath his boot.

Brilliant green birds lifted into the air as we passed, and settled in the date palms. The maintenance men were still sat on the rubble. They didn't look as if they had moved an inch in the last six hours.

'Jesus, look at these poor cunts, still hard at it,' pointed Dai, 'no respite, working their fingers to the bone. Giving them rocks a damned good sitting on, they are. Can't be easy having to drink all that *chai*, hey Abdul?'

Laziness aside, I wondered why anyone would want to sit all day next to the crater at a proven enemy aiming point for mortar fire.

It still came as a surprise to me that in the Green Zone, behind the walls where Iraqis were not allowed to go, there was a community of locals who had lived in the palace complex before the war and had remained there ever since. They were Saddam's clerks and cleaners, chauffeurs and gardeners, working now for the Americans and relieved, I was sure, to be protected from the world outside. If Dai was right and everything the CIA planned leaked out, here was a large pool of potential fifth columnists.

We had passed the PX, turned left at the blasted shell of the Ba'ath Party former headquarters, passed the site of the old Haji market and the CSH, then hung a right to walk down to the river. We stopped to watch two Iraqis moving a car. A vintage Chevrolet had broken down and a guy with another car had stuck a tyre between the two vehicles to push it. Each time the rear car braked, the Chevy shot forward, the tyre fell out and they had to chase it down the street. It was like a scene from the Keystone Cops, the drivers yelling and throwing their arms in the air.

Dai lit another fag. 'Wankers,' he remarked.

'Probably haven't got a rope,' I said, and he shook his head as he looked back at me.

'No, mate, they're just wankers.'

Iraqis often had a cock-eyed way of doing things, but I never mistook this for a lack of intelligence. It was an irony to me that Iraq was the cradle of civilization and could with a stretch of the imagination claim to have planted the seeds that led to the Renaissance.

When in the seventh century AD the Arabs conquered what today is called Iraq, they found highly developed architecture and schools of mathematics, medicine, astronomy and natural science many of which predated the Greeks. After establishing Baghdad as their capital, the Abbasid caliphs created a team of scribes and filled the library with translations of Greek writers, including Aristotle, Euclid, the mathematician, and Hippocrates, the Father of Medicine.

Unfortunately the subsequent obsession with Islamic scholarship and interpretation of the Prophet's precedents would take up much of the time, intellectual debates and Arab thinking by the time of the Renaissance, but the work of early scholars influenced Muslim philosophy and, for five centuries, Arabic replaced Greek as the language of scientific enquiry. When Christian scholars followed the crusades to the Holy Land, they were shocked to discover that the Arabs had made greater strides than them in mathematics, astronomy, navigation, chemistry, architecture, even gardening. Then, for reasons of interest only to historians and academics, as the light of scientific and technological enquiry grew brighter in Europe, it dimmed further in the Arab world.

An obscene quantity of priceless treasures were lost when the Baghdad museum was pillaged, but the early Christian and prehistoric sites in Iraq remain preserved in the dry air. Between battles and water-maintenance checks, I had come across temples and fortresses dating back six thousand years. You put the AK on safety and, when you study the fine work of these long-vanished craftsmen, you wonder how much we have evolved since the Euphrates and Tigris rose in what they say was the great flood and deposited the ark on Mount Ararat.

I was sure Colonel McQueen was going to try to take in St Elijah on our excursion to Mosul – not far from Ararat, now I come to think of it – but he at least had it easy since the monastery lay within the protection of FOB Marez. The sites I had wanted to see were all in hardcore insurgent areas. We had passed the turn-off to the Aqar Quf ziggurat a couple of times when driving out into the Western Desert from Baghdad. That might have been safe to visit, but the moment had never been right to take a detour and see this amazing monument, already 1,500 years old by the birth of Christ and only a few centuries younger than the Etemenanki ziggurat at Babylon, the one most closely associated with the legend of the Tower of Babel. However, there is virtually nothing left of the Etemenanki, and the other great Iraqi ziggurat at Ur, from the twenty-first century BC, is unfortunately so reconstructed that I believe nothing of the original can be seen.

Sammy had planned all the time I was in Baghdad to take me to Samarra to see the Malwiya, the soaring, conical-shaped minaret attached to the Great Mosque. The structure was built by the Abbasids in the ninth century AD and combines the ideals of Islam with the architecture of ancient Babylonia, the sheer walkway circling the tower making the climb to God a humbling experience. When the US Department of Defense created a set of cards to educate the military on the importance of respecting Iraq's cultural heritage, the Malwiya was one of the featured sites.

Dai clapped his hands, ending my musing. The Keystone Cops had got the car away on about the ninth attempt.

'We could have put that on YouTube,' he said. 'Hang on a second, I need a leak.'

We wandered into the nearest palace building that stood open, without any security or military banning access. Many of the palaces had been turned over by the CF, for example to be used by the Jordanian embassy. This was one of the few that still had busy offices filled with Americans in both civilian dress and desert-camouflage BDUs.

We made our way along a pink and pale green marble corridor with murals depicting idealized desert scenes, an extended caravanserai of dancers, traders, camels and sturdy men with bold moustaches and an uncanny resemblance to the former tenant.

'Where's the gents' room, mate?' Dai asked a guy in fatigues hurrying towards us.

'Make a left at the end,' he said and kept going.

A scene on the mural showed a group of Arabs in fancy headdresses meeting a group of Africans in white *djellabas*.

'How's Africa treating you, then?' Dai asked.

'Weather's fantastic, food's all right, but I'm getting a bit bored of it if I'm honest,' I replied. 'I'm with a good team although one of them's a Frenchie who gives me more drama than the locals, as you can imagine.'

'I can.'

'Medical's a pain in the arse. I'm popping malaria pills every day, and you need to stay close to the cities to get anything like decent treatment for even simple ailments,' I continued. 'Otherwise, out in the country, if you get a toothache you can fucking die from it while they're out praying to the sun for you to recover. Nice people by and large, bearing in mind they've just come through a shitty civil war. The further you move away from the coast the worse it gets.'

'Heart of darkness, mate.'

'If you think it's bad in Afghanistan, you can forget the Congo.'

'Best way to forget is to not think about it in the first place,' said Dai. 'Never fancied Africa, myself. Always thought it was a dump.'

We took a nostalgic leak in one of Saddam's gilded lavatories, and by the time we left the palace, the sky was turning orange as the sun went down behind the west wall. We carried on down to the river, down a ramp to where Cobus was waiting with a line of parked-up cars. To my surprise I saw Tanya was with him.

Dai went straight into his boxing routine with Cobus and I thought if these two heavyweights ever stepped into the ring it would go the full fifteen rounds. Dai bobbed about, effing and blinding. He feigned a right hook followed by a left jab, gave Cobus a slapping and Cobus roared with laughter.

'Fokken Welshman, I eat you . . .'

'Not with no fucking teeth, you won't.'

Another slap. Two back from Cobus. One more from Dai.

'You know something, I've got friends with kids who behave like this,' Tanya said.

I looked her in the eyes. 'I've got kids who behave like this,' I replied, and she paused for thought.

'How many?'

'Two girls.'

'Little angels, I'm sure,' she said, and her expression let me know she was glad I'd told her.

'Like their mother,' I told her. 'Must be the reason I married her.' I looked into her eyes, wondering what she was thinking. She didn't look disappointed, just thoughtful.

'I'm engaged to a lawyer back home. We're getting married in four months.' She replied in an emotionless monotone, looking to see my reaction.

'You didn't tell me you were engaged last night!' I was surprised, bearing in mind her body language and the crackling chemistry between us.

'Well,' she smiled, standing a little too close to me to be completely platonic. 'You never told me you were married.'

Dai finally stood back puffing and stared at Cobus.

'You must give up this smoking, Dai. It's going to kill you, man,' he said.

Cobus grinned and adjusted what I realized was his disguise. Our South African straight man was wearing black dungarees and there was a red and white *shemagh* wrapped expertly about his skull.

He had dropped his bag and now bent to open the long zip. He pulled out two grubby coats, one that I'd worn earlier in the day, and a couple of spare *shemaghs*. A lot of PSDs travel in matching cars and barge through the traffic like the cavalry. We kept a low profile. Our disguises wouldn't fool anyone up close, but from a distance, in a speeding vehicle, our silhouettes would blend right in with the locals.

Tanya carried a clipboard and a couple of bags with some goodies from the PX for Sammy's family. She was standing so close to me I could smell her hair.

Cobus held up a dark green double-breasted coat with half the buttons missing.

'You're having a laugh, mate,' said Dai.

'I have no sense of humour,' Cobus replied, smiling still.

'I'm supposed to be on fucking leave.'

Good soldier that he was, Dai always whinged but then always did what had to be done. We dressed and turned to the three vehicles. There was a black M-class seven-seater Mercedes dented in the driving door; the predictable white Nissan Patrol furred in dust; and a bronze Toyota Isuzu the colour of the desert.

Tanya walked over to them and kicked a couple of jerry cans.

'The vehicles have been sat here for a week now, and the locals have siphoned all the gas out, so I took the liberty of filling a few jerry cans for you guys.'

'Not bad, darling,' Dai said. 'Did you do it all by yourself?'

'Sure did.'

He shook his head. 'You lot are taking over. Next fing you know, there'll be a bloody woman in the White House,' Dai predicted. 'Still, couldn't be any worse than that wanker you've got at the moment.'

'It may come as a surprise to you, Dai, but I happen to like Mr Bush.'

'No accounting for taste.'

'He's cute,' she said, 'I always like strange men,' and turned with a wink in my direction.

She now shoved the clipboard under Dai's nose. There were the inevitable Department of Defense forms to sign in order to allow us to fill up from the fuel depot in the Green Zone later on. I started thinking again about how little back-up infrastructure we had for our team. Lifting Sammy out of Baghdad looked easy and, in my experience, the easier a tasking seems, often the harder it turns out.

Cobus stared up at the sky. The first stars had begun to appear, their light dimmed by the smog like the light of knowledge.

I'd made a mess of my turban. Tanya fixed it for me.

'There, that should do it,' she said, and pulled on my lapels to reach up and plant a kiss on my cheek that ended up on the corner of my lips. I could smell her perfume; it was musky, feral, sensuous.

'I guess I'll see you when I get back from Basra,' she said. 'Shame you're married,' she breathed gently in my ear.

Funny, that's exactly what I had been thinking.

She marched off with her clipboard, papers signed, job done. I stared.

'Oi, Casanova, you fucking coming or what?'

Dai and Cobus were already fuelling their vehicles. I ran over, dumped my pack in the back seat, grabbed my jerry can, popped the funnel in and started doing mine. We were surrounded instantly by the strong odour of petrol fumes. I glanced over alarmed as I realised that Dai was still smoking his cigarette.

We climbed into our individual cars and, after a quick radio check, drove off through the Green Zone to the fuel dump. The paperwork was fine and we filled up the vehicles and the jerry cans stacked in the back of each. We would need every drop to get up to Mosul, with potentially few refuelling stops for the convoy. Each car also held spare weapons – for Sammy and his brother – plus ammunition, medical packs, the lot.

With that job done we did another radio check to each other, then pulled out and headed over the 14 July Bridge. The plan was all to go in one trip, since the 14 July Bridge exit was at the start of Karada and it was literally a two-minute drive to another safe house where we were planning on stashing the vehicles. With the three of us as individual drivers in different vehicles mixing with the traffic, it was highly unlikely that anyone would even look twice at us.

The second safe house was a shophouse, with a little shop on the ground floor and an apartment above it, where Sammy's cousin Gabir and his family lived. It was near the river, beyond the Shia market where car bombs and suicide bombers had left more than 100 dead and injured during the previous twelve months. After thirty years of enforced harmony under Saddam, Sunni and Shia neighbours eyed each other suspiciously now that he'd gone.

It was useful that the shophouse was close to the Mashooen family. On the day of the bug-out, the three vehicles, already packed, would arrive quickly and remain only briefly outside the safe house – a time when the hustle of eleven Sunnis with their baggage and all of us whitefaces armed to the teeth would be hard to conceal. Colonel Ibrahim would probably be informed in about two minutes. Even if he was unable to prevent the escape, he would know Sammy was on the run and it wouldn't require Sherlock Holmes to work out where he was going.

I was running this through my mind as we crossed the 14 July Bridge. We shot by the growling generator powering the harsh portable floodlights of the checkpoint, through the long shadow of the last guntower and came off the traffic circle to slide through the empty streets.

We accelerated to a steady 100 klicks. After nightfall the militia and criminal gunmen went about their murderous deeds: al-Qaeda planting IEDs; Mahdi elements assassinating Sunni 'traitors and apostates'; bandits robbing, kidnapping and killing for revenge and reward. US patrols were sporadic, and during the hours of darkness the streets belonged to the bad guys.

Cobus gave calm directions over the radio. No more swearing or banter from Dai. With each of us driving solo we were totally focused, trying to see in all directions at once. We followed the long loop of the Tigris and turned left into an unlit street of warehouses. Gabir's store faced the water and wasn't overlooked by other buildings. It was dark, shadowy, silent. Cobus had obviously called to say we were on the way because as soon as we pulled up the door slid open. Barely braking, Cobus drove straight in, his headlights beaming a sudden flare of light into the dark garage. Dai and I drove right in behind him, squeezed up bumper to bumper.

Gabir was inside with Sammy. The door shut behind us and we killed the engines and lights. The store was lit by a couple of oil lamps, the light dancing with the sudden movement, the smell of fumes nauseating in the confined space. Sammy had a wide grin and, when he put his arms out for a hug, Dai lifted him clean off the floor.

'Fuck me, you're getting fatter,' he said.

'No, Mister Dai, you are getting older,' he replied. Sammy glanced at us in our *shemaghs* and turned to his cousin. 'You see, Gabir, now everyone is Iraqi.'

Gabir was pixie-like with a neat moustache, a pointed head and small dark eyes that flicked from face to face like a startled bird. I wasn't sure if he was more nervous of storing the vehicles in his garage or of us, the foreigners, bringing them. Gabir was a middleman, buying and warehousing goods. In the complex rationale of Sunni–Shia hatreds, as Fara's cousin, he wasn't the same bloodline as Sammy and remained nominally safe from Colonel Ibrahim's net. At least that was the thinking.

'Tea time, Mister James,' Sammy said.

'Just James, please,' I replied.

He threw up his plump hands and I followed him into the office, a cubicle little bigger than a telephone box to one side of the garage. There were two chairs, one piled with battered files, and pinned to the wall were handwritten bills of lading. The papers on the desk had been swept to one side and in the centre stood three tulip-shaped glasses Sammy filled with scalding mint tea. There was a plate with cakes 'made by Fara'.

'Please, you are my guests,' said Gabir.

We ate cake. We burned our fingertips on the glasses as we sipped sickly sweet *chai*. Dai pulled out a packet of Marlboros. Smoking American cigarettes was like owning a piece of America. As smoking declines in the West, the tobacco giants follow the tanks into the Third World and plant their billboards.

He tapped out a couple of cigarettes and passed the blue flame of his lighter over the fizzing ends of the two fags Sammy and Gabir stuck between their lips. He closed the Zippo and opened it again to light his own. They said in the First World War that the third light was unlucky and soldiers are notoriously superstitious.

As we finished our tea we decided to leave the weapons and ammo in the vehicles. It was just asking for bad luck for Sammy to take them home. He ran the chance of getting picked up by an American patrol and being taken in. He drove around with a rifle anyway, for which he had a permit. But explaining away half a dozen rifles and two thousand rounds would be a different matter.

Gabir assured us, through Sammy interpreting, that the garage was secure; only he had the keys to it. Sammy and Gabir would spend the rest of the night packing the vehicles up in advance with the Masshoen family baggage.

I grabbed the bags we'd brought along from the PX and handed them over to Sammy. There was plenty of candy for the kids, cigarettes, shampoo and all sorts of goodies that Tanya and Mad Dog had bought up.

'This should keep you going,' I said.

'Mister James, please . . .'

'Don't thank me, thank the United States government.'

'The American, they are too kind,' Sammy said, and I thought, *If they'd been a bit kinder they would have looked after their interpreters and I'd still be on the beach playing frisbee.*

We moved back out into the street, hands on our AKs under the coats. The street was deserted. The moonlight was bright, revealing in the shadows Cobus's other car, a black Nissan, a white van with Arabic logos and Sammy's yellow Toyota, the back left side drilled with holes from where my own Spartan guards had tried to gun me down over a year ago.

'Still going?' I smiled looking at the old car, remembering a hundred trips to the range in it.

'Like a dream,' Sammy replied. He looked from me to Dai and back again. 'Mister James, Mister Dai, I still cannot believe it, you are here.'

'Neither can I, mate,' said Dai in disgust. 'I'm on fucking R&R!'

'OK, guys, let's go. We are going to Aradisa Idah now.' Cobus was already in the Nissan, in the driver's seat.

Gabir offered me his hand and I took it.

'Thank you,' he said, glancing at Sammy, and it was strangely moving the way he cupped my hand between his palms.

Gabir slid the door back. We slung in our bags and piled in, Dai in the back, me up front. After a hurried goodbye, we took off. Cobus accelerated along the riverbank and took a different route, keeping to the backstreets. We thumped over barely seen potholes, and crawled around alleys, but it was safer. After four years of war, a single car packed with bulky men tended to draw the eye of civilians and soldiers both. The streets weren't just quiet. They were dead. The shadows lay heavy. It was like there had been a plague, the people had died or fled and the buildings that remained were like stone footprints following on from the

Babylonians, the Abbasids; as if all that ever remains of a people are their empty buildings.

The darkened glass of the car windows framed fleeting cityscapes. A row of gutted houses, a stretch of empty land littered with the shells of bombed and burned-out cars, the light above the oil refinery like a strange planet. A line of new electricity pylons loomed up like demons – like nude, giant girls that have no secrets, as the poet Stephen Spender wrote. By day companies that had won juicy contracts would lay copper cables and at night ali-babas would dig them up again. The War on Terror wasn't just an open bank for hired guns, it was a licence to print money for the reconstruction companies and thieves alike.

Finally, after ten minutes Cobus judged we were far enough east and we got back on to the main street.

'Truck approaching at speed,' Dai said from the back.

Cobus pulled tight to the sidewalk. The truck hurtled by at 150 klicks, the grim *jundhi* behind the wheel choosing speed as his ally. Trucks usually travel in convoy with armed guards and circle the wagons at night. A lone trucker at that hour was either mad or up to mischief.

I recognized the area; we were about ten minutes away from our old patch. I prepared myself in advance for the *déjà vu* experience of coming back through the looking glass, but already a part of me knew that I was going to be less affected. I had already significantly re-acclimatised to being in Baghdad, not least because we were back in the danger zone and had to be totally switched on.

I couldn't believe my own ears as, without thinking, the words just came out of my mouth. 'Quiet, isn't it? So far so good.'

You never, ever tempt fate.

'Oh, for fuck's sake,' muttered Dai, 'that's just asking for it, isn't it? I can't believe you just said the fucking "Q" word.'

Cobus sat grimly at my side, window down an inch, and clenched his jaw, his wide shoulders blocking my left view.

'Rooftops left,' Cobus said. 'Three men.' He accelerated.

Wow, I thought, *Fate works fast.* But nothing happened. We left them behind.

They'd taken a look at us and let it go. Perhaps we were moving too fast? Perhaps the *shemaghs* we were wearing had helped? Perhaps they'd buzzed their chums further down the line?

I thought about Tanya Carillo for two seconds, and then got back into my zone and focused on my arcs again.

My window was down a couple of inches, enough to let some air in, and thank God it wasn't the dusty season, when you breathed the stuff in like a fine mist. The air tasted musky, sensuous, with only a hint of diesel and mud. Nothing moved except the moon slipping like glass across the sky. We were making a wide circle to approach Aradisa Idah from the north.

I noticed a black BMW approaching from behind in the mirror and let Dai know. He swivelled around and knelt on the back seat, so as to bring his weapon up quickly if necessary. Cobus kept an eye on them through the side mirrors.

'Four men inside,' said Dai.

Cobus slowed down to let them pass. They drew up alongside, had a look in at us then dropped behind again. Cobus sped up and they accelerated as well.

'Ach, these oaks are up to some shit, man. I will try and lose them. Dai get ready to wave them off if we cannot shake them.'

Cobus rammed his foot down and swung the car left and right, feigning that he was going one way, then going the other. We screeched off the main road, looped around a block of buildings and came back on to the highway. Cobus floored it and we gained a couple of hundred metres before they came back out behind us. They accelerated steadily and this time in the rear-view mirror I saw two men emerge from the windows on each side, holding AKs. We all swore at the same time.

'Give 'em a couple of warning shots, they might be cops,' I said.

I started opening my window fully to get some shots off if necessary. In a sudden contact you wouldn't bother, you would just fire through the door or the window, but this looked to be a long chase and I couldn't fire straight out the back window with Dai sat right behind me. Also there was no point in making a mess of the windows now to draw attention to us later on. It's also noisy as hell, if I am honest, and I didn't fancy going deaf.

Dai leaned out of his window and waved a red torch from side to side, then fired a couple of shots into the road in front of the rapidly gaining car. Cobus hit the four-way flashers on for a few seconds as well.

The reaction was immediate. The other car switched its headlights on full beam in an attempt to blind us, and the two gunmen on each side opened up. Their accuracy was awful and nothing came near our car. Tough for them. It was big boys' rules now, and we were free to return fire. They were about to have a bad day at the office.

'We cannot outrun them, their car is faster,' Cobus said.

'We can't lead them to Aradisa.' I looked at Cobus.

'*Ja*, and we can't ride around all night or we'll bump into more of these assholes. They're already on their cellphones now.'

I considered whether we could take them on in a rolling firefight, but Dai was leaning out of the right-hand window right behind me, since he was left-handed, firing to the rear. I couldn't shoot out the back or lean out past him, so of the three of us he was the only one able to fire.

'Cobus, pull over and we'll shoot them up.'

'That junction up ahead, I'll do a U-turn to the left and stop for a snap ambush as they come past us.' Cobus pointed ahead.

I nodded and screamed our plan out of the window to Dai, who was rapidly plinking single shots back at the BMW, which had dropped back slightly but was keeping pace with us. It was weaving from side to side in an attempt to throw off his aim, but the only effect of this was to make it impossible for the enemy gunmen to shoot anywhere near us. It was a shame that we were not in a faster car, or we could have just left them to it, but they kept doggedly on our tail.

'Roger that,' Dai shouted back.

He gave them five more rapid and dropped back into the car. He moved to the other side of the back seat behind Cobus on the left, legs splayed wide, feet braced against the upcoming turn. Lightning-quick he dropped out his magazine and put a new one in.

The junction was approaching fast as Cobus gunned the engine and we pulled ahead. I checked that my AK selector was all the way down on automatic, pulled the bolt back slightly to check chamber and then smacked it firmly forward. We were less effective than we would have been had we had an LMG with us, but at the same time I almost felt sorry for the car behind us.

'OK, brace yourselves!' Cobus slammed on the brakes, then hit the clutch and the handbrake as we screeched into the junction.

We slid in a perfect 180-degree U-turn. Cobus dropped the clutch and we came back up the other side of the road before pulling into a dead stop.

It was a good position. The central divider between the two sides of the road would prevent the other car from simply driving over and ramming us. As soon as we stopped I hit my door, got out of the right side, ran forward and leaned over the engine of the car, facing to the left – the front of the car is good cover as the engine and the tyres are about the only things on a car that will stop bullets.

Dai and Cobus poked their rifles out of the left-hand windows and we sat and watched over our front sights as the enemy car approached from our front. Forced to react to our unexpected manoeuvre, the BMW driver was braking to make the same turn. If he had thought about it for two seconds he would have stamped on the accelerator and zoomed through, but instead he slowed right down and the mistake would cost him.

Our positions were now reversed. They were Shia gunmen. I could see the standard issue black balaclavas clearly now. Only one guy in the back seat had a clear shot at us, and he was too busy pressing against the G-force as the driver slammed his brakes on. He got off a two-round burst, nearly straight up in the air, no danger to anything but the moon. The driver had his hands full, and the gunmen on the other side of the vehicle couldn't bring their weapons to bear on us.

The BMW passed less than 10m away, point-blank range, and the three of us opened fire. The AK is relatively easy to control on full auto, especially at that range, and not a single round missed the target.

There were four seconds of deafening carnage as ninety high-velocity rounds tore through the doors, windows and bodies in the other car. Broken glass, metal fragments and blood sprayed out of the other side of the BMW. Then there was silence. I was already moving back into the car and jumped into my seat even as Cobus finished firing, dropped his rifle on his lap and accelerated off down the street. My ears were ringing and every sound was muted, as was normal after the first round goes off and you're not wearing ear defenders.

I reloaded, as did Dai, and then reached over and put a fresh mag on to Cobus's weapon for him and cocked it.

'One up the spout, mate, safety catch is on.'

'Thanks,' he replied.

I looked back in the mirror. The BMW was still moving, but the driver's foot had slipped from the accelerator pedal and the vehicle rolled to a halt on the other side of the junction, drifting into the shadows away from the street light. Blood and glass were strewn along behind the vehicle.

Job's a good 'un, Les would have said.

132

Cobus floored it back the way we had come and we made it back into Aradisa Idah, our old sector of the city. We needed to get our Nissan out of sight ASAP in case the Shia had called in our description and location.

Wide awake, and looking at every window and side street, I grimaced as we passed the old neighbourhood checkpoints we had set up, that had kept the community safe from the ravages of the gangs for nearly two years. Without us white-eyes conducting snap inspections they had fallen into disrepair. The roadblocks had disappeared, possibly used for firewood and construction, or more probably stolen by other locals for some reason too bonkers to understand. Instead of alert sentries, ready to step out and challenge any stranger, there were only a handful of old men, huddled around glowing braziers against the night cold. They didn't even look up as we drove past, and we slipped back into Aradisa, unnoticed. Soon we were back up to the river and approaching the empty road through the plantation that led to the SF villa.

Cobus stopped short in a shadowy stretch where we disappeared under the trees and got on the phone to call ahead and make sure that they were expecting a vehicle to turn up. Always wise to double-check, in case a jumpy gate sentry decides to make your day.

'*Ja*, we are just down the road. Your front gate is warned off? *Goed*. See you in a minute.'

Dai and I kept our eyes open, left, right and rear. It was almost totally silent, unusual for Baghdad. Cobus put his phone away, put the car in gear and we rolled forward slowly with our lights dimmed.

A Kurdish guard at a crude guardhouse halfway along the road checked our ID passes, then spoke into a walkie-talkie while waving us through. As we approached the outer wall of the villa, the front gate opened and a mixture of armed Iraqis and American soldiers checked our IDs again. I did not recognize any of them from before, but if they were following the same routine; the Americans would be from a separate unit on a fairly easy guard detail, securing the location as a home base for the Green Berets to operate from.

As the gate shut behind us, I thought of Tanya again. I was feeling increasingly guilty that I could find someone so intensely attractive when I was a married man, but I liked to think of myself as the kind of guy that would remain faithful to his wife. Still, I had to admit to being secretly happy that some force beyond my control, destiny maybe, was keeping me out of the Green Zone tonight. It was much easier to remain virtuous when I had half a city full of insurgents and murderous militias between myself and any temptation.

CHAPTER 12

THE GREEN BERETS are part of US Special Forces and perform much the same role as the SAS in counter-terrorism, unconventional warfare, specialist reconnaissance, etc. *ad infinitum*. In Iraq, they often lived in the community, the better to carry out their missions of mayhem.

When we had set up shop in Aradisa Idah, so had a Green Beret 'A' Team or 'ODA', a dozen men who, as far as we could work out, were conducting all kinds of covert chaos. Specialists in mountain warfare, I remember, they had found an unexpected bonus for their skillset, fighting in Fallujah, climbing up the sides of buildings to grenade from above unsuspecting insurgents who were waiting patiently for an American assault at ground level.

They were right on the Tigris River five minutes away from our old house in a well-defended villa whose former high-ranking Ba'athist owner had fled during the invasion. Their 18C engineer, a Nascar fanatic who was dumbfounded that none of us Brits had ever heard of Nascar, had fixed the place up nice and shipshape. More importantly, he had also built a quite excellent electric rotating sheep spit over the fire, which novelty greatly interested our South Africans due to their unfamiliarity with electricity. We had exchanged useful intel and maintained good relations, which usually involved a lot of barbecues whenever they were between missions. The day we were finally chased out of the old bus station by our Shia guards, we took shelter at their villa.

Cobus had told me that due to their frequency of rotation, six-month tours as opposed to twelve months, it was our good fortune that the current ODA knew us from the old days and was happy to put us up for a couple of nights. As we pulled up past the Humvees and the covert vehicles they used to drive around Baghdad, I saw that the team members were all gathered around the back at the barbecue pit. We were just in time for dinner.

'Magic.' Dai sniffed the cooking meat from the back of the car as Cobus parked up. 'It looks like the Septics have put on a right good spread for us.'

We got out with our packs and weapons, and dumped our coats and *shemaghs* in the car. Two large sergeants were waiting for us, Mark and Rick, whom I remembered from nearly a year and a half ago. They beckoned us over and we followed them through the front door of the villa, shaking hands and exchanging greetings. They were clearly in relaxed mode, in civilian T-shirts and fleece jackets, not even wearing pistols. Well, not that I could see. These two guys were living proof that strength comes in every shape and size. Rick's Austrian genes, combined with a punishing physical regimen, gave him a six-and-a-half-foot physique like Hercules with the chiselled features of a GI Joe action figure. Mark Amin, whose family came from Iran via Los Angeles, was a bear of a man just over five feet high and as wide as he was tall, with a low centre of gravity and arms too big for his sleeves. Disdaining the evening chill, he was wearing only a T-shirt and, despite the XXXL size, the sleeves were as tight as sausage skins on arms bigger than my legs. I'm not small, but each of these guys easily had fifty kilos on me, all of it muscle.

They showed us where to dump our stuff and we headed out the back door, taking a shortcut to the barbecue. We wandered through a dark passage narrowed by sandbags and out into an open courtyard that smelled of burning charcoal and sizzling meat. The rest of the team was out there, regular human size, and everyone raised a bottle and said their hellos as we walked around the circle, shaking hands and getting reacquainted. I pulled out the last and final bottle of whisky I had brought from London, and ceremonially presented it, to loud applause, to the team's officer, Davor 'A to Z'. We called him 'A to Z' because his Eastern European surname was unpronounceable and seemed to contain every letter of the alphabet.

They all looked lean and focused, and for a second I envied them. They were at the top of their game, successfully fighting the war of their lives, year after year, with a tempo of operations that most soldiers had not seen for decades. For career special-forces soldiers, life doesn't get much better. I was glad to see that all the same faces were there and that they had not taken any casualties.

At the same time they had a healthy interest in our lives, since the Circuit is the natural progression for someone who eventually does leave the Specops community for one reason or another. We didn't bother telling them about our little contact that evening. These guys had been on hardcore missions for months and – unlike a PSD, who might never fire a shot in anger – they had been firing thousands of rounds in the last few days. As one of the sergeants had said, when asked why he looked so tired, 'Man, I just been killing people all week.'

He hadn't meant to say it in a cavalier fashion; it was just a simple statement of fact. Our little gunfight was just five minutes in a week like theirs. So instead Dai and I happily lied our arses off about how many millions we had earned off our last few lucrative contracts. The more outrageous the story, the more they laughed. They knew we were lying, but part of them wanted to believe at least half of the fairytale. After all, if the money were not fantastic, why were we doing this as a career? It seemed a fairly shitty job, soldiering without the motivation of patriotism behind you. I hoped the fact we weren't getting paid this time around wouldn't surface, as it would be embarrassing.

'What brings you back, Ash?' asked Davor from the front, as if on cue.

'Your barbecued chicken,' I replied.

'We've got a leg of lamb roasting tonight.'

'Jim loves a bit of lamb, don't you, son?' said Dai.

'Oh, yeah, can't get enough of it.'

'Cobus made sure we got something for you,' Mark said, and I watched him stamp off, the ground moving beneath him.

Rick pulled a couple of beers from the ice chest and threw them to Dai.

Dai opened them both and we clinked cans. 'Never mind, son. They get hotter when you keep them waiting,' he said. He lit a Marlboro, then offered me the packet. 'Here, you want one of these?'

I shook my head. 'Shove it up your arse.'

He proffered the packet around the fire. Only Davor and one other took him up. The others that needed tobacco were chewing it.

I didn't need a fag after our contact out on the street, although traditionally I celebrated surviving with a cigarette. It was a habit developed as an army officer when I found that the adrenalin rushing through my body caused my hands to shake so much afterwards that even when perfectly calm I could barely write out the contact report. I had a couple of my favourite pipes and some tobacco in my pack, but I would wait until after I ate before having a pipe next to the fire.

Mark returned with a plastic bag. 'Said you'd appreciate this.'

I looked inside. Cobus must have remembered that I was still off the lamb and had provided me with a chicken.

'Thoughtful bastard,' I said to Cobus on my left. 'This must be in appreciation for us bringing civilization to your country.'

Mark sat down on a crate next to Dai, who immediately offered him a cigarette. 'No thanks, bro, I don't do that shit.'

'Yer having a laugh, mate.' Dai's eyeballs swivelled right to look at biceps the size of pumpkins dwarfing his head. He sniffed, unconcerned. 'Still, each to his own poison, I s'pose. I'd never do steroids myself. Shrinks the cock, dunnit?'

A soldier wearing an apron with a nude woman down the front cut the legs and breast off the bird and slung it on the grill, liberally coating it with barbecue sauce. Dai helped himself to some slices of lamb, a half-dozen sausages and a jacket potato with a dollop of butter. I started shovelling down coleslaw and sausages and potato myself.

A couple of Blackhawks thundered overhead, probably casevacs carrying some poor bastards back to the Green Zone CSH. There was now a constant thud of explosions in the distance behind the music banging out of a boom box. When Jimi Hendrix ripped into *All Along the Watchtower*, someone hiked up the volume and Davor and Mark went straight into riffs on air guitars.

I flopped down on a bench with my second beer and a picture of Krista and the kids came into my mind.

Hendrix was telling us that life is but a joke and who can argue with that? It's not easy to make sense of things. Winchester, Oxford, Sandhurst, a commission, I was the classic establishment figure bred for pips on my shoulder and stripes on my City suit. But the truth is that, even though I missed my family and our life in London, I felt just as at home in that courtyard in Baghdad, or sat on an RIB riding the blue swells off the African coast. Working in a law office discussing legal points and interest rates was killing me. It was death. This was life.

Dai was back on his feet, getting seconds.

'How's my chicken doing, you wanker?' I called.

'It won't be laying any more eggs, I can tell you that.' He forked a leg and a breast, stuck a potato on the plate and brought it over. 'Here, get that down you, son, you'll feel better.'

Dai sat back, lit up yet another cigarette and blew smoke up to the stars, then looked over at me as I started wolfing down the perfectly barbecued chicken.

'So, no problem with your appetite, you cold-hearted shit,' he sniffed, 'tucking into that scoff like a starving man just after you've walloped four poor cunts down the road.'

We both laughed.

'Speak for yourself, mate, I was only aiming high to scare them off,' I replied.

'Yeah, right. Still, not bad drills on your part, I guess they must have taught you something at Sandhurst.'

'What did you think, it was all tea with Princess Anne and ironing one's kit?'

He blew out smoke. 'How's that chicken?'

'It won't be laying any more eggs.'

'You . . . fucking . . . what's the word, pederast?'

'Plagiarist.'

'Yeah, plagiarist. Like that.'

'Funny that they tried taking us on, though, wasn't it?'

I looked at him and he looked back thoughtfully, knowing what I meant. Whether insurgents or criminals, Iraqis tended not to have the appetite for a stand-up shoot-out with PSDs or CF soldiers. The odds were just stacked too high against them, hence the predilection in the last few years for IEDs and indirect-fire attacks.

'I'd have thought all the nutters with a death wish had been killed long ago,' I added.

'New recruits maybe? Out to prove themselves?' Dai clearly wasn't worried about the unusual behaviour of our erstwhile and now presumably deceased foes. 'Still, that'll fucking learn 'em. They won't do that again, will they?'

Someone else had grabbed the other two pieces of chicken and

I dumped my empty plate on the pile. It was a good time to call Krista. Half past ten in Baghdad made it seven thirty in London. She'd just be getting ready to bath the girls before putting them to bed.

I wandered out of the courtyard and up to a terrace that would have had a romantic view of the river before the Green Berets added sandbags and razor wire to the walls. The villa was a fortress, a warren of arches, passageways and gardens shaded by palms, the mosaics in the corridors chipped and broken.

I keyed in the numbers. Krista answered on the second ring.

'Me.'

'James, hi. You all right?' It was always her first question.

'Never been better,' I said, 'ah . . . except when I'm home with you, that is.'

'Daddy, Daddy, Daddy.'

I chatted with Veronica in baby language, then Natalie got on the phone.

'Where are you, Daddy?' she asked.

'I'm up on the roof of a big house, Princess.'

'Isn't it dangerous?'

'You sound like Mummy.'

'Is it, though?'

'No, darling. Not at all. How's school?'

'It's all right.'

'What did you learn today?'

There was a long pause. 'I can't remember,' she said.

'Can't remember?'

'Yes I can,' she said and started reciting. 'Once nine is nine, two nines are eighteen, three nines are twenty-seven . . .'

This would have gone on but Krista must have wrestled the phone from her.

'That's lovely, darling, Daddy hasn't got much time,' I heard her say. She came back on the line and was immediately businesslike, although I could hear plaintive bleating from our youngest daughter, and I could see in my mind's eye Krista walking, bouncing Veronica on her hip trying to calm her down.

'Are you going to be back for Sunday lunch?' Krista asked.

'Maybe . . .'

At that moment, gunfire erupted out of the night and bullets hammered against the wall surrounding the old warehouse beside the villa.

'I heard that . . .'

'Uh, gotta go, sweetheart, people to do . . .'

'Be careful, darling, call me back when you're done.'

'Love you.'

I was talking to myself. The phone was dead. Krista would now read Natalie a story and all the time she'd be worried about me far away in a foreign darkness.

Everyone ran back into the villa to get tooled up. Our sentries on the riverside wall were returning fire, shouting in Kurdish and English. I couldn't see the firing point but was fairly calm, thinking that it must be across the river directly west of us, nearly 300m away.

Dai pounded along beside me. 'Fucking hell, Jim, you're a bullet magnet you are. You didn't say the fucking "Q" word again, did you?'

'No, mate, the bad men must have something contagious going around. Or lots of bullets they need to shoot off before the sell-by date.'

I ignored my AK, sprinted for the stairs and rushed up to the roof. The last time I had been in the villa the team had had weapons ready in all the firing positions as if the Easter Bunny had been around dropping off guns and ammo. As I got to the main balcony, though, I realised that I was surplus to requirements. The enemy firing point was a boat floating in the middle of the river 100m away.

Kurdish sentries had jumped down from the wall and had actually run to the water's edge to return fire. From the wall and every balcony on the main building, machine-gun fire flayed the boat from the SF team. The volume of fire was such that Dai wasn't even bothering to look for a weapon. He did, however, grab a night-vision scope and go to the other side of the roof to see if this was just a diversion for another attack from the other side.

The jihadis on board the boat must have been nutters to take on Special Forces in their own villa. Nutters or martyrs rushing into the arms of the virgins lined up in suicide heaven. The only thing going for them was the current carrying them to safety. They had almost missed the villa before opening fire and were heading around the long curving bend that would cut off our line of sight.

Davor was on a satellite link, giving a calm sitrep to headquarters. Rick was behind the firing line, coordinating fire and also on another radio making sure that the guys on the other side of the villa at the front gate were doing the same as Dai and Cobus, keeping their eyes open for an attack from the east side of the compound.

'Yes, confirmed hostile fire from the boat, at least two machine-guns. Fuck it, they're moving out of sight,' Mark said. He was on a walkie-talkie, yelling at people to move down the shoreline and keep up the fire on the boat as it rounded the bend. Apparently without success since Kurdish gibberish was the only reply he got.

'Goddamn, why don't these assholes speak American!'

I knew that most of the team if not all were fluent Arabic-speakers, but I guess that the focus at language school had not included Kurdish unless you were posted to the north.

'Don't you have any wheels?' I returned and his eyes lit up.

We raced back downstairs and this time I did pick up my vest and AK before following him out of the door. As I came out he was already gunning the engine of a Humvee facing south towards the end of the small island on which the villa had been built. I jumped in the back and he pulled off down the road. He was wearing PNGs and the headlights were off, so as not to give our position away to the enemy.

The Humvee had two weapons on the back, a .50 cal on a turret ring, and a 240 GPMG at the back. After fumbling around in the dark I gave up on the 240, stumped by the canvas dust cover firmly buckled around it. I just couldn't see the buckles. For some reason the 50 was uncovered, so I wriggled up into the ring and broke off the seal on the box of ammo ready in the cage next to the gun.

I whipped out the end of the belt, surprised at how stable the ride was as Mark zoomed the Humvee down the shoreline. We were hidden from the boat by a thick line of trees. I guess the previous owner of the villa had insisted on smooth asphalt being laid around his estate. I swivelled the gun to the right and went through the loading drill, feeding the rounds in, jerking back on the cocking handle, releasing the bolt, jerking back the handle and releasing the bolt again.

Job done, there was nothing more to do but wait while Mark continued down the road, looking for a decent firing position. I locked the bolt release on automatic and occupied myself by digging around in my vest for my ear plugs, which I always carried in case I ended up at the range. The .50 cal was a noisy bugger and my ears were still a little tinny from the contact earlier and then hearing the shooting from the roof. I found them, rolled them up and stuffed them in my ears just as we pulled up behind a lone fishing shack at the end of a spit of land.

'Here.' Mark was handing a set of PVS night-vision goggles to me.

I put them on and fumbled around. 'Shit, Mark, I've never used these Yank models, where's the switch?'

He reached over to my head, switched it on, then got back to uncovering the 240 and loading it up.

Immediately my world was illuminated in impressive detail. I could see the fishing boat clearly now, lit up by what looked like twenty lasers from the villa. But I had seen war at night before. What seemed like a crazy lighting show from a rock concert, I knew was careful and rapid scanning from a dozen or more professionals looking for targets. In the confusion of a dynamic assault you might only have lasers from the team commander and the 2i/c on each flank, using their beams to indicate left and right boundaries of movement for the team. But in this static defence everyone was free to use them for rapid target acquisition or indication.

I had no comms with the villa, but I turned on my PEQ2 laser on top of the .50 to let them know we were in position at the tip of the island.

I readjusted the turret ring and checked the gun was able to swivel freely. Then I waited. There was no movement from the boat. Having passed through the gauntlet of fire from the team up at the villa I would have been surprised if there had been any.

One by one the lasers all switched off from the villa. The boat was out of line of sight for them. Only Mark and I still had eyes on.

'Are we shooting or are we letting it pass?' I asked Mark quietly.

My eyes never left the boat and the barrel of the .50 never ceased searching out the shadows on its superstructure. As the MNF man on the spot, it was his call.

'Are you serious? We're going to light that sucker up. I can see an armed man at the back.'

I'm not really sure why we were whispering, because after waiting two seconds the boat was side on to us and Mark let rip with the 240. I followed an instant later. I let him shred what was left of the upper deck and worked my fire along the lower hull at the waterline. Even through the ear plugs it was deafening. Before I knew it I had run through my belt. I threw the empty can behind me and heaved a second box out of the rack and into the ammo mount next to the gun. Five seconds later I had reloaded, ripping back the cocking handle at lightning speed, releasing and doing it again. Even through my NVG I could see that the boat was in pieces and listing heavily, an ironic reverse image of my position just a few days ago, when I was riding a RIB shredded by pirate machine-gun fire.

I was mindful, after my own experience of abandoning ship and floating about, that survivors from a sinking boat can still get a shot off. I switched to single shot and scanned the surface of the river to the left and right of the boat. If there were any survivors in the water, which I seriously doubted, they were doing what I would be doing in their place; hanging on to the other side of the boat and praying like fuck that the boat would move faster down-river away from those lethal Americans. I also realized that throughout the whole contact I had not seen one of the enemy.

I bunked down on the top floor in the ladies' quarters. There were no ladies in the house. Less than an hour had passed. The girls were in bed and Krista sounded relieved when she answered the phone.

'Everything OK?'

'No,' I replied. 'I miss you.'

'A likely story.'

'I mean it.'

We were quiet for a moment.

'What happened, James?' she then asked.

'A couple of madmen floated down the river and took some pop shots at the house,' I replied.

'Why?'

'Why?'

'Yes, why do they do it? They can't win.'

'They're not trying to win, they just want to be a bloody nuisance,' I said. 'They're waiting for us to pack up and go home so they can fight each other for what's left.'

'So what about Sunday lunch?' she said. 'Alicia and Jamie want to know if we can make it.'

'Ummm, tell you what, ask if we can change it to dinner. I should be back but I don't know about the flights. Besides, if I get back early, then we can spend Sunday lunch with the girls, just the four of us.'

'OK, that shouldn't be a problem. I'll tell them we'll be over for seven.'

There was a pause. I could hear her breathing.

'What are you wearing?' I asked her.

'Oh, James . . .'

'Come on.'

'As it happens, I just stepped out of the bath when you called. I'm not wearing anything but a pair of earrings and some moisturiser. I thought I might put some high heels on and walk around naked for a while.'

'That's what they call cruel and unusual treatment.'

'You did ask.'

'Love you, darling.'

'Love you, too. See you soon.'

We did phone kisses and hung up.

I had a shower myself and then sat on my fold-out cot and sleeping bag, chatting with Cobus and Dai, catching up on news. Cobus cracked his bottle of whisky and he and Dai sipped theirs while I threw a glass back in one.

In spite of my good intentions, it was Tanya Carillo who visited my dreams that night in Aradisa Idah. It was weird and confused. Mortars were raining down over the Green Zone. I was looking for Tanya and, when I eventually found her, she was lying in a trench covered with blood.

Dreams to me are meaningless and I dismissed it as the light of morning pierced the shutters. The smell of freshly brewed coffee was seeping up the stairs and passageways. American logistics are phenomenal, and although the SF team were happy to source local food, the freshly ground coffee was a top-notch American brand that was definitely the best part of waking up. I drank two cups, shovelled in a mound of scrambled eggs with pita bread and was bright-eyed and beaming as Cobus, Dai and I jumped back in the black Nissan and slid out of the gate at 09.00, deliberately after the usual morning traffic bombs.

We were off to drop Cobus at the Green Zone car park, and then Dai and I would head straight out to pick up Seamus at the BIAP on the first flight in.

CHAPTER 13

SEAMUS HAYES HAD been working as a VIP bodyguard for a young but famous actress. She adored Seamus. She paid him vast sums of money. Obscene amounts. She asked his advice on tour dates and flower arrangements, new houses and new scripts. The star was very intuitive. Each time Seamus was on the verge of quitting, she gave him more money.

There's cachet having a military attaché on the staff.

Who's the guy with the big moustache?

My bodyguard. I don't go anywhere without him.

When I first met Seamus with Les in Baghdad they were both obviously cut from the same cloth, lean and fit from boxing and running marathons. Professional soldiers from the old-school British Army and hard as coffin nails.

Les had been too busy falling in love to send me a text but it was a relief to see him striding almost a head taller beside Seamus across the concrete concourse at BIAP. His back was straight as a ramrod, his green eyes glowed and there was a whisper of dark curls creeping over the buttons of his white shirt. As an appreciator of fine art and good architecture, I can without self-consciousness say Les Trevellick was a looker. In fact three girls in fatigues waiting to fly out watched him saunter by and you didn't have to be a mind reader to know what fantasies were playing in their heads.

Les Trevellick was an ex-Royal Engineer staff sergeant who could build or blow up anything and had done both the Para and Commando course, on which he became an instructor. Seamus Hayes had been in the Paras fourteen years and come out as a colour sergeant. They were both in their forties, like Dai, sharp as Gurkha khukris and fit as a butcher's dog.

Seamus and Les dropped their day sacks and greeted Dai and me with big smiles and firm handshakes. Although we'd kept in touch we hadn't all been together in one spot since the last time we had been in Baghdad.

'Any problems getting through immigration?' I asked.

'You know what they say, mucker, "Ask no questions, hear no lies."' Seamus laughed back at me.

Dai and I unloaded our bags full of weapons and ammunition for Les and Seamus to get kitted up. Neither of them had been working in a high-threat environment, so Dai and I had brought body armour and helmets as well as the rest of the kit. They filled pouches and checked weapons while ripping the piss out of me with the Rupert routine, beloved of all soldiers, which presupposes all officers are not particularly bright, inbred, upper-class toffs called 'Rupert' who have difficulty distinguishing *rrr*s from *www*s, and who possesses the minimum intelligence required to shoot pheasant and quaff port. As I got behind the wheel of the car there was horror on every face.

'Fuck me, Wupert's dwiving. Are we even going to make it out of the car park?'

'Ha ha. Just get in the fucking wagon or you can walk to the Green Zone.'

There was more piss-taking along the lines of how I was the worst driver in Baghdad, a reputation I had gained the year before (extremely unfairly, I would like to point out).

After passing through the BIAP checkpoint, I accelerated along Route Irish, heading for the Green Zone, the metallic clacking as everyone made weapons ready echoing in my ears. I don't know how the others felt, but with the rest of the old Brit team back together, zooming through the morning traffic, eyes flickering left and right, it felt like I had never been away. I also relaxed, letting go of a tension in my shoulders that I hadn't realized was there until that moment.

Driving around with just Cobus, or just Dai, was pushing the limits of prudence. Now that Les and Seamus were here, I understood how much I had come to rely on them and felt a rush of renewed confidence. We could pull this off in our sleep. We knew this city and the threat environment like the backs of our hands. And, if things did go wrong, there were worse people with whom to face trouble than three hard-as-fuck, armed-to-the-teeth, ex-British Army senior NCOs.

'Dicker up on the bridge,' said Dai.

We all noted the potential dicker and then looked around to see what he might be triggering. I screeched into the inside lane as we were approaching the bridge and shot back into the centre as we exited, a cacophony of horn blasts and Arabic blasphemy following us down the highway. Insurgents pay kids and widows small sums to watch the road and warn insurgents with RPGs, and jihadis with their finger on IED remotes, that foreigners are passing.

In the time that we had been in Iraq there had been lethal contacts on Route Irish nearly every day, even at the peak of the US security efforts with Bradleys and Abrams tanks dug in nearly every 100m. We kept our eyes open. We all knew people who had been shot up on this road.

We chatted as we watched our arcs, bringing Seamus and Les up to date; saying that we'd be staying in the old SF villa in Aradisa, that the SF guys were all right, that Mad Dog was down in Basra but would be back up the next day to join us on our ride up to Mosul. We did not talk in detail about the tasking;

there would be a time and a place and this wasn't it. Travelling through Baghdad was always risky and now was the time to concentrate on the road and make sure we got back to the zone without any dramas.

'Oh, and don't forget to tell them about your girlfriend, lover boy,' said Dai. He explained that I had fallen for McQueen's new sergeant, to howls of derision from the back seat.

'And you a married man as well, that's disgusting. I thought officers were gentlemen,' Seamus scoffed.

'Don't worry, mate, once she gets a look at me you won't have to worry about it any more,' added Les. 'Poor thing don't stand a chance – I mean she's not made of wood, is she?'

The traffic slowed to a crawl.

'Talking of the old trouble and strife, how's the family, Ash?' Seamus added.

'Couldn't be better. Two girls. They want a puppy now.'

'Don't get a dog, mate, tie you down worse than wives,' said Dai, and he turned to Les. 'Listen, how's the new lady?'

'Shagging him out,' Seamus answered for him.

'Still,' said Les. 'Nice way to go.'

'I didn't think you were going to make it,' I said.

'Me? Wouldn't have missed it for the world.'

'No one's told him we're not getting paid for this lark,' said Dai.

'Not getting paid! You fucking joking?' screamed Les. 'Oi, Rupert, stop the wagon, I'm getting out.'

I hardly needed to be told to stop. The traffic had backed up. Cars were crawling into a bottleneck, trying to get around a stationary truck parked in the inside lane. We all became even more alert and studied our surroundings intently.

Les pointed at a man beating a carpet out on a balcony to our right. 'Hello, old Abdul's having trouble getting it started this morning.'

It was an old joke but we all still chuckled anyway.

'Fuck me crossways,' said Dai. 'There's something you don't see every day. Look at that cunt.'

A red Toyota hung in a tangled mess from the grill of the truck like a dead gazelle in the jaws of a lion. Two filthy flip-flops lay in the debris beside a tall old man with a bushy grey beard stretched out on the tarmac in a bloody dish-dash. There were splashes of blood and chips of glass strewn across the road. Three women swathed in black were hollering and cackling.

'The *jundhi* must have scarpered,' said Seamus.

We were close to a row of buildings – half-built or half-destroyed, it was hard to tell – definitely not a good place for white-eyes to be stuck in a jam. The side windows were down far enough to let in the stench of rotting garbage, decaying animals, burning tyres, human waste.

At night, Baghdad takes on a certain charm with the boxy buildings and brooding palms creating a cubist landscape. The darkness hides the turmoil, the remains of motor cars, sacrifices to the highway pushed to the wasteland beside the road, as someone in time would remove the red Toyota, its parts like human organs would be salvaged, and the shell would shelter orphans and widows and scavengers too poor to warrant a bullet from the insurgents and militias who ruled the night. This time of morning there were no shadows to veil Baghdad's ugliness.

There was in the Nissan an air of caution, not fear, but out there in the chaos that had evolved since 2003 everyone was afraid – afraid for their lives, of the neighbours, for the future. Men were afraid to express opinions, and where the religious fanatics held sway women were afraid to open their mouths. Iraq was no longer a land where Sammy and Fara could bring up their children and have decent lives.

That's what had brought the guys back to Baghdad. They were men with a firm sense of right and wrong. I am sure if Mad Dog had asked Seamus or Les or Dai to lead a team to escort Sammy and his family out of the city, they would have done so. It just came about that he had asked me.

Usually I tried not to dwell too deeply on my work as a security contractor, about who I was, what karma I was accruing, as Krista once said. Now, at least, I was sure I was doing the right thing. I owed it to Sammy. I had no idea of the genuine reason for the invasion but, as General Mashooen had rightly said, Iraq has always survived the invader and toppling Saddam would be beneficial to the people in the long term. The oil, after all, would be there long after the Americans had left.

We did our rubber-necking. The old guy was dead. One of the women had got to her feet and was slapping the side windows of the vehicles passing her by. Her unveiled face with blue tattoos marked her as belonging to some tribe beyond Baghdad, her distorted features a portrait of horror and alienation, of blind fear. The old guy was probably the breadwinner, the women – wives or daughters – were trapped in the steel river of impatient cars with passengers armed with loaded guns and perilous journeys ahead of them. There were no Good Samaritans on that road. In any event I could see the IP coming up the road, blue lights flashing and horns blaring. They would take care of this.

We pulled into the Green Zone via the BIAP gate and zoomed towards the embassy.

'There's the old parade ground, and the tomb of the unknown soldier,' said Seamus looking out the window as we passed the Crossed Swords. 'Mate, I cannot believe we are back.'

And I knew he was experiencing that strange sense of homecoming to this foreign country that had become part of us, yet which none of us had expected to see again.

'It'll be good to see Mad Dog again, and that bloody thieving Yaapie, Cobus,' added Les.

'I'll just give 'em a call, mate, and let them know that we're on our way,' said Dai, getting out his Iraqna mobile.

'Hello, Cobus, it's me. Yeah, we're in the Green Zone, just coming past the Crossed Swords, mate . . . Yes both of them . . .'

There was a long silence on the phone. In the rear-view mirror I watched Dai's features harden. He tapped me on the shoulder.

'Jim, drive straight to the Cash, mate, Cobus is waiting for us there.'

Momentarily befuddled, I took the wrong road and had to back up and do a U-turn to get back on track. After all the chit-chat, no one spoke again until we reached the Combat Support Hospital. Cobus was standing out in front by himself, no body armour, just his pistol in his belt and a daysack on his back.

'Cobus, you OK?'

'*Ja, ja,* I'm fine.'

He didn't smile as he shook hands with Les and Seamus. He took a breath and glanced at each of us in turn.

'It's Colonel McQueen,' he said, then he looked at me. 'And Tanya. They were both wounded early this morning. The convoy didn't even get twenty Ks out of Baghdad. It was completely destroyed, man. Every vehicle shot out. All the PSDs dead or wounded. It was another military convoy brought them back in.'

We stood there in shock. No one spoke.

'She's asking for you,' added Cobus, motioning at my rifle. 'You must leave your long here in the wagon. *Net hand wapens* inside.' Pistols only.

I felt like a fist was clenching my guts. I unslung my rifle, took off my body armour and put them in the car. Cobus was saying that McQueen was seriously injured and had already been case-vaced to the BIAP, military side. He was probably already on a plane to Ramstein *en route* to the US military hospital at Landstuhl.

He led me into the CSH, around a few turns, which I memorized absent-mindedly.

'How badly wounded is she, mate?'

'Not too bad.' Cobus put on a brave face. 'Broken leg and some shrapnel, she'll be fine. But they need the beds here since there are more serious casualties expected all the time because of the Surge. She wants to see you before they move her down to Basra or out to Germany.'

'I'll leave you here, man. Meet you back out the front.'

I entered a large bright room with white walls and neat charts. She was the only occupant. She looked up with a faint smile. I was shocked at how pale she looked.

'Oh Jesus, don't look at me like that.' She smiled. 'I'm not dead – just got a broken leg. I only got two hours' sleep last night, this is what I look like in the morning without makeup!'

'You look as beautiful as ever,' I assured her.

'That's enough of your Brit charm, Ash,' she said. 'I gotta tell you about the colonel.'

I pulled up a chair and took her hand. I gently squeezed her fingers as she told me what had happened. The convoy had left at 3a.m., a bunch of containers on trucks driven by local *jundhis* and escorted by McQueen, Tanya and an American civilian contractor team. No military vehicles, only big GMC Suburban SUVs, one armoured and the rest converted into gun trucks.

'The PSDs were a bunch of complete idiots,' she said bitterly. 'They were all wearing their do-rags instead of helmets, those stupid little goatees, bare arms with big tattoos, knives and grenades strapped all over them . . .'

'Like Rambo,' I said.

'Without the brains. Instead of doing anything constructive like going over the route, they were too busy checking out their reflections and making sure they looked like bad-asses. They were a fucking joke,' she continued. 'One of these guys was wearing his shades and it's like fucking 3a.m. and still pitch black.'

'Where d'you find these guys?'

'I don't, Ash, they've got a contract. Colonel McQueen always used to tell me how professional you guys were, and I could tell it with Cobus driving us around. I mean, he never used to show off or tell me how tough he was.' She stopped to sip some water, tears of outrage in her eyes.

'Cobus is a pro,' I said, thinking to myself he was more like a wolf amidst sheep.

'You said that right. Jesus he could have had all of these guys for breakfast.' She put her glass down. 'So anyway, once these asshats all finished hitting on me, checking out my tits and ass, and telling me their "street names" and trying to impress me with their warrior-code bullshit, we finally got on the road.'

I listened in silence as she calmed down and coolly told me the tale of their nightmare journey.

They had set off first to Abu Ghraib to pick up the trucks from the depot. They were mortared in the depot and fought off a ground assault. They were mortared again and finally got their small convoy out of the gate and headed back to Baghdad to circle around the highway to the south. The PSDs – the asshats, as she called them – had done nothing during the assault but cower in their vehicles while Mad Dog had picked himself bleeding off the floor, rallied the depot sentries and directed fire at the enemy.

I would learn later that he had already suffered serious injuries by this stage, but was determined to get the convoy down to Basra. Securing the perimeter, marking out the unexploded mortar shells and rounding up the terrified civilian truck drivers had wasted precious time.

'So it's already like 06.30 hours, probably nearer seven, dawn is on the horizon, and the colonel is seriously pissed because we haven't even left yet. He stuck me in the armoured SUV with a couple of PSD shooters to bring up the rear of the convoy and took the lead with the other PSDs in the front gun truck. He ordered me to holler on the radio if the rear trucks started to lag too far behind, then we headed out the front gate.'

They had circled the city and started making their way south.

I knew the road, and understood the relief they had felt as they passed safely through the bandit town of Mahmudiyah.

'Oh, and this PSD next to me in the vehicle, a guy called John Hunt, that same dickhead wearing the shades, he was a real whiner the whole time. He's this really short, chubby, wimp with serious small-man syndrome. He kept wanting me to call him by his street-tag, "Blade", but I refused. Even the other PSDs thought he was a jerk. Hunt had been mouthing off in the Green Zone about what a bad dude he was, but after the mortars he was literally crying and kept asking every five minutes if we should just cancel the convoy and head back to the Green Zone.'

She was doing another radio check with McQueen when the world exploded. Daisy-chain IEDs buried on the roadside devastated the convoy and blew half the vehicles off the road in front of her. Even as she screeched to a halt, enemy machine-guns opened up on the surviving vehicles.

'I was in shock. There was no return fire at all,' Tanya said. 'The colonel, well I was waiting for him to give orders over the radio, but he wasn't saying anything, nor answering me when I called. I didn't know what to do because our immediate action was supposed to be to drive out of it, but all the vehicles were stopped. I mean, they were all on fire apart from us. It took me a while to realize we had to get out and fight.'

'First rule, return fire,' I said.

Her eyes searched mine for understanding, and she relaxed, obviously seeing it there. The unexpected is just that, unexpected, and it often takes time for the brain to forget about being surprised and overloaded with new information.

'So I cracked my door, poked my rifle out past the armour and started firing back at the AIF,' she said.

It was a brave reaction, but a trained operator would have crawled over the passenger seat to debus from the vehicle on the side facing away from the enemy, then got away from those bullet and RPG magnets as fast as possible. Tanya was a clerk, not an infantryman, but she was still a US soldier and determined to hit back.

It was then, she said, that she had seen movement in the tree-line off to the left-hand side of the road, the enemy pouring bullets into the convoy. The American contractors still standing were firing and moving off to the right-hand side, away from the enemy fire. The Iraqi civilian drivers had either run off immediately or were dead. Colonel McQueen was still on the road, running up the line of the convoy towards the rear, and checking the cabs of each vehicle for casualties.

Then a secondary explosion on the road had picked him up and thrown him nearly 10m.

One of the PSDs had turned back and run to McQueen, a Kurdish ex-Peshmerga, Tanya had realized.

'I yelled at the shooters in my car to get some goddamn fire down and cover them, and we all started firing. I could see the Kurdish guy is now pulling big chunks of smoking shrapnel out of the colonel with his fucking Leatherman pliers!' she said and a hopeless smile crossed her lips. 'In the meantime, this fucking contractor, Hunt, is shrieking next to me so loudly I nearly shot him to shut him up. He was always giving it to us how impor-tant he was, and how he was "the man", and now we're in trouble he is literally weeping and snotting all down his shirt. That fucking asshole never fired a single shot during the whole contact.'

As the Peshmerga started dragging McQueen away, Tanya had emptied her magazine out at the enemy positions, aiming at their muzzle flash and smoke. She stopped, dumped her mag and reloaded.

'I don't know how many I got. I'm pretty sure I dropped a couple of AIF, and then a couple more went down. At least some of the firing stopped, so I reckon I either hit those guys or made them change position. Then an RPG hit the front of the SUV and blew me the fuck up,' she said matter-of-factly.

'Thank God you're here to tell the story,' I said.

She was gripping my hand tightly, belying the calm expression on her face.

'And then what happened?'

She had woken up in terrible pain. The armoured passenger compartment had shielded her, but the front of the SUV, including the engine, had vanished. Her left leg was broken and full of shrapnel, and she couldn't move. Piercing agony ripped through her as she tried to shift her leg.

She looked to her right, where the PSDs who were still alive had bunkered down in a ditch and were pinging a couple of shots back across at the enemy. With growing horror she realized that she was the only person left on the road. On her left, an assault line of insurgents was walking steadily towards the burning convoy, firing into the vehicles.

'I couldn't find my rifle. I thought it must have been blown out of the SUV, and there was dust and smoke everywhere.' Tanya's voice was steady but the smile had gone now. 'I looked out again and I could see that maggot Hunt crawling away with my fucking rifle. That shithead left me there and took my weapon.'

I made a mental note that this John Hunt was someone I would do my best to find and have a word with.

'Hunt stood up to run and got shot about a hundred times,' she said, saving me a job. 'He went down like a sack and lay there crying until he died. I called out the open door to those PSD jerks to come help me but no one budged from their positions. I tried to move again, but it hurt so much and I couldn't reach down and free my foot.'

When she glanced back towards the ditch, she watched Mad Dog rise up from where the loyal Peshmerga had dragged him before being killed himself.

'I tell you Ash, the colonel looked like frozen shit warmed up,' she said and the smile was back again.

McQueen by this time had a long list of injuries: he had been hit in the legs, abdomen and back by shrapnel that had punched straight through his body armour and compacted half his vertebrae. He had lost the use of his right arm, which would be shattered permanently, his right eye and his right ear, and had severe facial injuries.

None of the contractors came with him. A full-bird colonel, fifty-six years old, wounded and half-blind, McQueen came up on to the road and attacked the insurgents alone. Firing his rifle with his left hand, Mad Dog staggered forward and managed to drop six insurgents before the rest realized where he was and took cover, pouring fire into the armoured chassis of the SUV. McQueen collapsed against the SUV, leaned around it and shot another two enemy before his rifle was empty. Almost dropping from blood loss, Mad Dog didn't try and reload, but let his rifle drop on its sling, grimly ignored the enemy fire and reached in to start freeing Tanya.

'I tell you what, I thought we were both dead.'

She looked me in the eye, and I was starting to think this was a bullshit story – there was no obvious way that they could plausibly have escaped this impossible situation.

'And then,' she paused for dramatic effect, 'I have never been so glad in all my born days. An army convoy came up the road the other way from the south, came straight on up right into the ambush zone and started machine-gunning the fuck out of those AIF. It was the most beautiful thing I have ever seen. So then the colonel pulls me out on to his shoulders. We nearly both fall down, and then he stands up, and there, right in front of us not four feet away, is a fucking I-raqi pointing an AK at us. I shit you not.'

'Jesus,' I breathed. 'So what happened? He let you go?'

'No! He starts laughing,' she answered. 'We are totally fucked. The colonel is practically dead and is blind and covered in blood with me on his shoulders and his right hand stuffed into his belt to keep it out of the way – and I don't even have a weapon . . . I mean, we are totally fucked, right?' She paused again. 'And then as the I-raqi brings the AK up to nail us, there are two loud bangs and I think to myself, Oh Jesus, he just shot the colonel and I'm next, but then the insurgent falls over with two holes in his face. I look down and I see the colonel is holding his M9 in his left hand.'

'Amazing . . .'

'He just turns around calmly and shuffles off back to the ditch, carrying me like a sack of laundry and shooting another two insurgents with his pistol on the way. It was un-fucking-believable.'

'Jesus,' I muttered. 'Good for you, Mad Dog.'

'He kept saying it was you, saved his life,' Tanya continued, looking at me thoughtfully, 'that you taught him how to do that.'

'Wow, really?'

I thought back to the months and months I had drilled Mad Dog on his pistol skills, drawing and double-tapping until we had calluses and blisters on our fingers. 'Northern Ireland drills' McQueen had called them, and I couldn't believe that those hundreds of hours had paid off and saved his life; in fact, both their lives.

'Anyway, I wasn't born yesterday,' I said. 'Do you really expect me to believe a science-fiction story like that? Why don't you tell me how you really broke your leg, falling over drying your hair or whatever?'

'You fucking asshole!' She spat in mock outrage and started slapping me, laughing.

'Excuse me, are you bothering my patient?' a cold voice behind me asked.

I turned around to be confronted by a strikingly beautiful woman, wearing a smile that was at odds with the cold tone. My mouth opened but nothing especially witty came out. I looked at her name tag, which read 'COX', then realized she might think I was looking at her impressive bust and jerked up guiltily. She gave me a look that told me she knew exactly what I had been thinking.

'You are obviously on the road to recovery,' she said to Tanya, having a quick look at her drug chart and ignoring me. 'We're going to be flying you out of Baghdad to Kuwait tonight. You'll probably be there a few days, but because of the surge they are trying to keep as many beds free here as possible, and in Kuwait and Ramstein. You could be back in the States in a week.'

'Oh my God, that is awesome, thanks Michelle.' Tanya beamed.

I was still goggling her, wondering if she was a nurse or doctor. She had a stethoscope shoved in a pocket and a pistol on her thigh, but no rank or any other identifying ID. I remembered last time I had been in the CSH, dropping off wounded and dead private contractors during another unhappy day in Baghdad, there had been a stunning nurse with whom Seamus had scored a date. It was astonishing to see such an attractive woman in a war zone like this – maybe to work in the CSH you had to be booked through a model agency or something. Rather belatedly I realized that staring at another pretty woman probably wasn't endearing me to Tanya at all.

'Don't excite her and pop any stitches,' Michelle warned me, resting her hand on her holster absent-mindedly.

She spun on her heel and walked out.

I looked back at Tanya. 'So you're off tonight? That's great news. On your way home. Wow, congratulations.'

She was looking at me seriously, still happy about the news she was heading home, but the smile was fading.

'There's bad news, Ash,' she informed me. 'The convoy to Mosul has been cancelled, and there's only Shaun and Scott in the office left. They'll have to stay and look after things until Colonel McQueen's replacement gets in.'

'Shit, I hadn't thought about that.'

'Look, you better go and get stuff sorted out for Sammy, and figure what you guys are going to do,' she added and yawned. 'I'm sorry, I am just bushed.'

We gripped hands again. This was goodbye. She was going back to the States to her fiancé and weeks of physiotherapy. I was going to get Sammy out of Baghdad and then head off back to my wife and kids, and apparently to Sunday dinner with some friends. It was hugely improbable we would ever see each other again.

'Want anything from the PX? Any snacks? A magazine?'

'No, I'm good.'

I thought there were a lot of 'what if's in her expression.

'Take care of yourself out there.'

'Will do. Don't worry Tanya, we'll have Sammy up to Mosul in a jiffy and be back in time for tea and medals.'

That got a laugh out of her, breaking the sombre mood. I kissed her on the cheek, said goodbye and walked out of the room.

That was the last time I saw her.

I wandered back down the corridors of the CSH towards the front, the smell of antiseptic strong in my nostrils. It reminded me of the Franco-German hospital in Split, Croatia, fifteen years ago where I had taken so many of my soldiers, become men before their time, eighteen- and nineteen-year-olds with pale, sweating faces and swearing in their pain and confusion as we clumsily lifted them out of the backs of our Land Rover. It had been a far less high-tech hospital, but there had been the same sense of relief when you entered; the same recognition that here was a place where professionals worked, where you could be saved.

I remember visiting the wounded from my company in a tented ward they were sharing with seven Pakistani peacekeepers with horrific lower-leg injuries. The Pakistanis had all been injured in the same incident when a single mortar shell had exploded on the other side of their wheeled APC. The shrapnel had gone horizontally under their vehicle and scythed them down like wheat. Virtually all of them had frames of titanium and steel rods bolted down their shins, holding their legs in place until the bones could knit together. With plenty of egging on from my Dukes, a couple of the Pakistanis were trying to get out of bed and walk, under the misconception that, with the metal rods, their legs were as strong as before.

The men collapsed screaming, amidst much hilarity and laughter from both the British and Pakistani soldiers. A French nurse came in attracted by the noise and started shrieking for assistance from her colleagues. The other nurses ran in, shocked, and gave us dirty looks while they lifted the men back into bed. Our offers of help were ignored, and the nurses disappeared in frosty silence. They were pretending not to speak any English and my basic schoolboy French was not up to any decent conversation.

Afterwards I went around to chat to two Dukes who had been injured by a booby trap as they had cleared mines. Private Kelly had lost two fingers from his left hand and had suffered nerve damage down the left-hand side of his torso. Private Bird had lost three fingers and most of his left hand and his right hand just above the wrist. Both men also had severe shrapnel damage to their arms. They were both cheerful and well drugged.

'Fuckin' hell, Boss, did you see that Paki go down? What a stupid cunt.'

'Who is it you are being calling stupid cunt?' shouted the Pakistani back happily. 'I am not the one whom the wife is being fucked at home by the large black man, isn't it?'

'Come over here and say that, Gandhi,' said Kelly, 'I've still got one hand and both feet to kick your arse, you fucking cripple.'

'Well, I came around to check on your morale, but there doesn't seem to be much of a problem there.' I smiled back at him. I stood in front of Kelly since he could not turn his head very much, but I was facing the both of them.

'Just don't start any trouble and get yourselves kicked out of here,' I admonished them.

'S'all right, Boss, they're awright, they are,' slurred Bird at me. He was heavily sedated. 'That Saleem over there, he's got about twenty fucking cousins in Bradford. Thass just down the road from me.'

Bird's voice was barely audible and even as I watched him he drifted into unconsciousness.

'How's he doing, Kelly?' I turned back to the first man. Is he coping all right? I suppose he has been out of it too much to really think about the future.'

'He's OK, sir. We was just talking last night about it and he reckons he's lucky it came off so low, at the wrist. That Jerry doctor reckons he's an ideal candidate for false hands, you know, them prosthetics,' Kelly replied. 'Besides I was taking the piss that he wouldn't be able to wank again. He doesn't care, he told me. He had a chat with his missus on the phone yesterday and she told him that her big hero won't ever have to worry about that part of life. Lucky sod.'

Yes, that was Bird all right. One lucky sod. I looked down at his bandaged stumps. *How did a man with no hands use a telephone? In fact how does he do anything? How does he feed himself, or brush his teeth or wipe his own arse?*

Every soldier, and every officer for that matter, has thoughts on being wounded. And whether they talk about it or not to their mates every man knows that there is a personal limit beyond which it is better to be dead. For many it is commonly the loss of one's genitals. 'If my wedding tackle's gone, Boss, just shoot me,' is a phrase I had heard during many such a discussion. For others it was their legs; they just did not think that they could face life in a wheelchair.

It is a common enough topic of conversation amongst men whose lives involve both danger, potential sudden and violent maiming or death, and often long, tedious periods of boredom in which to question the many disadvantages of their chosen profession. For me the fear was of being blinded. I thought that if I lost my eyes, then I would prefer to have been killed outright. In that respect both Kelly and Bird had been lucky, if you could call it that. The visors on their helmets, the only two mine-proof visors the company possessed, had protected their faces and necks from the angle of the shrapnel, right down to the top of their body armour.

I had very nearly been blinded by burning petrol during a riot in West Belfast. The flames had hit my chest, engulfed me and shot up inside my visor. Only a snap-second reflex had clamped my eyes and mouth shut, stopping me from searing my throat and lungs. Through my eyelids I could see white heat and smell my own skin burning as my eyelashes melted instantly.

For many people the memories of accidents or horror are visual. For me the main sensation was smell, the smell like barbecued pork that I will never forget. The petrol had only soaked the surface of my smock, but the flames had flash-burned my face. The men around me extinguished the flames very quickly and I carried on shouting orders throughout the rest of the incident. That night, despite the strong emollient cream from the MO the pain came and my face started peeling off in huge strips. By morning I looked like something out of a horror film, but with a bit more cream slapped on it was soon good as new. Like a good officer I necked back codeine and ibuprofen and soldiered on. In later years I was often complimented on how young I looked for my age, and I would laugh it off as the benefits of fresh air and exercise, whilst mentally crediting those lovely people in Belfast for my involuntary face peel.

As I walked back out into the sunlight, I thought back to Private Bird in Split. I had been there the morning that they were being flown back to Brize Norton in the UK for further medical treatment. Bird was lucid and in a bit of a slump.

'What can I do, sir?' His eyes were starting to fill up and he looked away. 'I mean, what job can you do with no hands? I was going to be a fitter in a garage. I'm twenty, for fuck's sake, Boss. What have I got to look forward to?'

I looked down at his bags to give him a bit of dignity while he recovered himself. *How does a man with no hands pack his bags?* To be honest I was having a bit of trouble speaking myself, what with this big lump in my throat and all.

'You'll be surprised, Birdy. You still have a couple of fingers left on one hand, as well as all the ligaments in your forearms and that is good news for all the new prosthetic hands that are about these days. And you have the love of a good woman, and your family is waiting to see you, aren't they?' I looked up at him and he nodded, still looking away from me out of the window and swallowing hard. I looked back at his bags. *How does a man with no hands unzip his flies for a piss?* I suddenly thought. I wondered how much use he would regain from his left hand.

'Besides which you are going to have so much compensation money you won't know what to spend it on.'

'Aye, you're right, Boss, I am just being stupid.' His voice was muffled.

'Paul, listen to me,' I leaned in close and turned him to face me. 'I am not going to bullshit you and tell you how good everything is going to be. I mean, you have lost your fucking hands, right?'

He nodded back at me angrily through unshed tears.

'But I will promise you one thing. That the recovery will be hard, that you have months if not years of physiotherapy ahead of you and that at times you will be more depressed than you ever thought possible. The thing is that I know you can do it. You came what, fourth or fifth in the company cross-country competition?

'First,' he replied indignantly.

'That's right. And your team came first in that shitty four-day competition we had over the hills in Yakima.' I nodded at him. 'You have guts and determination, bags of it and you are going to need every little scrap of it over the next few years. The only difference is that no one is going to know about your hard work but you and me, and the only reward you are going to get is not some trophy, but a better quality of life for yourself. You understand?

He nodded.

'I haven't got a clue what therapies there are,' I continued. 'Or how good these new fake hands are going to be. You're going to have to find that out for yourself. But you promise me that you are going to give it everything you have, because any opportunity that comes up I want you to give it the best chance of succeeding. You are fitter and more physically robust than any civilian that gets an injury like this so you will recover faster. And you are more motivated so you will learn quicker and succeed where another man might fail. Right?'

He nodded again, eyes dry now as he looked up at me with a bit more of his old self about him.

'Always remember you are a Duke, one of my men. And when your stumps heal up get your arse out and start running again. I don't want you turning into a fat lump. You keep a bit of pride about yourself and things will seem much brighter.'

'Yes, Boss, you're right,' he said and grinned. 'I am sorry about that. I just felt a bit low this morning thinking about it all.'

'It's OK, Bird, and you're right if you're thinking it will be bloody hard, but just don't forget to ask yourself if you're the kind of man that's up to it. I reckon you are, so don't get depressed, because that's not going to get your hands back, is it? Just get over it and get on with it. I don't want you wallowing around in self-pity like Kelly over there.'

We both looked over at Kelly, who was trying to impress one of the French nurses with his tattoo collection. That got a laugh out of him at least.

'All right, Birdy?' Corporal Helstrip came up to the bed and peered around me. 'Malingering again? Fuckin' ell, Boss. Some folk will do anything to go home early.'

'Go fuck yourself, John,' snapped Bird.

We all laughed. I went off to chat to Kelly and left the other two to say their goodbyes. Later on, someone would tell Bird that after the explosion it was Corporal Helstrip, their section commander, who was first to react and reach their bodies. He had sprinted down the cleared path, heedless of our shouts to beware any further mines. After putting rough tourniquets on both Kelly's and Bird's forearms he had picked Bird up and was halfway back even as the two platoon medics went running up with the medpack and the other sections stayed in place, weapons in the shoulder, ready to provide cover if the Croats up on the hill tried putting any fire down. A big, hard man and a rugby player for the battalion, Corporal Helstrip had been crying like a baby as he gently carried Bird's limp body back to safety, the both of them covered in his blood.

I was thoroughly depressed as I met up with Seamus, Les, Dai and Cobus all sat around the car as I came out. Cobus had filled them in on the situation, and by common consent we went up to the palace to sit and discuss our next move over lunch.

As we sat in Saddam's palace and ate our chilli-burgers and Freedom fries (I had passed on the dubious hygiene of the salad as I was trying to avoid the usual trial of a bout of Baghdad Belly) I wondered what had become of Private Paul Bird. The last time I had seen him had been years ago, when he was well on the way to recovery but still prone to the occasional lapse into depression.

How does a man with no hands kill himself? Plenty of places to jump, I suppose.

Krista once asked me if I remember the riot and being on fire, whether I still had memories of the flames. I told her no, because at the time my eyes were squeezed shut, saved by my blink reflex.

On quiet evenings sometimes, if I am in an introspective mood, when I close my eyes my nostrils flare at imagined petrol, and I remember the smell of my face burning.

CHAPTER 14

W HEN FARA STUDIED in Paris, she stayed with a friend of her father, a diplomat. When that friend was unexpectedly reassigned, Fara persuaded her father to allow her to share with two other girls in an apartment close to the cafés and theatres on the Champs-Élysées.

The experience shaped Fara's life. Living in the city of love, running off to see new plays and screenings of films by François Truffaut, discussing art and politics in the Café de Flore, where Sartre and Simone de Beauvoir had in their time filled the air with Gauloises and opinions on existentialism and free will.

With Sammy's status as an air-force hero, through the dictatorship Fara had continued to live with a form of freedom that suited her. It wasn't Paris, but she had her memories, her children, and she wouldn't have dreamed of wearing a headscarf in the modern city of Baghdad. I recall her once saying that in a veil a woman is inviting men to imagine what lies beneath: she is flirting. Fara enjoyed chatting in French with a younger man in a way that was perfectly normal and innocent in the world in which I had grown up and she had grown to admire.

Her *joie de vivre* had been shattered that day when the fundamentalist militia told her to cover her face and leave the school where she had been teaching. In the new Iraq you were either with us or against us, a member of the *umma*, a believer, or an apostate. The middle ground occupied by people like Fara had gone. She despaired at what was happening in her country, the fear, the distrust, the schism dividing Shia and Sunni. I recalled her saying, 'We are being Talibanized, James,' and the phrase had stuck in my head.

Cobus had given orders that no one was to leave the house. There was a price on Sammy's head. If a member of the family were seen in the street, someone would inform the police or the local Shia militia, which were generally the same thing; not because they believed Sammy was a traitor. They would do so for the reward.

After discussion with Cobus, Sammy had also given strict instructions that no one was to mention to either friends or family the plan to flee to Mosul until after the escape was successful. Far better that they fled first and then once in a safe place they could call and inform those close to them where they were.

It was Sammy's nature to indulge Fara. She was used to getting her own way. Now, for the first time in her life, she felt penned in, trapped like the songbirds you see in bamboo cages on terraces and rooftops in Iraqi houses. Fara was still angry that she had been barred from the school and it irritated her that she was unable to make her weekly visit to see Aunt Zahrah, the surviving sister of her mother. She knew the next time she went might be the last time, that it would be to say goodbye.

Fara had put off the journey to Mosul in the belief that the revenge killings would stop, that life would get back to normal. The day I appeared in a *shemagh*, that belief withered and died. She knew that they were leaving Baghdad and would never return.

Early Wednesday morning, at the same time that Colonel McQueen was setting off for Basra, Fara slipped from her room while the rest of the family was still sleeping. She hadn't gone to bed with a plan. Sometimes in our dreams plans make themselves, we create reality the way we would like it to be. She showered, applied her makeup and dressed in her favourite suit. It wasn't from Paris, but the tailors in Baghdad are unusually skilled. They take the designs from the pages of *Vogue* and copy them exactly. In the suit, Fara was herself again.

She went downstairs to the place where they had stored the two bags each they would take on the journey to Mosul. From her sister-in-law's bag she borrowed an *abaya* and *hijab*, the black, full-length robe and headscarf. Combined with her suit it would keep her warm this chilly morning. Although there was a risk that someone might recognize her, she believed it to be far less risky than covering her face with a veil. In a time of suicide bombers and mob paranoia Fara did not want to draw attention by appearing to be someone attempting to conceal their identity. With a string shopping bag over her arm, she set off for Aunt Zahrah's house, a twenty-minute walk through Karada.

Zahrah was delighted to see her favourite niece and made Fara sit down and have breakfast. Her delight changed to horror when Fara shared with her the family plan to flee to the north of Iraq as part of an American convoy.

Aunt Zahrah was shrill and unreasonable in her outrage. She had never liked Sammy, and had never accepted that he was good enough for Fara. How could he expect Fara to travel to Mosul in some dirty army truck with a group of unknown foreigners? She ignored Fara's protests that they would be travelling in very comfortable American SUVs. And what about the poor general? At his age. It's all very well for the children and that plump brother and his wife, but Sammy really could not expect her, Fara, to be humiliated by the indignity of being moved around like cattle or those terrible al-Qaeda prisoners who all deserved to be shot.

Aunt Zahrah hammered home her case. It was the wrong time of year to leave Baghdad. It had been snowing in the north. The roads were impassable and frozen. The children would die of flu. What kind of mother was she? The filthy Kurds would rape her and steal her precious possessions. Why didn't Sammy think about these things? He had never provided properly – Aunt Zahrah overlooked that it was Sammy who had bought the very flat she was living in with money he had earned from Spartan, a fact she brushed aside when Fara reminded her. She was in full flow and greatly enjoying herself. No ridiculous trifles such as mere facts were going to stop her rant now.

The thing is, she insisted, an army truck is going to be draughty, cramped and wholly unsuitable. She had once driven in one in 1973 and the bumps had damaged her hips so that they still hurt, even now, when she walked to the market. Had she not told Fara the story a hundred times?

Eventually Fara calmed her down, and persuaded her that Sammy had arranged for three luxurious SUVs crammed full of luxuries to transport them up to Mosul in comfort, warmth and style. If Zahrah did not believe her she could go over to cousin Gabir's shop garage and see them herself. To prove it, Fara gave her a packet of caramel-coated popcorn, a special treat and part of the goody bag that McQueen and Tanya had pulled together for Sammy's family.

Still suspicious, sulking that she had not been asked to help with the arrangements – had she not moved the entire family from that shithole in Habbaniyah to the upmarket Mansur district? – Aunt Zahrah allowed herself to be mollified as she munched on the sweet popcorn. But she was still annoyed.

Fara promised that as soon as they were in Mosul she would call right away and let Zahrah know that they were all safe. The two women embraced and Fara went out to pick up a few treats for a picnic on the way up to Mosul. It would be a long drive and everyone would be sure to appreciate something to eat and drink in the cars, even if they could not stop and get out.

When Fara left her aunt's apartment, it was mid-morning with the spring sun breaking through the gloom.

The *abaya* and *hijab* she was wearing symbolized for Fara the repression and humiliation of women. A movement backward in time. In using these garments as a disguise to pass through her own neighbourhood, she felt as if she were striking a blow against the hated Shia fanatics. Hatred was in the air like a virus, spreading through Baghdad in a plague of ethnic cleansing and the obscene intimacy of mutually shed blood. So keen had Fara been on her small act of revenge, she had forgotten these dangers and neglected to think of the consequences.

It was a pleasure being out in the fresh air and she strolled through the market, filling her bag with vegetables, dates, a bundle of mint. She was feeling content for the first time in weeks, glad to be out and about, glad that she had made the effort to visit Aunt Zahrah and say goodbye. She was even becoming optimistic about their new life in Mosul. As she selected vegetables she hummed to herself.

While Fara was shopping, her Aunt Zahrah suddenly had a thought. It was all very well Sammy arranging for these fancy vehicles, but who on earth was going to drive them? His brother? Almost as useless as Sammy. The general? He was over eighty and frail. She was furious. It was typical of the man not to think of these basic fundamentals, which is why they should have called her in the first place. What they should do is hire a nice clean taxi and – typical – it was up to her, Zahrah, to make the arrangements. She would call Abeer al-Mazyad. *Her* driver, as she liked to say.

Aunt Zahrah got straight on the phone to Abeer and Abeer went to her apartment to discuss the confidential nature of the job she was proposing. A single woman and a married man would not normally meet alone in these intolerant times, but this was different. As the Arabs say, everyone has the same religion when it comes to money. They drank tea. Zahrah drove a hard bargain, and Abeer went home to tell his wife that, within the week, he was going away for a couple of days to drive Sammy Mashooen and his family north to Mosul.

Women in Iraq had taken to wearing veils, but the men don't always wear the trousers. Mrs al-Mazyad went mental. What was her husband thinking? She had never heard anything so outrageous in her life. Leaving her alone while he runs off to take criminals to their luxury second home in the mountains? Didn't he know the roads were plagued by al-Qaeda, *mujahideen*, foreigners, or even worse, the *Amerikeyeh*?

When Abeer told his wife it was safe, they were going with an American convoy, travelling in armoured American vehicles hidden at Gabir's shophouse, she hit the roof. How could *they* be so selfish involving *her* husband in *their* devious schemes? If the Americans were escorting them, it was proof they were collaborators and traitors. Couldn't he see that? It had been all very well for Abeer, a Shia, to suck up to them when the Sunni wielded the whip. The world had changed. Saddam had gone. The Shia had no need to bow to anyone but Allah. And when Abeer was killed out there, ferrying around his Sunni friends, who would look after her and the children? God would damn all men who were thoughtless pigs and who never looked after their families.

Furious with her stupid husband and almost weeping with self-pity, Mrs al-Mazyad went straight to the market where, over bartering for bags of rice and raisins, she bumped into her two sisters and best friend, who provided perfect shoulders to cry on. Like her, they were outraged. They went straight home and told their husbands, this juicy droplet of gossip flowing like the Tigris in the rainy season through the streets and, like the rain, sprinkling across the neighbourhood indiscriminately.

I had been at Tanya Carillo's bedside all this time, holding her hand, trying to focus on Tanya, and thinking about what we were going to do now that the convoy to Mosul was off the agenda.

The moment I exited the hospital, I saw that Cobus was still updating the others. The mood was grim.

Above: Mad Dog next to a PSD vehicle hit by mortar shrapnel, the morning of his last convoy.
© Colonel Steve McQueen.

Above: Damage caused to an armoured PSD vehicle after a buried IED strike.

Above: Mad Dog's view from his casevac helicopter. He sat up, snapped the photo then laid back down on his stretcher for the medic to carry on treating him. Nutter. © Colonel Steve McQueen.

Above: With Dai on a rooftop – Saddam's unfinished mosque can be seen in the background.

Above: A 1st Cav trooper on the range, smiling even though he just lost $10 in our weekly shooting competition. Note he's crossed out the 'or Alive' part of Osama's 'Wanted' poster.

Above: Me on the M249 with the 82nd Airborne – note the homemade 'hillbilly' armour plating and sandbags on the floor to soak up shrapnel.

Above: Typical damage from a 'walker' suicide bomber. Fragments have shredded the cargo and driving compartment.

Above: An example of a much more severe blast and thermal damage from a vehicle-borne IED outside the Assassin's Gate.

Above: Visiting some friends just before heading for the Jordanian border. Note the M203 – a combination weapon capable of firing 5.56mm and 40mm grenades with devastating accuracy and an excellent force multiplier for small teams.

Above: An Iraqi Police (IP) checkpoint. We're using the CF humvee as cover!

Above: A picnic break near Fallujah. I'm with Sammy's youngest son.

Above: Bird's eye view of the rats' nest of buildings typical of Baghdad suburbs. This is a good example of the terrain through which we were fleeing. © Colonel Steve McQueen.

Above: A tense moment approaching the Sunni 'Sons of Iraq' checkpoint near Fallujah. We were hoping that they would be friendly as most of them are former insurgents and we had no military support. If they decided to take us on, fighting our way out would be difficult if not impossible.

Above: A Sons of Iraq mobile patrol on a pickup truck.

Above: An oil wellhead on fire after an IED – an example of the many hundreds of incidents every day caused by IEDs.

Below: Bullet damage to one of our SUVs. Hit by twenty rounds, there were amazingly no casualties.

'Mad Dog going to make it?' asked Seamus.

'He's a tough SOB.'

'Fucking cunts,' said Dai. 'How's the girl?'

'She's doing OK.'

'Let's get our arses up to the embassy and grab a coffee and work out what the fuck we're going to do.'

It was a pretty crappy reunion. Seamus and Les had been looking forward to meeting up with Mad Dog, who with Cobus had been holding the fort and striving to maintain what we had all built up. Now it was unlikely that they would ever see McQueen again. We drove to the car park, parked up and locked our longs in the wagons. I had already told them about the increased IDF threat, so we kept on our body armour as we trooped morosely into the chow hall and grabbed a table.

We sat for a moment in silence. I thought about Tanya lying in the narrow cot, her slight body barely making a bulge below the sheets. I took a breath. Four years of hearts and minds, twenty thousand fresh troops in Sadr City, and the death toll just kept rising. They had even managed to shoot the legs out from under Mad Dog. And I'd thought he was bulletproof.

'Fucking country,' said Les, and I guessed the same thoughts had been going through his mind.

'There won't be a convoy going to Mosul,' I said, stating the obvious. 'It's going to be dodgy, thin-skinned vehicles and only four of us.' I paused again. All eyes were on me. 'If anyone wants out . . .'

No one spoke for several seconds. Dai then expressed the opinions of them all.

He leaned across the table. 'Fuck off, Ash.'

'I had to ask.'

'You've asked. Now get on with it,' said Seamus.

I'd anticipated the response, but it had to be said. We were a team, not a unit. Even the army gets paid.

'I still reckon we go for it. Stick to the original plan. Just because we're not running with a convoy doesn't make a difference. Sammy and his brother can both shoot.'

'Don't forget Mad Dog's convoy just got the crap shot out of it and they had a hell of a lot more shooters than four white-eyes and two Iraqis,' Dai butted in.

I thought about it for a moment. 'But that's the point. *It was a convoy*. Lots of tasty-looking lorries in a line with high-profile PSD vehicles escorting it. That's a target begging to be hit, a civilian contractor convoy without military back-up. We will look totally different. The highway is still full of civvy traffic. As long as we stay within sight of each other and don't all line up on each other's tail, we will blend in with the local traffic.'

They all took that in. It was a good point. We would be indistinguishable from the rest of the vehicles. There would be no reason to ambush us.

'Ash is right,' said Seamus, and there was a chorus of assent.

'But I think we need more firepower,' said Les. 'If the shit does hit the fan I want some machine-guns, especially if there are only four of us.'

I remember in the old days when each rifleman had an SLR and each section had a GPMG, that the GPMG represented 70 per cent of the section's firepower. A couple of belt-fed guns would be a massive force multiplier for us, especially at ranges over 300m, which we might well encounter away from the cities.

'Cobus, you still in contact with that guy on the black market who can sort us out with some weapons?'

'Sure, hang on a second, let me just take this call.' His phone was ringing. He tried answering it but reception was notoriously poor in the embassy chow hall. 'Wait one minute, I'll be back.' He jogged outside to answer the call.

'OK,' I continued, 'we get hold of a couple of PKMs, maybe rifles with decent sights on them, then find out when another convoy is due to head up north, there's probably one a day, and we can just follow it up. If there are any ambushes they will try it on with the convoy in front of us. We can just hide in with the local civvy traffic.'

We immediately started on a lively discussion debating the potential tactics since there would only be four of us. Whether it would be wiser for all of us to be in one heavily armed gun truck, or split into two pairs so that we could have one PSD car front and back, bookending Sammy's family, or even split up among the family members so that each of us could be driving a vehicle and at least rely upon each other's driving skills.

We decided that we would use two cars, two of us in each, and maybe even take a couple of family members with us in each car. Sammy and his brother could drive two cars certainly, and we were debating who could drive the third, his fifteen-year-old son who was already driving all over Baghdad, or Fara, Sammy's wife. Possibly if we took two family members each in the PSD wagons, we would only need two vehicles for the rest of the family anyway.

'Guys, there is a serious problem.' Cobus was back in from making his phone call, and the grave tone in his voice shut us up immediately.

We all looked at him surprised. His face was ashen under his tan.

'That was Sammy on the phone,' Cobus continued. 'His cousin Gabir has been killed by the police. The IP raided the house and the garage. They have taken our vehicles . . .'

'Fuck,' I said.

'They shot Gabir during the raid, said he was storing weapons for the insurgency.'

'Oh fuck, the cunting vehicles. How the hell did they know?' asked Dai.

I couldn't believe it. Seamus and Les turned to us curiously. Having only just arrived we hadn't yet briefed them on Gabir's shophouse.

I turned to explain. 'We stored three SUVs at Sammy's cousin's garage in Karada – all loaded up with our weapons, ammunition, medpacks, radios, spare tyres, petrol, you name it.'

'They were packed with all of Sammy's worldly goods, as well,' added Dai.

'Without those vehicles the whole operation is fucked,' I said. I shook my head, then echoed Dai's question. 'How the hell did they know to raid it? Did someone spot them loading the baggage?'

'It was Fara.'

'What?' I said.

This was becoming a pantomime.

'She compromised Gabir's location. Worse, she's compromised the whole escape.' Cobus looked ill.

He told us that Sammy had received two phone calls. The first was from a panicked neighbour of Gabir, saying he'd seen Gabir being executed in the street by the police and he was looking after Gabir's wife and children. The second call was from Fara's Aunt Zahrah, a total bitch, demanding to know what had happened to her driver, who had just been arrested because of Sammy.

After calming her down, Sammy had debriefed Zahrah and found that Fara had been to visit her that morning and told her of their plan to escape from Baghdad. The aunt had then arranged off her own back for her own driver, Abeer, to help drive the family to Mosul. Abeer told his wife and she in a rage grabbed her shopping basket and marched straight out to the Shia market. Within twenty minutes, the IP had arrested Abeer and put a bullet in the back of Gabir's head.

Knowing how Baghdadis gossiped, Sammy understood immediately what had happened. Abeer's wife had managed to tell half of Baghdad about the escape plan, and as soon as the Shia realised she was talking about the ex-wing commander, they had lifted Abeer immediately to get the details out of him. The fact that Fara had told the aunt about Gabir and that the aunt had then told the taxi driver was a tragic and unnecessary embellishment to the conversation. Gabir had died because these stupid women could not keep their damned mouths shut. Sammy had been beside himself with rage on the phone with Cobus.

'Sammy has asked us if we can meet him at Gabir's place. He's on his way there now.'

'Yes, of course we can,' I said. 'We'll take two cars. Cobus take Dai with you.' I nodded to Seamus and Les. Cobus was driving a white SUV, common in Baghdad, but a white SUV packed with more than two people looked like a vehicle on a mission. The three of us in a saloon car would draw less attention.

Cobus got his vest on and we trooped down to the car park. My mind was racing. Two facts were in play. Firstly the Shia militia really were in deep with the IP; in fact, the two groups might as well have been interchangeable. Secondly, more importantly, they now definitely knew that our plan was to get Sammy to Mosul.

I had thought that, once up in Mosul, in a Sunni area where the family was well known and had deep roots, they would be safe. The problem was that I now thought we might not make it even halfway there, even if we got out of Baghdad. Searching for Sammy's family in a city of millions was virtually impossible for the IP or the Mahdi Army, but placing ambushes on the single highway north would be a much easier task.

'Cobus,' I said before we got in our cars. 'Fara never told the aunt where the safe house is right? Otherwise they would have lifted Sammy by now.'

'*Ja*, that's right.'

'I'm thinking, Mosul is out now. It will be nearly impossible to get them up there. The militias and the IP will be looking for anyone heading north.'

There were grunts of agreement from everyone.

'We need to think of somewhere else for them to go. Let's talk to Sammy about it when we pick him up. See if he's got any other havens stashed away in his back pocket.'

CHAPTER 15

IT WAS LUNCHTIME, middle of the day, and we didn't bother going for the disguises. We peeled out of the car park and headed down the road towards the traffic circle with the statues of the heroic Iraqi soldiers in the middle. We screeched through it, turning left, giving each other quick radio checks when suddenly, halfway up the 14 July Bridge, Cobus slammed the brakes on in front of us and we nearly piled into the back of him.

I looked past him. I could see that the Bradley parked there actually looked alive for once, hatches buttoned down and turret pointing towards us. There were three US soldiers walking towards Cobus and they meant business. All three had weapons tight in the shoulder, eyes looking through sights and barrels directed straight at Cobus.

They were spaced out so as to give each other and the Bradley clear fields of fire. One of them signalled the others to stop and moved forward to Cobus's window alone. Cobus had his hands up in plain sight, but the soldier still didn't shift his muzzle from Cobus's face. I could see them talking and then Cobus showed him his pass from around his neck and the man relaxed and signalled the others to stand down.

'What the fuck is going on?' muttered Seamus in front, next to

Les. Les was driving, wanting to get back into the Baghdad groove, and to be honest was a much better driver than me. I also wanted some time to think.

Cobus drove off slowly, and we started up and pulled up to the soldiers, who waved us down. We stopped with the windows down and passes ready to show.

'What seems to be the problem, officer?' asked Les, smiling.

The soldier appreciated the humour and grinned back.

'Sorry about this, fellas, but you should all be aware that there is a white SUV driving around the International Zone, full of bad guys. They've shot up a couple of people, so tell your buddy up ahead to approach checkpoints with caution, and you guys keep your eyes open driving around inside the zone.'

'OK, thanks for that. Have a good one, stay safe,' said Les and we pulled away. 'Fucking great, that's all we need. Some nutters driving around raising hell up, *inside* the Green Zone.'

Up ahead, Cobus saw that we were moving and he accelerated as well. Once past the second Bradley we all made weapons ready. Seamus cocked Les's rifle.

'There you go, mate, one up the spout, safety catch on.'

'Cheers,' grunted Les as we swung right and left through the chicane of concrete T-barriers. Once past them we accelerated fast towards Karada. On the other side of the road, heading into the Green Zone, was an Australian military packet, a green and brown camouflaged LAV in the lead, its turret swinging left and right in a non-stop oscillation, seeking targets.

We shoved through traffic and in no time we were pulling up outside Gabir's shophouse.

'Fuck me,' said Les.

His window went down. We passed the warehouse, drove on 50m and swung in a U-turn to drive back again. We parked up both wagons in front of the building and debussed.

'Seamus, Les, you guys stay out here and watch the street,'

I said, and heard the reassuring rasp of metal as one safety after the other was taken off.

The doors to Gabir's garage were open and smoke was pouring out from a burning car outside the back, in an alley.

Suddenly Sammy was next to me, coming out of a doorway where he had been waiting. I gripped his hand firmly as I exited the car, then got both hands back on my rifle and turned to look at Gabir's shophouse. I saw the large patch of blood on the street, still drying. Up the road, Cobus had remained next to the 4x4 while Dai had debussed and crossed the road to take up a fire position in a doorway.

I turned back to Gabir's place. It was an ordinary-looking two-storey building, the same as all the others in the street except for the fact that people were hurrying in and out like it was the entrance to the souk. Two women wrapped in *abayas* stood opposite, but disappeared quickly when we appeared. A crowd of thickly moustached men, some with *shemaghs*, were milling around the door leading to the apartment. A van was parked outside, the back doors open, and two men were loading a table with ornate iron legs.

Everything that could be taken was being taken. I noticed Sammy shaking with anger and squeezed his arm. Sammy's face swelled in anger. He went forward and started screaming at people and slapping men in the face.

As soon as people turned and saw us, five large Westerners in body armour, carrying rifles, they dropped whatever they were carrying and fled. Sammy was ranting and raving with a gold pistol in his belt, and to Iraqis a pistol is a sign of authority, a prestige item amongst the Ba'athists, and thirty years of conditioning had developed an almost spinal reflex of fear at the sight of someone who might be a secret policeman or government agent.

I was thinking we might have to fire a couple of warning shots but it wasn't necessary. In less than a minute the house was empty apart from two men arguing and shouting with Sammy.

'What's going on?' I said, making sure that both these guys could see Cobus and I pointing AKs at them. 'Take it easy. Go slowly,' I said.

He took a deep breath, controlled himself. 'Yes, Mister James, I am ready,' he said. 'This man . . .' He indicated a man with a thick moustache who looked to my Western eyes to be late fifties, but was probably only forty. 'This man is a friend, the neighbour of Gabir. Also a cousin. He is trying to stop the ali-babas from stealing everything. He and his brother have taken many of the things from the house and stored them in his house.' Sammy took another deep breath.

'Where are the wife and kids?'

'Still inside, they have locked themselves in the room and will not come out.'

I thought quickly. 'OK, Sammy, tell him it's dangerous for him to be seen being friendly to us, tell him for his own safety he has to get down on his knees with his hands on his head and pretend to be our prisoner in case the Shia militias are watching. Tell both of them, now.'

Sammy spoke rapidly in Arabic. Understanding dawned on both their faces and, when I shouted angrily at them and waved my rifle, they both dropped to their knees and clapped hands on top of their heads. Sammy got out his gold pistol and pointed it at them as well. It was just in time; in my peripheral vision I could see a small but rapidly growing crowd up at the corner of the main street, gathering to see what was going on.

'Ask him to tell us what happened.'

Sammy and the man talked rapidly for a couple of minutes while I got more and more worried about the enemy turning up.

'Fuck it, Sammy, we have to go. Tell him if you have any more questions you will call him on the phone later. We have to move. Now.'

I slung my rifle and picked up the cousin and slapped him about a bit and kicked him into the open door of the house. Then I grabbed his brother, roughed him up, shouting abuse at him and smacking him on the top of the head for the benefit of the crowd. He cowered away and I shoved him into the doorway as well.

We checked the ground floor. This house was totally inoffensive and stripped of everything other than the items that had been broken by the looters in their rush to get in.

We climbed the stairs. A door at the top of the house was locked. We could hear sobbing from inside. Sammy knocked and whispered. He kept knocking, he kept whispering, and I had to control my urge to kick the door down before Gabir's wife was finally persuaded to open up. She was with her young daughter, who was cowering behind her, and her son, a boy of about fourteen with the faint stain of his first moustache on his top lip. He stood in front of his mother and stared at me, jaw set.

Sammy took the woman in his arms. She rattled out a stream of Arabic, then started wailing. I understood nothing. When the woman crumpled to her knees, her son lost his composure and fell weeping beside her. It was a private moment. I shouldn't have been there to witness their terrible grief and couldn't even begin to imagine how I would feel if something happened to Krista or one of the girls.

Sammy translated. The police had come for Gabir and dragged him out of the house. He had not fought with them, only protested his innocence. The neighbours came out of their houses to watch. Like the guillotine and public hangings in days gone by, police brutality is entertainment if it's happening to someone else. When a big enough crowd had gathered, the cops held Gabir down and shot him twice in the back of the head: 'resisting arrest'. They took his body away. An unusual courtesy, but I supposed criminals and traitors didn't get a family burial. It would also make any honourable funeral impossible if the body were dumped in the river or the desert where it would not be found.

Sammy sniffed back his tears.

'Does she know who shot him?'

Sammy asked her a quick question in Arabic. She shook her head.

'No.' He paused.

The cousin, standing behind us, piped up and jabbered away. Sammy quickly got hold of a piece of paper and started writing.

'Yes, the cousin, he saw them, he know the policemen. They are all living here in the neighbourhood, these are the names and the police station where they work.' Sammy wrote quickly, and put the paper safely in his pocket. 'Gabir died for me, Mister James. For my family.'

'I know. I'm sorry, Sammy.'

'What can I do?'

'I don't know,' I said.

Tears welled up in Sammy's eyes.

'I will kill these men. We go now. We must go and kill them.' He clenched his fists. 'I am sorry, Mister James. Of course we cannot, but their names, I will remember until I can come back and kill them.'

We were quiet for a long moment, a small group in semi-darkness in the heart of chaos.

'Bring them with us,' I said instinctively. 'We'll sort something out.'

'We take them?'

'Three more makes no difference.'

After another burst of Arabic, Sammy explained that his cousin's wife had her parents and sisters in Karada. This was her home. She could not leave.

'OK, but we have to move now,' I said. 'Every second we are here it is dangerous, for them as well as us. Say goodbye, Sammy. Tell them you probably won't see them again.'

I moved to the top of the stairs and waited for Sammy to say goodbye in private. The woman was sobbing hysterically. I looked around the house, which only an hour ago had been a home to a happy family, and was now a bare shell, stripped clean. The neighbours had watched a policeman in uniform perform the *coup de grâce*, those two shots starting the race to rob Gabir's widow. One day his son would discover who had robbed his family, and one night he would kill them, an eye for an eye. On this primitive framework Mr Bush and Mr Blair planned to build their vision of democracy.

We ran out of the house and with a quick shout to the others we all piled into the cars and headed off. I took Sammy in my car, with Les driving, leading the way. Seamus had joined Cobus and Dai in the vehicle following behind. We revved the engines, beeping our horns and barrelling through the scattering crowd.

We turned left on to the main road and almost immediately there was an IP checkpoint with three police pickup trucks parked on the sides of the road and half a dozen policemen in navy-blue body armour, armed with AKs, stopping cars in the middle.

They flagged us down. I worried suddenly that one of the policemen would be one of Gabir's murderers and that Sammy would not be able to control himself. If that happened it would all kick off very quickly.

'Stand by, stand by,' I sent over the radio to the SUV behind us. I could imagine them going to full alert, training their weapons on the cops around us.

Les and I were in the front, smiling grimly at the approaching policeman, showing our ID cards. Les had one hand on the steering wheel, one hand on his lap holding his pistol, and I had the muzzle of my AK resting on the window, my left hand still on the pistol grip.

'Sammy, you just keep calm, OK?'

'It is OK, Mister James, this man, I know him, he was one of our guards, he is *Sinneh*.' *Sinneh* was how the Iraqis pronounced

'Sunni'. I was slightly surprised that a Sunni had managed to get a job in the police, but I supposed that it was possible after all.

The policeman was right at my open window now and I *salaam alaikum*ed him. I didn't remember the man's name, although his face seemed familiar, but he obviously recognized me and his face lit up with pleasure.

'*Alaikum salaam*, Mister James.' He peered into the cab and smiled at Les. 'Mister Les, hello, hello, how you are very much?' he asked in mangled English.

Then he looked into the back of the car and his face fell when he saw Sammy. '*Salaam alaikum, Abu Qusay*,'

I recognized the name the Iraqis had given Sammy. It meant 'Father of Qusay' and was a customary name change for all Iraqi men after the birth of their son. Back in the old days, even though it was not normal to do the same with a daughter, Sammy had tried calling me 'Abu Natalie' for a while but it kept making him laugh so we had gone back to 'Mister James'.

Sammy and the cop chatted away in Arabic. The policeman looked back at the other cops and said something to Sammy. Sammy picked up a *shemagh* from the back seat and quickly wound it around his head and face. I picked out the policeman's name, Tariq, from the exchange.

'Why is he so worried, Sammy?'

I looked at Tariq curiously. I had deliberately turned my muzzle away from him, but the man was visibly perspiring despite the cool of the day. Little beads of sweat had popped out at his temples and forehead.

'He say that he and two others are *Sinneh* in this patrol, the rest they are *Shia* and they are looking for me. He does not want any shooting. He remember you, Mister James, he remember you shoot very well.'

I remembered back to the days of range practice when Sammy and I had drilled the guards, shift after shift of training cadres, trying to improve their usually abysmal shooting accuracy. Because we were never sure how much we could trust our own men, Sammy and I finished the day at the range with a little play-acting routine that would always be the same.

Sammy would gather the entire group and ask if they would like to see Mister James shoot at all. They would all shout loudly that of course they would. I would feign embarrassment, but eventually let myself be persuaded to show them if I could hit the target. Then they would all cheer loudly as I readied myself, and then the cheers would die out in puzzlement as Sammy walked down-range to the targets. The men had been firing on man-sized targets all day, six feet high and two feet wide.

Sammy leaned over and placed an empty coke can on the ground, and the men burst out laughing. This was obviously a joke on me. By the time Sammy walked back, the laughing had died out. I readied my AK and started firing rapidly on single-shot. For me, after a few months having spent every day on the range, it was a relatively simple process to shoot the can and then keep pinging it as it bounced around the end of the range 30m away. For the men who had been struggling to get half their shots anywhere on the big screens it was nothing short of miraculous.

The first few shots would attract shouts of amazement. After ten shots they would usually clap. After twenty rounds they weren't laughing or clapping any more. In fact, there would be dead silence as I finished off firing through a thirty-round magazine. For my finale I would let the empty rifle drop on its sling, quick-draw my pistol and nail the can with one last shot. Some classes would clap. Others would just remain silent until Sammy rounded them up on to the trucks to get back to our headquarters.

Sammy had made the message clear. Don't get into a shoot-out with the white-eyes because you will die. The objective went beyond just impressing a class of ragged students. We had thousands of guards coming through our range. All of them were local Iraqis who loved to gossip. The message would soon spread out into the neighbourhoods of south-eastern Baghdad; don't fuck with the PSDs living in Aradisa Idah, there are easier targets out there.

I looked back at the nervous policeman, who had just realised that the SUV behind us was full of Western contractors as well. I don't know if he could see that it was Seamus and Les, but the colour drained out of his face and he really started to sweat. He looked back at me. I smiled at him and his eyes bulged.

'Good to see you again, Tariq, stay safe,' I said. Sammy translated for me. He was now completely hidden by the *shemagh*.

'*Inshallah*,' Tariq replied. He swallowed and waved us through. We drove past the checkpoint and I started scanning the street ahead. I looked back once and saw one of the Shia IP looking after us, talking on his radio.

'Where to, Ash?' Cobus came over the radio.

'Aradisa, mate. We'll head to the SF villa. Can you give them a call and let the front gate know we're coming?'

'*Ja*, will do.'

We needed a place to regroup and think out our next move, somewhere secure. We needed guns, we needed vehicles and we needed a plan, and I was hoping that the Green Berets would be able to help. More importantly, we needed to get off the street as fast as possible.

CHAPTER 16

BACK IN THE SF villa we dumped our body armour and rifles, stretched, had a quick toilet break and then convened a little council of war over mugs of English breakfast tea. A reliable pillar of the British Empire, tea was not only a vital source of caffeine and antioxidants but also of inspiration and moral fibre.

On the drive through Aradisa I had already prompted Sammy to start thinking about where else he could go with his family. He had agreed with me that now the plan was compromised, it was highly likely that we would be ambushed and chased down long before we even got halfway. In addition, my suspicions as to the security situation there were validated when he confirmed that the foreign al-Qaeda fighters and other fanatical Sunnis not keen to join the Awakening councils were rumoured to be regrouping in the north.

'So, Sammy, any relatives anywhere else?' said Seamus.

Sammy bunched up his shoulders and shook his head.

We all knew the basic geography. If the north was out, so were the east and the south. To the east was nothing but desert and then Iran. It would be an even guess as to who would be more hostile to Sammy's family, the desert tribes who killed anyone not in their tribe, or the Iranian Shia. To the south was the Shia heartland, where people had been busy hunting down former Ba'athists and kicking out the Sunnis, so that was not an option for this pale-skinned Sunni family.

The only direction left was west, into the heart of the last Sunni-dominated region, Anbar province.

'So are you thinking about Anbar?' I asked. 'Ramadi? Fallujah? Do you still have friends near Habbaniyah?'

'No,' said Sammy. 'I used to have the house in the Habbaniyah, but the people there they have steal it and live there now. They are very bad people.'

We all looked at each other.

'I have another thought.' Sammy seemed embarrassed, as if it were difficult for him to say. 'I would like to take my family to the Jordan. There are many Iraqi there. We will be the refugees.'

'That's a great idea!' I exclaimed, and the others agreed whole-heartedly. There were smiles all around. 'In fact, the more I think about it, it couldn't be better.'

Sammy still looked uncomfortable, and we all quietened down.

'What's wrong, Sammy? You can't work there or what?' asked Dai straight out.

'No, this is not the problem. I can find the work, I am very clever man. You remember I know how to fix it the car. But the problem . . .' He hesitated again and then forced himself to speak. 'The problem is I do not have the money for the visa. I know it the man who sell the visa, but the money is 100 dollars each.'

There was silence and we looked at each other again.

'Is that it?' said Les. 'You daft sod, how long does it take to get them, then?'

'He can get them in two, maybe four, hours . . .'

Even as he finished speaking we were opening up our wallets and pass-holders. In our line of work you wear certain items on the body at all times, your pistol, and you also take your ID cards, your pass-port and a wedge of US dollars in case you need to run with what you have on your body. Everybody put in 300 dollars each.

'There you go, mate.' Seamus stuffed the bundle into Sammy's hand. 'Now, where is this guy. Do you need an escort to get there?'

Sammy was suffused with embarrassment, but at the same time he was amongst friends and there was no point refusing something he needed to save his family.

'Thank you,' he whispered, barely able to speak. 'No, I will take it to him myself. He is a very good man.' He regained his voice and wiggled his finger with emphasis. 'He is a Christian man.'

Sammy had a very high regard for the Assyrian Christians. I remembered him telling me that if you took your car to a Muslim mechanic to be fixed, you had to stand there and watch it being repaired, in case the mechanic sold it to someone else while you were away. But a Christian mechanic was a different kettle of fish altogether. 'You can take it your car to a Christian garage to fix and leave it. Even two or three days; it will still be there.' Sammy had shaken his head in amazement.

After some discussion we agreed that Sammy could probably go on his own. The Christian's office was in a relatively safe part of town, if such a thing could be said of Baghdad. We gave him the keys to the saloon car, a battered thing that most importantly looked nothing like Sammy's trademark yellow Toyota. I told him to go back home and call us once he had obtained the visas.

Sammy went around all of us to shake our hands and say thank you for the money. Les was the last one and Sammy grabbed him and managed to plant one big hairy kiss on a cheek before Les lurched away.

'Fuck off, you fruit,' he yelled, loud enough for the Kurds and National Guardsmen at the gate to turn around to see what was going on. 'Not while I still have life in my body.'

Les took up a boxing stance and Sammy danced away laughing, surprisingly light on his feet.

'Right, let's see who we can talk to about guns and cars,' I said to the others.

'There's Mark,' said Dai, and we went and caught him as he was walking between buildings.

He stood, feet planted like two tree stumps. 'You look like you're gonna ask me a favour,' he said as I approached.

'You're a bloody mind reader,' I told him.

'He grinned. 'Do what I can.'

'We lost our vehicles, taken by the IP.'

'Assholes.'

'Can't get out of Baghdad on foot,' I said.

'What you looking for?'

'Three covert rigs good enough to get us to the border.'

He didn't ask which border; a Special Forces sergeant, Mark Amin knew the drill.

'Let's go,' he said.

We followed him out to a yard where a mass of cars and minibuses were lined up like it was a car lot. The Green Berets regularly had to dump and rotate vehicles to avoid being compromised. I left Dai, Les and Seamus to pick out some wheels and went with Cobus to see Rick in the concrete guest-house that had been turned into an armoury.

'Hi, Rick, how's it going?' I walked through the door and then looked around me. 'Holy shit.'

Cobus was speechless.

'Holy shit.' I said again. I couldn't think of anything else to say.

'Impressive, ain't it?'

Rick pushed his big form off the chair where he'd been sitting and his carved features broke into a grin. We shook hands and, when he sat down again, he carried on fiddling around with the working parts of a .50 cal he had stripped down on a table in the middle.

Arrayed on the shelves around us was a display, a museum, an Ali Baba cave of armaments. Cobus and I stood rooted to the middle of the room, gaping in awe. One of the walls, as expected, was racked with American weapons, although if I am honest

I wasn't expecting that many. The SF team obviously could choose M4s and M16s, depending on what they wanted, but there were also specialist weapons, a few silenced MP5s, shotguns and half a dozen sniper rifles. Most of the floor was taken up with support weapons, 240 GPMGs and M249 SAWs, two more .50 cals and a couple of Barrett M82s. The whole of the back wall was shelves and shelves of ammunition, including anti-tank rockets, grenades, and a stack of over a hundred mortar bombs.

'Mortar?' I enquired.

'It's dug in out the back by the swimming pool,' Rick answered. 'It's not obvious, you guys probably haven't seen it.'

'Check these out.' Cobus nudged me.

The third wall was amazing. It was encyclopaedic. These were obviously captured or seized weapons from locals. There was twenty-first-century, state-of-the-art Belgian hardware, and there were hundred-year-old British Lee-Enfield .303s. There was a batch of Second World War LMGs, including Brens and MG34s. In pride of place, just above a museum-quality MP44, was a silver-plated, lever-action Winchester cowboy rifle, completely impractical but beautifully ridiculous. Both Cobus and I ignored a pair of Uzi and HK MP5 submachine-guns and walked over to a shelf of pistols.

'Jesus, these must be worth a fortune,' I remarked. There were Nazi-stamped Lugers, Mauser Schnellfeuers and a host of other peculiarities, many garishly plated in gold, silver and chrome.

'Fuck, can you see me with these, man? They weigh a ton.' Cobus had grabbed a pair of .44 Magnum revolvers.

'They look tasty, but we got four bullets between the whole lot of them,' Rick said. 'Most of the rest we ain't even got the ammo for.'

'What can you spare?' I asked, expecting the same generosity I'd found with Mark Amin. 'We're desperate for a bit of firepower.'

Rick shrugged his massive shoulders. 'Sorry, buddy, no can do,' he said. 'They're on our books now. We have to account for everything we seize, all serial numbers, date taken, all that shit. Although some of them get destroyed and some of them we sabotage and put back on to the market to trace. The rest we have to register for our own safety.'

'How do you mean?' Cobus asked. I was wondering myself. It wasn't as if there was a working government here, let alone anyone licensing firearms.

'It's to avoid any American unit building up a store of unaccounted-for weapons, for two main reasons,' Rick explained. 'First to reduce the risk and temptation of guys trying to smuggle this shit back home. Nothing gets taken back to the US unless it was shipped out on our original manifest. Hell, I could even bring my own personal USP from North Carolina, but I would have to leave it here in I-raq. You can't take anything back.'

'And the second reason?' I asked.

'To prevent any accusation that we shot up some unarmed civilians, then tried to cover it up by placing unregistered weapons on the bodies afterwards and claiming that they shot first and we killed them in self-defence.'

'Makes sense,' I said, and turned to Cobus. 'Looks like we have to check out our own black-market guy, I suppose.'

He shook his head and looked glummer than ever. 'I called on the way in after I spoke to the guys on the front gate here. It's the fucking surge. The Americans are hammering the militias and there are no guns for sale, not anywhere.'

We stood there in silence. We had to make our way through a combat zone with militias and surge marines locked in a duel to the death, with a family of Iraqis hunted by death squads, with nothing but a ragtag, *de minimis* collection of AKs and Swiss Army knives. And that was before we began our journey through the badlands to Jordan. The despair must have shown on our faces.

'Hold on, guys.' Rick could see that we were stuffed for ideas. 'We use a local dealer to slip weapons we've fucked around with back into the market. He owes us, big-time. He always has stuff. Let me call the LT.'

Five minutes later we were sitting around the main dining table, listening to a one-sided conversation as Lieutenant Davor spoke on the phone to the arms dealer. His Arabic was fluent. I was impressed.

'OK, *inshallah, shukran jazeeran, hallo*.' He hung up and looked at us. 'He'll meet you at six tonight, just after sunset. Do you know the old range you guys built?'

'Sunset? Does it really get dark that early?' I replied.

'Yeah, just don't forget this is 6p.m. Iraqi time. He may turn up any time between six and eight. He's got just the stuff you need. Usual arrangements.'

'What are the usual arrangements?'

'Don't worry, I'll fill you in later.' His brow furrowed and he gave me a strange look. 'You know, you might have dealt with this guy before, because he deals with us exactly the same way you described getting your guns from your guy.'

I mulled that one over. 'I've got to be honest, mate, I can't think of all the Baghdad black-market arms dealers I'm good mates with off the top of my head.'

'Well, maybe there's just not that many ways to deal in guns and the word got around.' He shrugged his shoulders. 'Anyway, who wants a coffee?'

The 'usual arrangements' were the methods by which two parties strange to each other would exchange guns for money. Although often seen as a little theatrical, a certain amount of cloak-and-dagger precautions were necessary if each side was putting their lives at risk. The seller knows that the buyer is coming with a large amount of cash, and presumably doesn't have many guns, which is why he wants to buy some. The risk is therefore to the buyer, who may simply be robbed of his cash if the seller decides he is the one holding all of the guns and can get away with it.

The risk to the seller is that he is doing something that the security forces may decide to clamp down on. In a war zone, if you're an underground arms dealer, your clients aren't going to be government forces, they will be the rebels and criminals.

Each side has to ensure that there is a carrot and a stick: an incentive for the deal to go ahead as agreed, and at the same time a deterrent of a suitably violent and terminal nature to ensure good business practices. At the same time, just as important as the handover itself, each party needs to ensure that their routes to and from the place of business are as hard to ambush as possible.

Rick joined us with a pot of steaming coffee. We sat around their dining table and discussed what help they could give us in general and, specifically, what help they could give us before we met up with the arms dealer. After getting the go-ahead from Davor, Mark went back out to look at the armoury to see if there was anything taken recently that was (a) not yet on their books and (b) had some ammunition with it.

'There must be something, and ammo shouldn't be a problem,' Davor said. He then almost looked embarrassed. 'The last team told us when you left you gave them a dozen rifles and thousands of rounds of ammo, so we owe you something.'

'That's not forgetting all that good intel we shared,' I added.

At least the wheels weren't a problem. They were looking to dump half a dozen vehicles and were happy to give us two at least, since it saved them the hassle of going out and abandoning them around the city. Mark and the boys had picked out an SUV with a powerful engine to use as a gun truck, and a reliable minivan, with rows of seats like a bus, that would take most of Sammy's family in comfort.

As for the rendezvous location, the range was isolated with a single road leading to it. This was a problem and a potential ambush risk, but one of the large fields around it bordered a highway, and the SF had previously loosened the barrier so that they could access the field off the highway. That would be our exit.

We arranged to accompany the SF out to the range so that they could test some weapons an hour or so before sunset. Then they would mount up and drive back from the range, leaving us hidden inside the high earth berms that made four sides of a square. Other than the black-market dealer, no one would be expecting us to be there.

'Let's wait for Sammy to come back. He can do the translation if we need it,' I decided. 'Cobus and Les, you two can drive the pickup vehicle. Seamus and Dai, you can be the fire support. I'll be with Sammy in the middle.'

Cobus called Sammy to let him know we needed him to come back as soon as he had the passports. As I sat back with a second cup of coffee, my thoughts wandered to Tanya and Mad Dog. I was getting pissed off with the whole operation. This wasn't how it was supposed to be.

It was supposed to be a simple job, in and out, a quick road trip to Mosul, job done. Now half the team were out of action. Tanya and Mad Dog were wounded, Mad Dog seriously, the two sergeants in Mad Dog's team were unavailable and the convoy cancelled. Poor old Gabir had been killed, leaving a grieving wife and two kids, and all of our kit and vehicles had been stolen.

The original plan was shot to hell and, instead of our military escort up to Mosul, we were going to be making a break across the desert to Jordan with no support and hoping that Fallujah would be so occupied with the surge that we could slip by without any trouble.

Things were getting too complicated, there were too many variables in play and the city was a lot more violent than I had been expecting it to be. The last thing I needed now was to be taking any more risks by walking into a deal with some Iraqi black-marketeer with whom I had never dealt before.

CHAPTER 17

THE SUN SET quickly and Sammy and I sat next to each other for warmth, little seats dug into the sand berm behind us. Without power in the neighbourhood, the blackness of full night fell quickly, broken only by the flaming tower at the Dora oil refinery across the river. I was glad of my fleece, the *shemagh* around my neck, and gloves. The heavy body armour was a welcome source of warmth, too. Off to the side, the engine on our car pinged as it cooled down.

A kilometre or so to the north, the gunfire had already started in Sadr City. It was distant enough that the non-stop crackle could have been a fireworks celebration, but I knew that, in streets, houses and the cramped interiors of armoured vehicles, both soldiers and insurgents were swearing, sweating and shooting at each other in a fierce firefight that would last until dawn. Invisible helicopters thudded overhead, totally blacked out, on their way to unknown missions.

For Sammy and me it was just another pleasant, calm and deceptively quiet evening.

'So, any problem with the visas?' I asked, rubbing my gloved hands together for warmth.

'No, no problem at all, Mister James,' he said and paused. 'You are I need an Iraqi passport?'

'What?' I was momentarily puzzled by the grammar and the question. 'Do I want an Iraqi passport?'

'Yes, my friend he make it for fifty dollars.'

'Must be fake.'

'No. No. It is real. He work in the Ministry. You give him the photograph and fifty dollars. One hour and you have the passport. Any name you want. You are want which name? Osama bin Laden? George Bush?'

We both laughed.

The SF team had departed half an hour ago in a cloud of dust, bumping over the waste ground back to the main road, dropping off Dai and Seamus in the tree-line at a point invisible to anyone watching from the nearest buildings. We had been on the range, shooting for just over an hour beforehand, and I didn't think anyone here would be professional enough to notice that the number of vehicles coming out of the SF villa was more than the number heading back.

We had all mucked in together to help the Green Berets save time on their maintenance, sorting the headspace and timing on a couple of .50 cals and the gas settings on their 240s, before settling into a very interesting shoot, watching them practise their drills.

Before going down to the range, Cobus had suggested that we have a friendly wager with the SF on a shoot, like the old days, but, after watching them double-tapping Coke cans effortlessly, I was glad that I had vetoed the idea. These guys had clearly been on the range constantly over the last year. We hadn't.

Instead we put the time to good use practising our basic shooting skills, and I was pleased to see that the muscle memory and the hand-eye coordination was not all lost. Every few rounds there was a noticeable improvement in accuracy and speed, and after thirty minutes we were virtually back to 90 per cent of what we used to be.

As for weapons not yet registered that the SF could spare us, there were only three; a Bren gun and two of the .303 Lee-Enfield rifles. We declined the Bren since they only had a single box of one hundred rounds and the gun would have gone through it in seconds. Out in the desert, however, the .303s would be invaluable as long-range sharpshooting weapons. One was a Second World War vintage No. 4 rifle, the other was a hundred years old, an SMLE. We had used up twenty to thirty rounds on each one, zeroing them, one for Les and one for Seamus. Although Dai had been a sniper, he preferred the firepower of an AK and would wait to see if the black-marketeer had something more to his liking.

I checked my Kobold again. It was twenty minutes past six and I was just thinking of asking Sammy to call the dealer when my phone vibrated. It was Davor.

'Ash, sorry, buddy, we have to pull out and go on a mission now.'

In the background I could hear the noises of the team moving equipment.

'Oh shit. That's bad news,' I said.

This was more than just bad news. If anything went wrong with this deal, our agreed action was that Sammy and I were to take care of whoever was within the berms of the range, and Dai and Seamus would pick off anyone outside the berms from their overwatch location. Then we were to hold in place and call in the SF, who could be there in three minutes in heavily armed Humvees. They had numbers, machine-guns, snipers, night vision sights and the necessary skills to use them all. If we needed to go on the run, then the Green Berets had already marked in the range as a predetermined target, or 'DF', for their mortar and we could call in fire behind us as we fled. Now that they had to go, we would be left on our own.

'And another thing,' he informed me. 'Because of all the classified shit we have back at the villa, I can't let you stay the night if we're not there. But I told the gate guys to let you pick up your stuff and then show you the armoury so you can pick up whatever ammo you need for your new toys. Take what you need.'

'Thanks, Davor, I appreciate it. Thanks for putting us up the last couple of nights, mate. Good luck tonight. Stay safe.'

'Sure thing, buddy. One day we'll all have a drink and laugh about this. Bye.'

'Bye.'

Shit.

Shitshitshitshit. I considered quickly calling the dealer and calling the whole thing off or at least postponing it. We needed more backup. Our ace in the hole had just disappeared.

As if on cue, my walkie-talkie clicked three times. That was Seamus's signal that the dealer had arrived. Unbelievable timing. Sex and comedy, I reminded myself. It's all about timing.

Seamus would be waiting with his earpiece on for me to get back to him. I scrambled quickly up to the top of the berm and peered at the distant tree-line. There were vehicles on the way with their lights off, all blacked out.

'Seamus, can you talk? Over.'

Two clicks on the radio. *No.*

'Did they drop off a cutoff team at the tree-line? Over.'

Single click. *Yes.*

'Near you?'

Single click.

'How many men?'

Two clicks.

'Machine-gun?'

Two clicks.

'Rifles.'

One click.

That would not be a problem for Seamus and Dai. I drew in a breath. Les and Cobus were parked up, blacked out on the other side of the highway in a palm plantation, waiting for instructions.

'OK, listen in, Seamus and Les. There's some bad news. I just got off the phone with SF. They have had to pull out and will not be supporting us. Both of you, acknowledge. Over.'

Single click.

'Roger, Out.'

Les and Cobus were no doubt filling the cab of their car with some good Anglo-Saxon and Afrikaans swearing.

I slid back down to where Sammy was waiting and he handed me my rifle. I brushed off my trousers and checked chamber. I had a seventy-five-round drum magazine on my AK, thinking that if it kicked off at short range inside the berms then I needed immediate firepower. The two of us walked over to the front of our car and waited.

I could hear the vehicles coming now. My nerves were pinging. If things went wrong now, there would be no cavalry to come and get us out. I thought about Krista suddenly. Shit, she was waiting patiently for me to come back and spend the weekend doing family stuff. And here was I in some war zone, in the middle of the night, having arranged a meeting with an unknown number of possibly enemy nutters and no friendly forces to bail us out.

The vehicles stopped outside the berm, as previously agreed. They had parked on the side of the range where they could not be seen from the road, lights off, engines running.

Sammy's phone rang. That would be the dealer, as we had agreed. I could not understand the conversation that followed, but the three most important words were '*bes wahed sayarra*'. Only one car.

'Seamus, how many cars came in?'

Three clicks.

'OK, they are about to come in. Les, stand by to move.'

'Roger.'

Engines revved outside and gravel and dirt crunched under moving tyres. I adjusted my grip on the AK. If more than one car came in through the gap in the berms, Sammy and I would open fire on it. I told Sammy to be ready and then walked several paces away from him, so that they would have to split their fire if they wanted to take us down.

One car appeared out of the night and slowly rolled between Sammy and myself before stopping. The two of us separated a little further still, angling to each side of the car.

The door opened and a Shia militiaman got out. He was wearing an overcoat and a green headband that I could see clearly even in the dim moonlight. I nearly shot him by reflex and thanked God that Sammy hadn't done so. The man approached with his hands out to the side.

'Mister James, do not shoot.'

'Who's that?' *Who the hell is that?* I was speechless. And I didn't stop aiming my rifle at his belly.

'Mister James,' he said and walked right up to me.

When I saw his face, I dropped the rifle on its sling.

'Oh my God. Ali. Is that you?' I grabbed him. 'Ali?' I hugged him and we were both jumping up and down laughing.

Ali had been one of my most loyal staff and, more importantly, a friend during the eighteen months I had been in Iraq. As the former Spartan armourer and weapons buyer, it suddenly made sense that he had slipped into this line of work after we had left, and also had contacts with the American SF.

I held him at arm's length and looked him up and down.

'Thank you, Ali. I saw you that last day, trying to stop them. It was very brave of you.'

The last time I had seen Ali, he had being trying to stop the mutinous guards charging down the road, shooting at our house – and worse, shooting at us. Ali and one other Iraqi had tried to pull them back, shouting at them to stop, but in vain. I was glad that he had survived. He had been a loyal and deadly companion, accounting for several enemy in the old days, and I had always been happy to choose him as a bodyguard if I headed out on quick errand.

Sammy approached and the two men shook hands, kissing each other on both cheeks.

'*Salaam alaikum, Ali.*'

'Wa alaikum salaam, Abu Qusay.'

There was no Sunni and Shia here, just two old comrades-in-arms. They were obviously delighted to see each other and chatted away in Arabic.

I got on the radio. 'All's well so far.'

Both Seamus and Les sent me one click back.

That was the agreed signal. If five minutes had gone by without a sound from me, they would have known that Sammy and I were being restrained and unable either to fire our weapons or to use our comms. That would have been the signal for them to start using their initiative, probably in a noisy and violent manner.

I didn't even consider bringing them in to see Ali. No matter how pleasant a reunion it might have been, I had no idea who was in the other two vehicles. I had been betrayed before. I was very happy with my fire support where it was, hidden and ready.

Ali reached inside his car and beeped his horn twice. That was obviously his signal to his team outside that he was fine as well. We then went round to the back of the vehicle to see the guns.

The selection was impressive, but this was no time for browsing. I pulled out four M4s and three M16s. They were obviously items recovered from the battlefield and, apart from the fact that I wanted them, something emotional in me rebelled against leaving them for potential use by a future enemy against other CF. If the former owners of the weapons had been killed, I was sure the ghosts would be happy for me to use them on insurgents.

Having said that, I considered then discarded two M249s in favour of two PKMs. I needed something that could reach out potentially to 800–1,000m, and nice as the Minimis were, we wouldn't have the space to carry both types of machine-gun. I also remembered seeing boxes of belted PKM ammunition in the Green Berets' armoury.

'You like the FAL, yes Mister James?' Ali pronounced 'FAL' as one word, not spelling out the letters, and held up a gleaming old

FN FAL rifle for me with a scope on it. Yes, I did like the FAL. It fired 7.62 NATO and would be a good sharpshooter's weapon.

'Do you have Dragunov?'

'No, Mister James. I sorry, now for Dragunov is very difficult. The bad man is fighting the American.' Ali softly pointed a thumb back over his shoulder, towards the sound of gunfire in the distance.

'No problem, Ali. Thank you.' Then I coughed. 'Umm, about payment . . .'

Ali stopped me straight away. He called Sammy over to translate. They spoke in Arabic for a minute, then Sammy turned to me, his eyes glistening.

'He say: Mister James, you are a very good man. You are come here to the Iraq and you are look after him very good for one year. He always remember that you take it care of him and his family. Now he will take it care of you. He will not take your money. Take the weapons, they are yours.'

Ali grinned at me.

'You are my brother,' he said.

'*Shukran jazeeran,* Ali.' I shook his hand and hugged him again.

'*Afwan.*'

'But I have a present for you, *Ta'al.*' I led him over to the back of our car. I opened the boot and flipped open a blanket. The contents glowed under the internal light of the boot. 'For you.'

Ali gasped in pleasure and a huge smile broke out under his moustache. Displayed on the blanket were the silver Winchester rifle, two gold-plated Browning pistols, a gold-plated Luger, three Glocks and four .44 Magnum Smith & Wessons. The Green Berets had given us the pistols because they had no .44 ammo, and plenty of 9mm but no magazines at all for the other pistols. Iraqis love shiny things, especially weapons, and the pistols were especially prized. He could sell them for a lot of money. The Winchester, realistically useless but very pretty, he might keep himself or sell to a rich collector.

He immediately picked up the two gold Brownings lovingly. Then, quick as a flash, drew two of his own Brownings from under his coat, ejected the extended twenty-round magazines and loaded and cocked the two gold ones. He flipped on the safeties and admired them lovingly before putting them back in his belt. His own pistols he put into his coat pocket, then wrapped up the rest in the blanket. Sammy looked jealous of the gold pistols – he was Iraqi after all – but there would be no taking the weapons into Jordan.

We loaded up the goods, and once both parties had finished packing we prepared to say our goodbyes. Sammy and Ali spent a long time speaking in Arabic. They shook hands, kissed cheeks and came over to me.

'Goodbye, Ali.'

'Goodbye, Mister James.'

'I will not see you again, Ali.' I said, and he nodded, understanding that this was goodbye. 'Take care of yourself. And thank you. Thank you so much. You have been a good friend. Again. I will never forget you.'

'I know you will not come back to the Iraq, Mister James. It is very dangerous now. You must go back to your home.' He shook my hand for the last time and bid me to go in peace.

'*Ma salaama.*'

'*Ma salaama.*'

He got back into the car and drove out, bumping up and down over the ruts. There was a pause and then a rumble of sound as the other two vehicles swung around and followed him out, then they pulled on to the road and drove off towards the distant buildings. One vehicle lagged behind slightly and I guessed that it was picking up its cutoff group.

'OK, all call signs, the deal is done, the other party has left and we'll give it two minutes before moving. Les, I'm going to call you on the mobile to discuss next move. Seamus, acknowledge, over.'

Single click.

I wanted to wait a couple of minutes just in case there was anything funny being planned, just to let the night settle on us again and let our senses stretch out – listening, mostly – for any suspicious activity.

I called Les and explained that, with the Green Berets unable to let us stay at the villa without them present, we would go back only to pick up our stuff and some ammunition. Then I anticipated the best move would probably be to head out to the safe house and spend the night with Sammy's family before heading out to the west first thing in the morning.

Cobus would come with us to the safe house, but then he needed to get back into the Green Zone. He would not be coming with us to Jordan.

That was about two minutes, so I called in Seamus and Dai, and, while the two of them walked across from their lie-up position in the trees, Sammy and I repacked our new weapons. I didn't want to show too much light out there in the middle of nowhere, but we would need to check them out properly before mothballing our AKs.

'Fuck me hard,' announced Dai as he walked into the range, patrolling with his AK butt in the shoulder. 'I've got a bladder like a space hopper, mate. Let me have a quick slash before we go.'

'Can't you wait until we get back?'

'I've been busting, mate. I must have had five cups of coffee before we came out and they went right through me. I couldn't do anything because them militia cunts were in the bushes right fucking next to us.'

'Just let him get on with it. Jesus, he's only been moaning like an old woman the whole time,' Seamus said. 'So, Rupert, what did you get?'

I showed him the stash of weapons in the back of the car and he whistled appreciatively.

'That's a right good deal there. I would have thought that lot would cost.' He rapidly did the maths in his head. 'At least six or seven grand. Them PKMs alone were going for around 900 bucks apiece last year. How much did it cost with the SF guns thrown in?'

'Nothing, mate. He only took the SF guns.'

'You're kidding, right?' said Dai from behind the car.

'Fuck me,' said Seamus in mock astonishment. 'What are you doing, mate? You can't still be pissing? Couldn't you find it?'

'It very tiny,' said Sammy, joining in. 'I have flashlight if you need.'

'I'm going to fucking do you, sunshine,' Dai replied.

We all laughed. Dai finally finished and, after being forcibly restrained from having 'just a quick cigarette', we mounted up and drove off across the fields to the hidden entrance on to the highway. I called in Les and Cobus and they appeared as if by magic out of the plantation to the east and joined us.

As we pulled off I wondered how Ali's life had been the last year. Also what his future would be. He had been a trustworthy companion and it sickened me to see him having to put on a militia uniform to get by and keep his family safe. I did not judge him. Trapped in a city like this, a country like this, and in a war with no foreseeable end and no predictable winners, I wondered what I would have done in his position.

I knew I would never see him again, but I had been deeply touched by his desire to reach out and help me one more time in the only way he knew. I felt some pride that our efforts with the community in Aradisa Idah had been worthwhile enough that many of the local Iraqis thought of us as friends. Now, I locked his memory away in one of the many chapters in my life I had left behind. It was time to get back into character and focus on the night ahead.

CHAPTER 18

GETTING OUT OF Aradisa Idah and into Karada district was a nightmare with the main roads blocked by queues of vehicles waiting to pass through Mahdi Militia checkpoints, or VCPs. Often there were dozens of militiamen dressed in a variety of coats and jackets instead of the usual summer uniform of black. But they all had the black balaclavas, turbans or green headbands that had come to represent the Shia in this neighbourhood.

I wondered why there were so many here, down in the south of the city, when presumably their brothers needed reinforcements up in Sadr City in the north-east. I could only assume these were the local gangs and they were making sure that no one got any funny ideas and stepped out of line in their neighbourhood just because the Americans had inconveniently decided to have a surge.

A ten-minute drive turned into over an hour after we had to stop, do a U-turn and double back on ourselves every time we saw a VCP. I wasn't worried about standing out. Many of the other cars on the road were doing exactly the same thing. The militia were not concerned about going after those trying to avoid the VCP. As long as they controlled that section of road and were intimidating everyone, that seemed to be their only objective.

We drove around the outskirts of Aradisa Idah into the palm groves that run 3km deep along the banks of the Tigris. Once, when a training session with my water guards had come under fire from some have-a-go jihadis, I crisscrossed the whole area hunting down the culprits with a platoon of paratroopers in their Humvees from the 82nd Airborne. It had been on Christmas Day, I seemed to remember, and I spent it kicking down doors and clearing rooms with a borrowed M249 SAW.

If there was a better place to lie low than here, I didn't know it. The zone had been owned by Saddam's family and for some reason – fear or respect – it had remained largely deserted. Among the groves Saddam had built some of the most spectacular mansions in Iraq, sprawling estates with swimming pools shaded by date palms – a sacred tree because Mohammed had survived on its fruit in the wilderness.

The villas had been hammered in the bombing campaign that launched Operation Iraqi Freedom, and the squatters who had moved into the area had plundered the ruins to construct lavish hovels with marble walls and gilt doors, the insides equipped with TVs and refrigerators, not that there was any electricity to power them. The squatters planted vegetables, kept goats and kept to themselves. They were too poor for al-Qaeda or Shia gunmen to waste a bullet on.

After driving around what seemed half the city, we arrived at the safe house, taking one last loop to shake any tail and make sure we hadn't been followed. The sound of gunfire to the north was constant and the sky was lit with flares, lines of tracer and explosions, occasionally punctuated by the loud hammering of automatic cannon, either from Bradleys or helicopters. The non-stop sound of intense fighting was grating on my nerves and I was glad finally to arrive.

Sammy called ahead and they were waiting for us. The gate opened and we drove straight in, parking up as Sammy's brother Abdul quickly closed and locked the gate. I noted that in one hand he had an old AK with no buttstock, an Iraqi standard.

Without a word being spoken, each of us grabbed armfuls of weapons and ammunition and started carrying them in and laying them out on the sitting-room floor. The mission was buggered but the team was running with the *Vorsprung durch Technik* of a new Audi.

Fara, General Mashooen, Ayesha and the six children had gathered in the sitting room. As they came to their feet among the cushions and mats they looked like porcelain figures, like the tiny islanders of Lilliput in *Gulliver's Travels*. I felt like a giant, shouldering my way in, bundled up in body armour with a coat over the top. The two youngest girls were clinging to Ayesha's long robe. Ayesha and Abdul looked afraid, of us as well as our unexpected arrival, their fear an almost tangible presence.

The general drew himself up straight, his hair immaculately parted and Brylcreemed back. He gave me that distinctive swift nod of the head and, as I met his old grey eyes, what I saw was the trust a senior officer places in a junior. You come out of Sandhurst with the confidence that you are the best in the world. True or not, it's what you believe, and it seemed suddenly as if all my training had been for this one task, to bring this family out of Baghdad.

'Good evening, sir,' I said in greeting.

'A pleasure to see you, Captain,' he replied.

I glanced at Les and Dai. 'General Mashooen,' I said. 'My colleagues, Les, Seamus and Dai. Cobus, of course, you know.'

'Thank you,' the general said. 'You are too kind. I remember you from last year.'

They nodded and all shook his hand before greeting Abdul and the others. No one offered to shake the hands of the wives although Fara regarded me warily with a smile in case I tried to kiss her again. Qusay, Sammy's son, stood as tall as he could and squeezed our hands fiercely.

Fara came towards me. 'What's happened, James?' she asked. 'You are here . . .'

I pulled off my coat. 'Let's sit down,' I said. 'Wait for Sammy.'

Dai handed out fags to the smokers. He loved Iraq because everyone smoked constantly and he didn't have to go outside just for a quick tab. The pouches down each leg of his sand-coloured cargo pants were crammed with what seemed like a lifetime supply of Marlboro.

The guys tossed their coats in the corner and sat cross-legged to one side like a line of Buddhas. Fara lit the oil lamps. The last light of day had faded and the people whom I'd thought looked like Lilliputians were magnified in shadow against the wall. I could hear the tinkle of glasses being placed on a tray in the kitchen below us. Other than that, there was silence.

Sammy took a deep breath and started speaking in Arabic to the family, outlining what had happened during the day. When he mentioned Colonel McQueen, their faces brightened with smiles, but then fell as obviously he related the story that Mad Dog had been badly wounded. Fara shook her head sadly. The convoy to Mosul was off. In fact the whole trip to Mosul was off. The new plan was to escape to Jordan to be refugees. Sammy looked to his father, who nodded his approval of the plan.

It didn't matter that it was Sammy who was fifty years old and had been running around in a war zone for four years supporting the entire extended family. His eighty-year-old father was still head of the family and nothing would happen if it did not merit his approval; that's just the way it was.

Sammy continued. I heard him mention Gabir and the women gasped. The general and Abdul both looked down and then the wives and the children were hugging each other with tears in their eyes. Sammy kept talking, and I could hear him referring to Fallujah and then Amman.

They all seemed to take it in, but then Abdul was asking about Gabir and how had the police known to search his shophouse. Sammy looked at Fara and she spoke softly in English. Tears rolled down Fara's cheeks and fell on the front of her green smock. I watched the stain grow as she switched from English to Arabic. She spoke quickly, gasping for breath, telling them the story of how she had told her aunt they were leaving for their country house in Mosul and Aunt Zahrah had decided to arrange a taxi with her regular driver, Abeer al-Mazyad.

'A Shia,' added Sammy. 'With a wife who talks louder and longer than the imams in the mosques.'

The puzzle slotted together instantly for the family. They could easily imagine what had happened when Fara left her aunt and Zahrah made that fateful call to Abeer al-Mazyad.

Suddenly Fara gave out a low cry and clapped her hand to her mouth. 'Zahrah!'

Sammy gave Fara the phone. She scrolled through the contacts. I heard the ring across the room, two rings and the line opened.

Her face brightened. 'Auntie Zahrah . . .' She went into Arabic, then screamed and dropped the phone.

I reached for it. The line was dead.

'It was a man, he sounded . . .' she said, and stopped, unable to describe his voice.

I glanced at Sammy. We knew exactly who it was waiting for that cellphone to ring. Sammy had no need to punish Fara. She would feel her guilt until the day she died. Sammy took the phone from her and dialled another number, walking into the next room.

Fara spoke to Ayesha and the younger woman looked relieved to have a task. On the table, dominoes stood like a miniature Stonehenge, the game interrupted. I watched Ayesha placing the pieces in a box, stacking them to face the same way, before hurrying off to make *chai*.

She returned shortly with a tray, kneeled before us and poured tea from a silver pot. We sat watching in silence, the tang of fresh mint rising into the air, and it felt as if we were taking part in the same Japanese tea ceremony captured in the prints on the wall, the girl's movements having some deep significance. Ayesha looked up at me as she gave me the glass on a small saucer.

'*Shekir?*'

'A little,' I replied, demonstrating with a narrow gap between my thumb and finger.

She added sugar and smiled. I hadn't noticed before – strange for me – but that smile changed her completely: her face came to life. She was a real beauty with small, delicate features and big dark Madonna eyes.

I burned my fingers and tongue playing out the tea ritual. I quickly held up my palm to prevent my glass being refilled. Everyone waited in silence while they were served their tea, and sipped it appreciatively.

Sammy came into the room with a grim look on his face. I looked at him questioningly but he shook his head. He would tell me later.

I cleared my throat and got everyone's attention by standing up. 'OK, we have to get ready to move tomorrow morning. Sammy, can you get your family to pack everything, then eat and then they need to get to sleep as early as they can.' I looked at the Brits. 'We need to strip down and clean these weapons and check that they are all good to go for tomorrow morning.'

Sammy got the family moving out of the room and Les, Seamus and Dai got straight to it, carefully laying out the weapons on top of their coats on the floor. The SF had been more than generous before leaving and had left a marked-out pallet of ammunition, MREs and cleaning products for us to take. We hadn't even taken half of it.

In a few seconds of clacking metal the M4s and M16s were in pieces, all carefully laid out and being inspected minutely with torches. We all knew that the M16-type weapons were suffering higher levels of stoppages than normal in Iraq. By some bizarre quirk of fate, the size of the average dust particle in Iraq was much smaller and finer than the 'standard' dust particulate used in US Army weapons-testing trials in the States. If you visited any American unit that had been in country more than a couple of days, you would always see troops with weapons broken down, constantly cleaning them.

The Brits started to lay out cleaning cloths, rods and fluid.

Cobus came up to me. 'OK, man, I have to move off now, back to the Green Zone.'

'Do you want us to escort you up?'

'*Nie*, it's one minute's drive, I'll be fine. Don't take the risk of coming in and out of here again and compromising this location. It's all we have left.'

We shook hands and said goodbye. I knew almost nothing about Cobus's covert actions in Baghdad – it was better that way – but I was sure there were a lot of Iraqis who said his name in their prayers.

'Give this to Sammy when you get to Jordan, man.' He tucked a wad of dollars into my hand.

'Sure thing.' I put it away in my pass-holder around my neck. 'And, next time you have a fucking problem, call some other poor sod to come to Baghdad.'

He laughed and slapped me on the shoulder, then went to say goodbye to the other guys. There was a lot of laughter and back-slapping.

'I'll call you when I get to the Green Zone to let you know I got in.' He waved and was gone.

Sammy followed him out to open and close the gate. I sat down with the others and broke down the FAL to start cleaning it.

'How are we going to zero these?' Dai asked. The SF had also left us half a dozen optical sights from various manufacturers. They were asked to test so many that they couldn't use them all. We had left them since we had no way to zero them, but a couple of these M4s had ACOG scopes already on.

'Well, they've all got see-through mounts,' I said, examining one of the uppers. 'We can do a rough estimate at first light, put them on a rest and look through the iron sights and then the optics and see if they are pointing at the same thing. Otherwise, first chance we get, we do a quick test-fire and adjust.'

We all got back down to cleaning and Sammy came back into the room to sit next to me.

'I have called to the neighbour of Zahrah and he has told me what has happened to her.' For once his perpetual smile was gone.

It was an old friend, I'd learned, a Sunni. The IP had taken Zahrah. They had told the neighbours that she was a spy working with al-Qaeda and was helping to plan the bombing of the local market. Sammy had been described as the senior al-Qaeda terrorist behind the spate of bombings across the city. It made sense if you wanted it to. Al-Qaeda was Sunni. Assam Mashooen was Sunni, a former MiG pilot in Saddam's air force, a man who might well bear a grudge towards the new Iraq.

He threw up his plump hands. 'People do not believe these lies,' he said. 'They pretend to believe, or they have trouble.'

'I'm sorry, mate,' I said to Sammy. 'Will the family be all right?'

'Allah will provide,' said Sammy in the tone of a non-believer.

If the justifications for war were created from dodgy dossiers, an out-of-date PhD thesis and a tapestry of lies, it was hardly surprising that the new Iraq was being stitched together from the same fabric.

Gabir would have been tortured before being dragged out into the street and shot, a demonstration of what happens to traitors, a show of power that could have been adopted from the Nazis, Stalin or Pinochet. Gabir would have told the IP everything. Fara's aunt would have filled in a few more details before the cops went after Abeer al-Mazyad.

Sammy looked depressed and I knew why. Iraqi insurgents captured in combat by the Americans would beg to be sent to a US camp, and not to be turned over to the Shia-dominated

Iraqi security forces. A middle-class Sunni woman taken in the middle of the night by a Shia police unit would be gang-raped before being tortured to death and dumped in an unmarked grave or into the Tigris.

So many similarly abused bodies were being recovered from the river, dozens every day, that *fatwa* had been declared on the fish normally caught in the river as part of the staple diet. The population of Baghdad, both Shia and Sunni, had been banned by their imams from eating the fish; it was now *haram*, since it had undoubtedly been feeding on human corpses.

Sammy had received another call. From Abeer the taxi driver. As a Shia he had only been roughed up lightly before being released, although that still meant the loss of several teeth. He had wanted to let Sammy know he was sorry and had soundly beaten his wife for all the trouble caused. I twisted my lips wryly, not knowing whether to feel satisfaction or exasperation with the local manner of doing things.

My phone rang. I looked at the caller ID. It was Cobus.

'Hello, mate. Back safe?'

'*Ja,* you guys take care. Let me know when you get to Amman.'

'Sure thing. Thanks for everything. Hallo.'

'Hallo.'

We both laughed and clicked off.

At the end of an hour working on the weapons, with a small interval to shovel down some MREs, we were good to go. We agreed that we would use the M4s in the cars but would have the M16s, with their longer effective range, ready to go in case we had to abandon vehicles and fight in the desert. One of the M16s had an M203 40mm grenade launcher under the barrel. We had twelve magazines of 5.56mm each and a dozen 40mm grenades for the 203.

If we ran through all of that, we still had our AKs and quite literally a mountain of decent Yugoslav 7.62mm ammunition.

We exchanged the AK magazines in our tactical vests for 5.56mm magazines and repacked the AK ammo into day sacks, each one with an AK strapped to the side. We split up responsibility for the other weapons. Dai would take the FAL, I would take the 203, and Les and Seamus would each take a PKM with two boxes of ammo for each. I thanked God we weren't on foot. There was no way in my old infantry days we could have humped this much hardware around.

When we had finished I got Sammy to call Abdul to join us in the sitting room.

'So how are we going to do this, Ash?' Seamus asked. 'Who do you want in which vehicle?'

We had three vehicles; a four-wheel-drive SUV, a minivan that could seat twelve, and a fairly powerful saloon car, a Peugeot.

'We'll lead off with the SUV. That will have myself, Sammy and the general.'

'Ahhh, Jim.' Dai cast an embarrassed look at Sammy. 'No offence, Sammy, but, Jim, Sammy's dad is fucking five hundred years old. He'll be about as much use a chocolate teacup, mate.'

'Yeah,' grunted Les, 'about as much use as a one-legged man in an arse-kicking competition.'

'Sammy and I will be the shooters if necessary. Sammy, I need to talk us through any Iraqi checkpoints. My ID should get us through any Coalition VCPs. The general's job will be to sit in the front passenger seat and look old and harmless.'

They all hesitated. It was true. A large SUV full of fit-looking men in Iraq meant trouble. Even putting a woman in the vehicle would only look like a feeble attempt to feign innocence. But an ancient white-haired man with a snowy white moustache and a *shemagh* would evoke sympathy and respect, obviously some elder being driven out by his sons, and too old to cause any trouble.

'In the middle I want Abdul at the wheel of the bus.' Les was probably the best driver out of all of us and I had wanted him to have this, probably the biggest responsibility, but we simply didn't have enough guns to spare him. 'You will have all the women and kids with you in the bus.' I pointed at Abdul. 'Your job will not be to shoot at all, just drive and get the family out of any trouble if we get into it.' Abdul nodded his understanding. 'You can have Qusay next to you. Can he shoot?'

'*Na'am.*'

'OK, but remember, if anything happens it is critical that you just keep driving. Leave the shooting to us, OK?'

'*Inshallah.*' He nodded. I gritted my teeth but didn't bother to push the point.

'You three are the fire support.' I looked at the other three Brits. 'Behind the SUV and the bus your car should be low-profile. Your job, if anything happens, is to zoom up to the best firing point and mallet the fuck out of whoever is giving us grief. I want you bringing up the rear. Firstly, so that if we get chased you can drive them off. Secondly, if we hit trouble from the front, I don't want you caught up in it. I want you a tactical bound behind; close enough to see us if we're in trouble, but far enough behind that you're not drawn in, or under fire yourselves. That'll give you the freedom to manoeuvre to the best position and lay down a shitload of fire.'

'Understood,' said Seamus.

'Roger that,' said Dai.

'OK, let's pack the vehicles up with the AKs and AK ammo, plus all the baggage. All the other longs, keep next to you until we mount up tomorrow morning. We'll head out as soon as it's light enough to see. Best get to sleep now. We'll need all the rest we can get.'

After shifting all the weapons and baggage into the cars, we trooped back and unfolded sleeping bags in the room Sammy had said we could sleep in. He had no mattresses for us, only a few rugs and blankets folded over to use as insulation and take the chill out of the concrete floor. It was late at night and the house was freezing cold.

Seamus was one of those guys who said, 'Yeah, I'm sleeping.' And he slept in an instant, training wired into his mainframe. The rest of the guys gradually nodded off too, relaxed and comfortable.

I tried to do the same but, when you try, when the guy next to you snores like a goods train, sleep evaporates and thoughts come whizzing in like rounds: the neighbours robbing Gabir's house; Sammy's silence; the metal embrace of twisted motor cars; Tanya squeezing my hand as she calmly told me how she had seen my friend Mad Dog shredded by shrapnel and flung so far across the road she thought he was dead even before he hit the ground.

I got out of my sleeping bag with a curse. There was no sleep in me, just a restless thirst I could not quench. I went and had a quick shower in cold water, washed my hair and changed into clean clothes. I would sleep in them in my sleeping bag and then get straight up in the morning and just put my boots on, ready to go. I realized I hadn't talked to my family that day. I dialled quickly. Tomorrow was going to be tricky and I wanted to hear their voices one last time.

Before calling Krista, I opened the shutter. I stood to one side, you can't be too careful, and peered out at a bleak landscape of rooftops. There was another power cut and the only light came from the moon rising over the Tigris, pale yellow like the last stages of a bruise. The clouds were slow and heavy with rain. Far out into the night the sounds of battle seemed muted, as if even the war was taking a nap. I knew this impression was deceiving and that, a kilometre or two away, desperate life-and-death struggles were taking place. With the callous pragmatism of the professional soldier, I had to admit that a selfish part of me was glad it was someone else out there and not me. I had a full belly, a warm sleeping bag waiting and I was about to talk to my wife and kids. Life was good.

I remained staring from my position beside the shutters while I spoke to Krista.

'You all right?' she asked.

'I am, actually, yes. I've got a nice view,' I replied looking over the rooftops, absently scanning for any stealthy movement. There was a dull thump in the distance, and I thought it must have been big for me to feel the vibration halfway across the city. 'How's things?'

'Awful, James, it's been raining like buckets.'

'Like buckets,' I repeated. Krista prided herself on speaking better English than me and it was so sexy when she made a mistake.

'Here, someone's dragging the phone out of my hand,' she said.

'Daddy, is it dangerous in Iraq?' Natalie asked.

'No, darling, I told you. It's as safe as houses.'

'That's silly.'

'No, it's not. Our house is safe.'

'It's still silly. When are you coming home?'

'In time for your birthday. How old are you going to be?'

'You know, seven. Seven sevens are forty-nine.'

'Seven. Gosh, that's very old. You'll be getting married to some old man soon. Excellent. You'll have to become an accountant and look after us all when you're rich.'

'Oh yuks, Daddy.' She had already promised me she would never ever get married. Then: 'What's an *accountment*?'

'Someone with lots of money.'

Krista got back on the line. We did phone kisses and I went back downstairs to my room. I was calm now, and looking forward to the morning.

CHAPTER 19

SAMMY, NORMALLY CHATTERING and throwing out directions, was lost in his own thoughts. I could see his eyes mirrored in the windscreen, staring without focusing on the beams of light before us. Odd rounds carried on the wind, a distant fizz and thump, enough to remind you that nowhere was safe. Ever. Even if you and your loved ones had learned to manoeuvre your way through those streets where footsoldiers from a dozen different factions, plus the innocent civilians – either bystanders or chosen victims – had left their blood and guts, there was still the daily struggle to survive the anarchy, shortages, shredded nerves, shifting loyalties, old and new hostilities, new restrictions that were no compensation for the new freedoms like voting along tribal lines and Internet porn. Married men who had barely seen their wives naked were relieving the daily tedium with buff, shaved Romanian girls a breath from childhood.

We had set off just before dawn. It was cold enough that my breath frosted and I was glad of my leather gloves. Les had sniffed in disdain. As a former Commando Arctic Warfare instructor in Norway, he had never let his men put on their gloves until it was minus ten centigrade. Sammy's family had been in a complete state, and it had taken a mug of steaming *chai* each before we could get them out of the house into the courtyard. All the children had visited the toilet and the two women had cried as they left their last refuge for this unknown journey. To combat the cold, the whole tribe were bundled up like Eskimos.

I was counting on the early hour and the cold to help us. As ex-British soldiers we could shrug it off like just another ice-frosted morning in Brecon. If the local militias were anything like the Iraqis I had worked with, then a chilly 6a.m. start would see them dopey or unconscious at their posts. We Brits had briefly assembled on the roof to sight in our weapons on a distant watchtower. It had aiming marks painted on to its sides as if for that purpose. The iron sights and the optical sights on top were lined up on all of the rifles. The proof would come only on firing, but I didn't want to have a quick couple of shots only to risk waking up any militia check-points that might have been set up just around the corner overnight.

After the initial fugue, Sammy's family moved quickly. Depressingly, most of their belongings had vanished with our cached vehicles in Gabir's garage. They appeared from the house, eleven refugees with wretched bundles. Despite having feared and hated the Ba'athist Party, the Mashooens had always been close to power. Now the *ancien régime* was being swept into exile. I recalled that London after the Second World War had been awash with banished aristocracy – from Romania, Bulgaria, Russia and the Balkans – a chessboard of kings, knights and courtiers.

It had rained overnight, and around the palm tree at the end of the passage was a puddle they had to step through to reach the cars. Baghdad is cooled by mini-monsoons mid-season when the heavens open up and wash the dust off the streets.

Fara, like Ayesha, was discreetly dressed in a grey *abaya* that didn't suit her but matched her appearance. She was ashen. I had never seen such a complete change in a person so quickly. Her eyes had lost their colour and sunk into her head. She was gaunt, her hands trembled faintly and her hair, always neatly held in a chignon, fell loosely about her cheeks.

'I am so sorry, Fara. There is no news.'

'It is what I expected, James. Thank you.'

She shook my hand and joined her children in the bus. I had hoped to get some news of Zahrah for her from our SF friends, but a quick phone call from them to various IP commanders had shown no log of Gabir's execution, nor the seizure of three vehicles from his shop in Karada, nor the arrest of Auntie Zahrah, who was undoubtedly dead by now. At least, for her sake, I hoped so.

Sammy was wearing a red and white *shemagh* and carried an old AK, his gold-plated Tariq stuffed into his belt.

'Mister James, Mister Dai, good morning.'

'Morning, matey,' said Dai. 'You've chosen a good day for it.'

'I didn't have anything else better to do,' said Sammy, and we laughed.

'Well, the waiting is finally over. Next stop, Amman,' I said.

'We say patience is bitter, but its fruit is sweet,' the general added.

He translated for Abdul and Ayesha. The children were like spectators at a tennis match, their gaze moving from face to face.

'Make no mistake, Sammy, we're going to get you out,' I said.

Sammy nodded his big head slowly up and down. 'We are more grateful than I can express,' he said. 'It only makes me unhappy that, while you save my family, there are other families who will be left behind and they will be less safe.'

We were quiet for a moment. I then told them how I wanted them sat in each vehicle, and how Qusay or Fara would have to take over driving the bus in an emergency.

'This is just back-up,' I said. 'I don't expect anything to happen.'

'In Iraq you must always expect the unexpected,' said General Mashooen.

He was right, of course, but I didn't want to spook them before the off. I glanced at Fara. Her dead eyes seemed to have come back to life.

'It is OK, James,' she said. 'I am sad because it is my fault Auntie

Zahrah has been taken. But I am strong. I am strong for my children.'

Her eldest son was sitting close as if to protect his mother and nodded as if to confirm what she had said. He was only fifteen but in Baghdad was already regarded as a man with his faint shadow of a moustache. If anything happened to Sammy, he would be the man of the family; even Fara, his mother, would be relegated to an advisory role. Our eyes met.

'I am ready,' he said in English, and I was startled, hearing his father's voice coming from him, though he had the more refined looks of his mother.

Jesus, is the world ready for another Sammy? I thought.

'You will have to look out for the little ones,' I told him.

He nodded gravely. 'Yes, I will,' he said, patting his AK.

On an impulse I shrugged off my tactical vest and indicated that young Qusay should take off his coat. My tacvest was a plate carrier and already had heavy SAPI plates in front and back. The soft Kevlar vest I normally wore underneath it I took off and strapped on to Qusay. He was a little tubby, like his father, but even so the Velcro straps nearly doubled around him. At least that way he would be protected from shrapnel. He put his coat back on over the top, looking very pleased with himself, and I put my tactical vest back on. Sammy started to thank me but I motioned him to be quiet.

'OK, let's go. Everyone mount up.'

Sammy made sure everyone was safely aboard the bus, before swinging himself into the driver's seat of the SUV. The Brits were already in the Peugeot, at the rear, engine purring, heater on, faces grim. I looked at them again through the windscreen, not as familiar friends but as an image of how they would appear to the enemy. I was glad that I was on their side.

Les saw me looking and made obscene hand gestures, indicating that I was a wanker.

I shook hands with the general before I sat behind him in the back seat of the SUV. The events of the last twenty-four hours seemed to have put an extra decade on his features and I realized with sudden shock just how old he was. It would be a gruelling enough journey for him across the desert even without the enemy. I suddenly felt the full weight of responsibility for Sammy's family hit my shoulders, an almost physical sensation. No turning back now, this was it. We pulled out of the safe house on to the street and drove off, leaving the gate open behind us.

A hint of light slid along the horizon. We hissed through the wet empty streets with the cry from the mosques calling the faithful to the first of the day's five sessions of prayers. The words echoed from tinny speakers from one minaret to the next, penetrating every corner of the city, every aspect of life. The voices sounded urgent, blending into an unintelligible stream, and I thought with sudden paranoia that the muezzin were throwing a curtain down around the city to warn their brothers-in-arms that we were on our way.

We moved through Karada without meeting any other traffic, but as soon as we turned south to try to get on to the Dora highway, there was a steady stream of vehicles changing lanes and edging into every available space. Abdul stayed a yard from my tail and I knew that Seamus, Les and Dai would be carefully watching over us from a few cars back. I grinned, knowing that well before we even left the city Dai would be bugging the others to let him have a fag if he wound the window down.

The traffic picked up speed. I kept my eyes glued to the rooftops, the windows, the overpasses, the husks of abandoned cars, the piles of masonry.

Weak sunlight lit the grey sky. Every shadow suggested danger. Every car that passed could hold fundamentalists appalled by my lack of facial hair, ghouls drawn out at dawn by the coppery tang of fresh blood. In the Green Zone, you could always catch it from a stray mortar if you were very unlucky. But 'outside the wire' the highways, residential streets, markets and mosques were a gauntlet of booby-traps, roadside bombs, lone gunmen, militiamen with grenades that came in wooden crates with 'US ARMY' stencilled along the side. Just as they say when it comes to money everyone has the same religion, when it comes to urban terrorism, the *mujahideen* were not prejudiced against using the weapons of the enemy. US-Zionist fragmentation grenades will do very nicely, thank you. Certainly more trustworthy than the crap being produced by the Libyans.

The Shia cops weren't out in the streets searching for bandits, jihadis or Shia brothers in the Mahdi Army, they were running around like headless chickens, inexperienced, disorganized, not bringing order but spreading horror, their job in the madness to hunt down Sammy Mashooen, a national hero, an innocent, a man the former water guards knew, and knew to be innocent of everything except the will to survive.

I kept my commentary over the net to Seamus's vehicle to a minimum. Abdul wouldn't have understood it anyway. We slowed. A military checkpoint was up ahead, joint US and Iraqi forces. I was impressed with how professional and with-it the Iraqis appeared to be. Long gone were the days of the half-hearted ICDC troops, often as much a danger to the Coalition troops as they were un-reliable. Cars peeled off into the suburbs. We joined the *jundhis* queuing to get through the VCP, the vehicles jamming up tight as we inched forward. Fumes filled the air. Drivers started leaning on their horns. Iraqis are always impatient and never in a hurry.

Then I saw in the rear-view mirror, a dozen cars or more behind me, a door open and a woman get out.

She shuffled slowly to the side of the road and I assumed that she was going to buy something from one of the market stalls, but she ignored them and just walked up the pavement towards the distant checkpoint. I kept scanning the rest of the traffic. There was no movement whatsoever. Each car or lorry that reached the checkpoint was directed off to the side into an inspection bay between concrete blast walls, inspected and then released on to the highway beyond. Grim-faced Iraqi and American soldiers clearly had no interest in cutting any corners and were doing the job properly.

The faces of the drivers around me did not show any stress or emotion, other than boredom and impatience at the slow pace of the traffic. The sun was above the horizon now, and a couple of Iraqi soldiers had wandered down between the cars, raising one hand palm upwards with all the fingers and thumb pursed together at the tips, the Iraqi gesture which translated into 'patience' or 'wait a minute'. Some of the drivers had wound down windows to talk to them, the rest monged in their cabs, still sleepy and not in the mood for anything. Many of them smoked. I could see the silvery blue curls coming out of some windows. I smiled, again thinking of Dai going through nicotine withdrawal. There was no way the two marathon runners would let him light up.

'Seamus, all OK back there?' I sent over the radio.

'Yes, mate. Reckon we should have gone the other way, though. This is taking fucking ages.'

'Better an American checkpoint than a Mahdi Army one.'

'Yeah, roger that.'

We lapsed into silence and I scanned around again.

The same woman I had seen earlier was level with us now, still walking slowly towards the checkpoint. I looked at her curiously. She was much younger than I had previously thought, no more than a girl, her face drawn and thin, far too thin for the large bulk of body humped up under her black coat.

And then I realized why her coat was so bulky.

My blood ran cold.

CHAPTER 20

M Y STOMACH FLIP-FLOPPED with dread. I could see the girl
making her way towards the checkpoint and knew what was
going to happen next.

We were probably only 50m from the gate, maybe 15–20 cars
in front of us, the curve through the chicanes allowing me direct
line of sight to the American and Iraqi soldiers standing around
in a cluster having a smoking break.

Sammy leaned back to look at me. 'Just like the old days, always
lining up,' he said. 'Now we have to line up to get out of the city
as well as line up to get in.'

I didn't respond. I was watching the girl. She hurried, paused,
hurried again. Did she have a moment's doubt? Did the words of
the imam ring hollow all of a sudden?

I felt nauseous. I lowered the window. Sammy did the same.
My eyes focused completely on the girl, every step seemed to me
to be tremendously significant. This was the twentieth-last step
this body would ever take. This was the nineteenth-last step she
would ever take, the eighteenth.

Training? Instinct? Hard to say.

A dozen scenarios ran through my mind. I had already looked
around. The traffic was solid. We wouldn't have time to drive out.
Debus? No. I couldn't even consider getting the nine family

members out of the bus behind us and herding them off the road in time. We had only a moment left. I was too far from the checkpoint to even shout a warning to the soldiers manning it.

A random crazy thought occurred to me that I should fire a warning shot over their heads and make them duck, but I discarded that one straight away, imagining the response. Or I could call the SF or Cobus in the Green Zone and get someone to look up the local Brigade Combat Team headquarters and warn the checkpoint that a suicide bomber was approaching them. But we had about ten seconds, not the twenty minutes that might entail even if it were possible.

Sammy started to say something but stopped, seeing my face. He followed my gaze and saw the girl. He looked back at me and there was a void behind his eyes.

'Sammy, get back to the bus, tell them to get on the floor now, get them as low as they can. All of them. Run.'

Sammy was gone, his door swinging shut.

'Seamus, contact, contact. There's a suicide bomber on foot approaching the VCP. Take cover, take cover. Wait, out.'

I could hear some shouting behind me and presumed it was Sammy.

'General, sir, there is going to be an explosion, please get down as low as you can.'

He might have been in his eighties but there was no problem with his reflexes. The general dropped in a flash, virtually tucking himself into the footwell of the passenger seat.

After my initial shock, my brain had kicked into gear and I realized that, as a 'walker', the explosives vest she had under her coat would be limited to the amount she could carry. The main threat would come from fragmentation and I had no doubt that the outer layer of her vest would be taped with hundreds of nails, screws and other bits of metal. With enough vehicles and bodies between us and her to soak up all the shrapnel we might actually make it.

I unbuckled my day sack and pulled my helmet out. My gaze was still riveted on the girl, time stretching painfully towards the inevitable outcome. I could not believe no one else had noticed her and seen her for what she was.

A lone Iraqi soldier, posted out in the traffic, turned as she walked up and held out his hand to stop her. I saw his face change as he looked down at her. He turned to run and I ducked my head down, slapping my helmet on.

I was waiting for the detonation and, when it came, it was still a surprise.

There was a colossal bang and the SUV rocked back on its suspension as the shockwave slammed into it. A cacophony of noise deafened me as hundreds of metal fragments shredded metal and glass, spraying off the buildings to the side. When the screeching of metal passed, I look up at an alien scene; everything before my eyes vanished in a cloud of debris and dust, buildings, cars, the sky. There would be nothing left of the bomber. Nothing.

In those first seconds after the blast, there is nothing but the blinding Iraqi dust billowing out across us. Sprays of blood and pieces of people rain down with the glass. My brain goes into overdrive. I am thinking faster than the normal human being but at the same time a precise calmness slams down on my thoughts with mechanical brutality.

My priority list flashes in my mind. I need an immediate status report on my people and vehicles. I need a route out for them from this ambush killing zone. I need to organize a defence against any follow-up from enemy forces.

'General, you OK?' I shout, grabbing his shoulder.

He answers affirmatively and I am already moving out of the back seat, buckling my helmet strap.

'Stay here, don't move.'

I pull the 203 after me and run back to the bus.

'Seamus, are you all OK? Send sitrep, over.' Sammy is already checking the family in the bus. The windows on the bus and even the ones on the SUV are untouched. We were far enough back.

'Yes, yes, all OK, over,' Seamus answers me.

'We need to get out of here. Try and start moving the vehicles around you so that we can get off on a side street, over.'

'Roger, out.'

I look back southwards past the SUV. The dust still swirls but is clearing. There is no movement at all. The cars nearest the girl have no windows and every vehicle around bears the tiny pinpricks of shrapnel and fragmentation. Of the soldier and the girl there is nothing left that I can see.

I look north, the way we have come and two cars behind the bus I see Les and Dai debus. They are also wearing their helmets and carrying M16s. Seamus stays at the wheel ready. They are already looking for an alternate route out. There is no need to start moving the Iraqi drivers. All the way down the line, people are frantically trying to reverse.

That's when the secondary device goes off. A car bomb 60m behind us that makes the girl look like a firecracker. I see the flash then I am hurled off my feet. It was the closest I'd been to a car bomb and the sheer magnitude was incredible, the explosion like the sound made plunging into deep water but magnified a million times, louder than anything you can imagine, a sonic roar as if the world itself has been ripped apart. This is a much bigger thump that whiplashes through the air and the earth. Cars, not just people, are picked up and thrown to the side. Another wave of choking dust and smoke flies out and surrounds us.

I don't bother using the radio. I pick myself up and run straight back to Seamus's car. Dai and Les are already on their feet, coughing.

The ground has moved, but the Peugeot has settled again. We are on the edge of the quake. We are witnesses, not victims.

'Fucking hell, that was close.' Les wipes his eyes and holds his weapon ready. He is shouting. We are all slightly deafened.

'Let's see if we can get out.'

The three of us start walking back northwards through the traffic, away from the military VCP. Seamus stays with the car but gets out to stand next to it. He pulls out one of the PKMs, his M16 on his back.

Seconds have passed and now there is movement; figures emerging in slow-motion like demons dripping blood, clothes ripped from their bodies, leaving charred rags, empty eyes, unfocused stares.

As your hearing returns, the film speeds up. The smoke climbs in a spiral, sucking the oxygen from the air. I saw a girl Natalie's age, completely naked, hair and flesh in flames, a scene recalling the napalm bombings in Vietnam. A woman in a smoking coat, face and hair uncovered, drifts by like a sleepwalker, the bloody rag of a dead infant in her arms like a sacrifice, an offering. Old men, lost children, women screaming, throwing back their heads and wailing wordlessly in misery and pain.

Time is out of joint. Only a few seconds have passed since the suicide girl detonated the first device, but my retinas have been scorched by more images than I can take in. Grey dust hangs in the air. It peppers your taste buds. You are swallowing history. You are stunned, in shock, immobile. You feel hollowed out, useless. You can do nothing. Absolutely nothing. Which burning child or haemorrhaging woman do you risk your life to help? You are programmed to save yourself, the people you're with, to complete your mission.

Family cars have become metal coffins holding blackened, un-recognizable people. Mercifully they are unconscious or dead as they burn. The smell of burning rubber and metal is overpowering. They burn tyres in the villages taken by rebel armies in Africa just to show they've been there, the eternal flame of destruction and death.

With the smell of rubber is the smell of roasted flesh, the sharp, chemical vestiges of explosives, and you can sense the cold coppery panic that passes through crowds when tear gas is fired into the air. I remember an old friend of my father who had been present shortly after the liberation of Auschwitz who said the smell of the concentration camps was the smell of concentrated human suffering. That was the smell at the south gate that March morning.

Dead bodies were strewn across the ground at the side of the road. Survivors were limping and crawling from the eye of the blast, burned, distorted, limbs ripped off. It was worse than the worst nightmare I'd ever had, Blake's visions of carnage and hell. Around the site of the car bomb all the vehicles had been shifted aside and were burning. In the spin of my thoughts I was trying to imagine how the bombing would be reported. Iraqis killing each other was barely worth mention; it was just a number, a statistic. If we four British contractors were among the dead it would hit the headlines. Behind the news, the death mask that holds our attention is the mirror image of ourselves.

I turned back towards the VCP and jogged forward again to Sammy and the bus. The vehicle in front of the SUV was empty and blocked the way forward. At least my head was clear.

I turned to Sammy and the general. They were shaken, numbed, eyes dead. I spoke slowly.

'Let's get the cars turned around,' I said. 'We're moving out. See if you can fit between that car and the concrete barrier and get on to the other side. The road's pretty clear behind us.'

Sammy's big features had frozen in a look of horror. His plump hands were trembling.

'You OK?' I asked.

He took a deep breath. He nodded slowly and his eyes sparked to life as if a flame had been lit behind them.

'Yes, Mister James. I am ready.' He glanced beyond me, at the burning vehicles and dead bodies. 'Such waste,' he said. 'Such waste.'

He climbed into the driver's seat of the SUV. I glanced at the general and he held up his palm.

'Thank you, Captain,' he said and I closed the door.

My hearing had fully recovered. I was thinking that actually the car bomb had cleared a lot of the road. If we could just shift a couple of cars we could all reverse out of this. Then the machine-guns and AKs opened up from the rooftops of the buildings around us. Rounds were coming in, pinging against the sides of cars, thudding into the dirt, picking out windscreens that hadn't blown in the explosion. I dropped to a fire position on one knee.

Dai had ducked down behind the engine mounting. Vehicles aren't the best shield in the world but are better than nothing. He scanned the buildings adjacent to the checkpoint. They were mud-coloured four-storey tenements with muzzle flare in numerous windows and along the flat roof. As the rounds came in I wondered who they were for. There was still no clear field of fire and the people wandering dazed through the smoke and carnage were Shia as well as Sunni. They were Iraqis.

The incoming was all over the place. You could see the little puffs of dust as they drilled into the dirt. You could hear the smack of each impact.

They were close, but not too close. Iraqi gunmen are excitable, driven by dogma not training. Thank God. Also, most of the fire seemed to be heading at the soldiers who had survived up at the checkpoint. That was the good news. The bad news was that we were stuck out in the open, in the middle of it all.

I looked to see how Sammy was doing. Using the raw power of the SUV he had shunted a smaller car out of the way and was now driving back down the side of the road, one set of wheels up on the pavement. I could see the ghostly figure of the general with his white moustache sat next to him. The bus followed on behind. We needed to clear a route out for them.

'Get in front of Sammy, we need to cover them and clear the route out. I'll cover you,' I shouted to Dai and Les.

They moved at the same time, bodies bent, making the target smaller, and took cover behind the molten chunks of steel to the left and right in front of Sammy. Once they had gone to ground, I got up and sprinted down the road. I took a knee at the corner of a building and peeked around. It was clear. I waved the others forward. Seamus watched over us all with the PKM propped on the bonnet of the car. When Sammy and the bus both pulled up next to Les, Dai and me, he threw the gun into the back seat and quickly drove around to catch up with the other two vehicles.

We were level with the seat of the explosion from the car bomb. The puddles left from the rainstorm were slicked in oil and blood. The wind was moving the smoke about. People were crying and screaming, wandering in circles with blinded eyes. There were limbs and body parts everywhere. Dust films your eyes and goes up your nose. I could feel the grit in my teeth and spat it out. The firing was all behind us now, the Mahdi Army and the joint US and Iraqi soldiers duking it out in a vicious short-range firefight. Even as I looked back a mixed squad of Iraqis and Americans stacked next to a doorway, then kicked it in and piled in to clear the building of militia. Impressive. Fighting a common enemy would be one of the things that bonded two nations together more than any politician's empty gestures.

More importantly, the road back to the junction 100m north of us was clear. I was about to tell Dai and Les to mount back up when firing rang out from ahead of us, in the direction I had thought was safe. A PSD convoy was passing through the junction, overt and heavy. Two Mamba armoured personnel carriers and two refurbished Saxons, the old British Army 'Michael Jacksons'. The turret gunner and top-cover PSDs on each vehicle were hunched down pouring fire into the buildings back at the junction.

To my dismay figures in black uniforms and *shemaghs* were firing back. There was an enemy cut-off group blocking our escape. Even if it had just been us, I wouldn't have risked trying to shoot our way through. With a bus full of women and children there was just no way. I looked back down the side street next to where the car bomb had gone off. Apart from the dead and the dying, it was empty.

I waved in Les and Dai.

'There's no way out through the VCP, and the junction behind us has a cut-off team.'

The two of them nodded. They had both seen the PSD convoy roaring through the junction.

'We're going to take this side street, and I think we can follow it all the way to the canal. We'll cut back into Karada and then into Dora from the other side. We'll escort them a couple of blocks on foot and then mount up once we're out of the danger zone. Any questions?'

'No mate, let's fucking do it,' said Les.

I ducked down behind a Toyota to look up the side road again, wondering if they had a secondary device up there, or another cut-off group. The Toyota's engine was spitting green and blue flames. The front seats were occupied by two dead, disfigured men and, in the back, among the pieces of luggage, was a white parrot in a bamboo cage. It was silent. It moved sideways along its perch, one way and back again. It stared accusingly at me, as if I had let off the bomb.

I lifted the cage through the shattered back window. 'Pretty Polly,' I said stupidly as I unhooked the catch. The parrot stepped out. It continued gazing at me, but it didn't fly away and I wondered if its wings had been clipped. It was a prisoner afraid to leave its prison, like most of the 7 million people in Baghdad.

'Shoo. Shoo,' I said.

But it just stood there, staring, and I wondered if the parrot was blind or in shock.

Dai Jones had thrown himself on the ground behind the car.

'Poor cunt,' he said. 'Go on, fuck off back to the Green Zone.'

He went up on one knee, made himself comfortable, elbows resting on the boot of the Toyota, stock rammed into his right shoulder, sniper eyes gauging distances, picking targets.

Les was on the other side of the road, to our left. Seamus ran up to join him, M16 on his back, holding the PKM across his chest. I looked back in surprise and saw Sammy's son, Qusay, behind the wheel of the saloon car. He grinned manically and waved. We were ready. I gave the signal and we all stood up and started walking slowly forward, rifles in the shoulder, front sights seeking out every doorway and window.

There was movement through the still-thick cloud of smoke and dust, and we all froze and went to ground behind the ruins of cars and their grisly occupants. I raised my rifle, eye glued to the scope, movements slow, steady, like a pendulum, muscles tight across my belly, years of training carved in every reflex. We hid ourselves and waited.

Coming through the mangled breaker's yard of twisted cars and dead and dying non-combatants were the militiamen of al-Sadr's Mahdi Army. It was hard to know exactly how many there were, but the numbers seemed to grow as they got closer, aim all over the place, spurts of orange flame leaping from the barrels of AK47s.

'Fuck me, there's hundreds of 'em,' said Dai.

'There'll be less later,' called back Les with a dirty laugh, and I couldn't help smiling at his black humour.

They were easy to spot in their black suits, most wearing black turbans or black balaclavas, others with green headbands spelling out religious texts from the Koran. Some of those militiamen had photographs of al-Sadr pinned to their tunics – it was blasphemy to show the graven image, but I guess as al-Sadr was a god that was all right.

The men of the Mahdi were fanatics with no safety vests – only the occasional green sash tied around their waist – zealots hyped up on faith; drugs, too, some of them – harder to fight when they keep coming forward with no sense of precaution or fear. These were the bullet chewers. Grunts in the Shia uprising. The holy martyrs fighting for the Shia vision of Sharia law: women veiled, girls ripped out of school, Fara Mashooen expelled from teaching, limb amputations, stoning, beheading, the great clock of time being turned back fourteen centuries.

I squeezed the trigger, aiming at the centre button on one man's chest-rig pouch and squeezed again and again. The guns of my three companions chattered in fury, announcing our presence with a deadly bouquet of lead.

CHAPTER 21

THE NEAR DISTANCE was lit by the muzzle flash from a score of rifles. They had no real idea of our numbers or position in the thick smoke and dust and were firing blindly at every car and building in front of them.

Steady. Squeeze. No hurry. Pick a target. Don't look to see if he goes down and stays down. There were too many out there for counting kills.

I heard the dead man's click as the mag expired, ducked my head behind cover and reached into my chest pouch to change mags.

'Magazine,' I yelled over the gunfire.

The arc moved to cover me. I changed mags. My hands were sweating.

'Back in,' I shouted.

The clatter and ping of gunfire in the mud-brick street was punctuated by moments of silence. It's hard to know what's worse, the crack of rounds coming in or the silence warning of fresh bursts still to come. What you hang on to is the memory of some grizzled training instructor who reminded you that when you hear the song of incoming rounds you know you're still alive and free to fire back.

'Magazine,' shouted Les.

I moved forward and ducked down again, seeking a better firing point. I was impatient to move forward and drive the enemy down another road so that we could get past. Staying where we were and fighting a battle of attrition was not an option. The US and Iraqi troops sounded as if they had their hands full back up at the VCP and some of these battles could go on for hours. Even worse if the army started doing well, they would drive the Mahdi fighting them back down here.

The momentary silence had gone. The day was alive with lead and cordite, the air whistling and cracking, ripping apart, a sound like silk tearing. Grit caked the corners of my eyes. My throat was dry like old bones.

'Back in,' Les yelled.

We had formed an inverse fan. Seamus was on the left, then Les, then Dai, with me on the right. We were fighting our own individual duels, but the shape protected us all. We could cover for each other as we changed magazines, as we advanced, switched positions and drew the militiamen into the bowl of fire spitting from our four scalding barrels.

We were picking targets in a continuous rhythm. At the same time, we were looking out for each other, a subconscious glimpse lasting the same fraction of a second it takes a single shot to cover the space between you and the target.

'Ash, above you,' Seamus called.

I ducked and a burst from his PKM took out a sneaky bastard trying to get round behind us on the roof above me. That's all we needed, for them to get clever and start using the rooftops. I mentally cursed Sammy's family bitterly. Without them we would have long since kicked our way into a building and be escaping out the back door into another street, out of contact and free to run. With a bus full of women and children we were stuck here.

As I turned back, I noticed on the edge of my vision a militiaman creeping up, keeping his head down. He was hauling what looked like a Dragunov, a Soviet sniper rifle.

He slid into position behind a vehicle thrown on its side. I dropped down on one knee behind a piece of wreckage. I watched the Dragunov slide through a gap. I didn't have a clear target, just the barrel, and knew that above was a head wrapped in a headband, a brain filled with radical Shi'ism, a searching eye, an itchy finger.

I squeezed once, twice, three times, and the Dragunov barrel jerked sideways. He was out of play.

In action, you fear getting killed, but you feel fully alive – as I've said before, it's the most extreme aspect of your humanity, courting death and dealing death.

I'm also thinking: I should have drunk some water before I debussed from the SUV. I'm going to get dehydrated.

Fuck it!

'Let's go.'

I moved forward towards the upturned car where the sniper had taken cover. Dai followed. I indicated to Les, then Seamus. We were closing the net, setting up a crossfire, drawing them in like wasps to a nest.

Rounds were coming at us like hail. I didn't want to think how lucky we had been not taking a hit. From the upturned car, I could see Sammy and the three wagons. They hadn't turned the corner yet, but were waiting for us to clear the road. The barrel of the Dragunov was still poking through the wreckage. I gave it a pull, but there was a dead man's weight on the other end and it wouldn't budge.

Dai found a protected spot on the other side of the car. It was a good defence position, the engine block thick enough to stop the 8g of an AK47 7.62mm round.

In a firefight, you have to lay down enough suppressing fire to keep the enemy from moving. We'd done that. We were still doing that. And they were still popping their heads up like a deranged army of black moles with flashes of green and gold, zigzagging through the rubble crying *Allahu Akbar*. Cartridge cases were pinging out from the bolt on my M16 like popcorn. My face was black with soot.

'Magazine.'

My fingers touched the blunt heads of the 40mm grenades in my chest pouch as I grabbed another full magazine. I'd gone through three mags and wanted the enemy to bunch together in nice convenient groups so that I could use the 203 to blow them up. I put a couple of grenades downrange at them, but they were widely spaced.

As soon as I was in, Seamus was out. We laid down a steady stream of fire while he changed belts.

'Back in.'

You acknowledge, but it's like spotting someone on an empty platform from a speeding train, Seamus a fleeting, impressionist image, left foot forward, knee and spine slightly bent, shoulders hunched, his right leg like a pivot. He had gained some height on the remains of a family car that had welded itself into the embrace of an upturned truck.

People made a fortune with scrap iron in the West. In Iraq, it got dumped and stayed dumped. The Mesopotamian desert with its biblical place names and the oldest artefacts created by man was a wasteland of blown-up tanks, burned-out trucks lost from American convoys, crashed bombers and choppers, and plastic bags that chased by on the wind like a strange species of rodents. In another two thousand years, anthropologists will study plastic bags and say we were a careless civilization.

We moved beyond the upturned vehicle. I saw the dead kid clutching the Dragunov, the headband ripped off, his face slack, an empty mask, the back of his head blown away by one lucky shot. Maybe he was enjoying those seventy virgins, how was I to know? It was the first confirmed kill I had actually seen after hundreds of rounds fired. He could only have been eighteen years old, maybe younger. Foolish and untrained. What sniper would close to within 30m of the enemy with a weapon he could hit them with from twenty times that distance? Or push his barrel out of cover for everyone to see?

Les pulled in closer. I saw two militiamen, boys in identical costumes, rush towards him.

Allahu Akbar. Allahu Akbar.

The boys were shooting from the hip as if their training had consisted of watching *Rambo* films. Les gave them the good news, one-two, one-two, four shots straight from the textbook, and they crumpled, dropping flat in their tracks. They hadn't got anywhere near us.

'Come on, you cunts, you want some?' I heard Les shout.

Still they kept coming. We were at the centre of the hurricane. Up until that point, our safety had relied on the churning smoke, the dazed figures trapped in the field of fire, the sheer ineptitude of the enemy. In Afghanistan, the Taliban had drilled their recruits in training camps set up by Osama bin Laden. The Mahdi in Baghdad was not the Taliban, and was even different to the militias down south in Basra. The Baghdadis hid in dark rooms and mosques throughout the city. They had no ranges to practise their marksmanship skills, no nice parade grounds for their victory rallies.

The Mahdi Army was more like the Salvation Army with Kalashnikovs instead of tubas and trombones. There was no need for training. Volunteers were driven by passion, by the sermons preached by their imams. There were a million Shia kids willing to die for their faith. It was the end of time. The time of the Mahdi. Martyrdom was a privilege. We were merely the tool granting that privilege. The foot soldiers of the Mahdi Army weren't firing at us, not exactly, not accurately; they were firing at what they had been taught we represented: the Infidel, the Zionist crusader capitalist conspiracy. To have taken a bullet would have been bad luck, a flaw in the flow of karma, like Mad Dog McQueen catching the full blast of an IED.

That feeling of being protected in the eye of the hurricane came to an end now. They were rallying around a makeshift barrier of cars parked across the full width of the road. Rounds were cracking back towards us. Seamus had dropped down from the heights to move forward. We were no longer a bowl. We were a line. The last line. The line where the attack has to stop. The gunmen who had been firing wildly into the inferno, running recklessly in to finish off the dazed survivors of the car bomb, had instead found a nasty and unpleasant shock in the form of us four Brits. But they were recovering now. From the rooftops I could see cautious peeks of balaclavas. I wondered who was directing them, who was sending them to their deaths?

I turned just long enough to catch a glimpse of the undamaged vehicles outside the main circle of the blast. Our three vehicles had found a gap into the alleyway off to the side, back near the main road. If we could hold on for another few minutes we'd able to withdraw and be out of there.

'Les, Seamus,' I screamed. They looked over. 'Sammy has found a way out behind us. We need to hold on long enough for him to get the wagons out and then we will withdraw.'

'All right, mate, roger that.'

I glanced back and, and at that moment, I saw a patch of white in the sky above.

'About fucking time,' Dai said.

I grinned. The parrot had taken wing.

'Heads up,' Dai screamed.

He took two shots and turned. I did the same. Christ knows how many kids had been killed out there and still they kept coming. My hands were burning.

'Magazine,' called Les.

We moved the nozzle of the hose a few degrees to the left.

'Back in.'

And back again. The incoming rounds spat into the dirt,

ricocheted off chunks of metal, roared and crackled. They were running through the rubble, weaving a path through the spilled vehicles and piles of dead and debris, firing wildly, and I thought if one of those blokes out there just ducked down, took a breath and concentrated his aim, we'd have caught it long ago.

Allahu Akbar, Allahu Akbar.

'Magazine.' Dai this time.

The spray moved.

'Back in.'

There was a lull. There is always a lull.

They come again. I could see their eyes now, the tails from their black turbans flying in the wind, expressions wooden like puppets carved with rage, that slipped from their faces as they fell, none of them getting more than two paces from the barrier of cars thrown across the road. They were cannon fodder running into our guns like soldiers in the First World War. An RPG cracked overhead, hitting the building 50m behind us and throwing dust across the street.

I turned at last to see the street empty, our vehicles gone. Sammy was peering around the corner at me, waving wildly, holding his AK. Jesus, I hoped he wouldn't get shot by Hank the Yank. With his *shemagh* and moustache he looked like an insurgent. Sammy started firing up at the rooftops over our heads.

'Les, Seamus,' I shouted across the road. 'In pairs, withdraw back to Sammy.' I point back to Sammy at the corner.

'Roger.'

'Jim, you move first,' Dai shouted to me.

I ran past him, slapping him on the shoulder out of habit, and took up a position near the middle of the road. I start firing rounds at gaps in the barriers, militiamen if I see them.

'Dai, Move.'

Dai rolls out of my line of fire to the side and runs straight back down past me, hugging the wall.

Meanwhile, on the other side of the road, Seamus has stood up and is firing out a hundred rounds from the PKM in one continuous burst. His massive frame holds the barrel down mercilessly and every round hammers into the barrier, through cars and bodies.

I trigger the 203 and the grenade thumps into the barrier and explodes, throwing up a gratifying dust cloud. I eject the empty and reach for another, slotting it into the breech as Dai starts firing behind me.

'Jim, move.'

'Seamus, move.'

I fire the 203, turn to the side and get out of the way, then run back down the pavement. On the other side of the street Seamus is doing the same thing. He slings the PKM on to his back as he moves and gets the M16 into his hands. I am busy sticking another 40mm grenade into the breech as I run.

Les and Dai are both kneeling behind a car in the middle of the road, firing straight up the middle. In two bounds we are virtually at the mouth of the alleyway, where Sammy still waits.

'Dai, move straight back to the cars.' I start firing my rifle.

No pause. He legs it.

Seamus drops down, shouts to Les and covers his retreat, firing repeatedly at the shadows and silhouettes emerging from the wreckage.

Les reaches the corner in two steps, turns back to cover Seamus.

He empties his mag and takes off. He is a marathon man. He'll do the distance back to the cars in three seconds.

I fire another bomb and run across the road, reloading.

'Les, go.'

And he runs like a deer, almost in Seamus's shadow. They were rivals. They both did those 26 miles in sub three hours and kept clipping off minutes every year they got older.

I am the last man at the corner. Everyone else is safely down the alleyway and we have made it, broken contact and are on the way out. The militia have had the stuffing knocked out of them on this road. Between Seamus's last long burst and my three grenades the barrier is shrouded in smoke and dust, and the enemy is in disarray. I pause, greedily, and unload one more 40mm bomb into the barrier before running to the vehicles.

Then, of course, I get shot.

I actually see the round that hits me. It's a ricochet that skips low on the wall about 15m down the street with a puff of concrete dust and there is a lighting fast blur of dark movement that I see as an after-image, after it smacks me in the stomach, pushing me backward. I sit down hard with an 'oof' of breath. My rifle clatters to the ground.

Fuck.

'Come on, Jim, stop showing off.' Dai is leaning out of the back window of the saloon, laughing. He thinks I have tripped.

I grab the 203, get up and run. Run past the Brit car, noticing Seamus is back at the wheel. Dai has his rifle up, covering the corner behind me.

'Faster, Ash, that's like running but fucking slower,' Seamus crows as I run past.

There was a burning feeling across my gut as I rushed past the van full of children and leapt into the rear of the SUV. Sammy accelerated and our small convoy raced off down the alleyway into a tangle of cars, some dragging barbed-wire coils from the barriers.

The vehicles on that section of road had not been damaged in the bomb blast and were trying to push through the chicanes before turning back to the city. No one would give an inch. Drivers were screaming from side windows and pumping their horns as they clattered like dodgems into the whirl of steel, each gap wide enough for one car blocked by two trying to shove their way through at the same time.

'Look at them. Iraqis,' Sammy said. 'They cut off their own noses.'

I glanced up at the chaos and continued scanning my arcs as

we bumped through the maze of alleyways. Sammy knew the neighbourhood like the back of his hand and we spent a bewildering several minutes turning this way and that, but always heading north, slowly but surely, back into Karada.

'This street it is only one-way street,' said Sammy, indicating that we were heading the wrong way. *Shit we don't have time for the tour. He's going to show me the house he was born in next.* My free hand was firmly pressed on to my stomach to stop the bleeding. I hadn't even looked at it yet. The adrenalin had kept me going as I ran. Now the pain was kicking in.

Sammy pushed and bumped his way through the traffic, the two vehicles staying close behind. Odd shots rang out from rooftops. Explosions detonated in the distance. The air smelled of smoke and death.

Forty-five long minutes after leaving the safe house, we drove back past it on the main drag through Karada. It seemed bizarre after the carnage at the checkpoint to see men in dirty white dishdashes at outdoor cafés and women in *abayas* strolling off to the Shia market, life continuing in one part of the city while for scores it had ended in another not far away.

Ten minutes later, using the alternate route, we headed south past the Dora refinery, straight up the overpass on to the six-lane highway. We looped west and then north over Route Irish. In another five minutes – if we were lucky – we would be on the main road that leads past Abu Ghraib and out into the Western Desert.

CHAPTER 22

I T STILL WASN'T easy to get my head round the fact that Colonel Ibrahim was collaborating with the militia in their hunt for Sammy. He knew Sammy wasn't a traitor. They had worked together. I could even recall having seen them having a laugh together, although over what I couldn't imagine. Arab relationships are intricate and paradoxical, filled with immense generosity and deep hatreds, profound wisdom and utter ruthlessness. The Italians think they invented the notion of the vendetta but blood feuds are as ancient as the Babylonians.

We all knew Ibrahim was smart, but it had not occurred to me until that moment that he must have been as slippery as a bag of eels to have reached the rank of colonel in Saddam Hussein's Sunni-led army. It was ironical, to say the least, that, as the local police commander, he was now leading the very water guards we had trained. That's what we were dealing with, the web of politicians, police, army and Shia militias furtively taking the levers of power and eradicating anyone from the past who might get in their way.

Ibrahim would have known from the Karada grapevine that the Mashooen family were preparing to flee Baghdad. The seizure of Gabir's storehouse with the vehicles had told him it was imminent.

I had hoped that Gabir and Zahrah's deaths would at least serve the purpose that two independent sources would have confirmed to the Shia, undoubtedly under torture, that Sammy intended to head north to Mosul. In that way their precious resources would have been used up planning roadblocks and ambushes on the route north.

However, after this morning's bloodbath someone might put two and two together and realize that the PSDs involved in the shoot-out were seen to have been escorting a couple of cars full of Iraqi civilians. Any police car now could be a potential threat, ready to inform Ibrahim of our location. We just had to get out of the city. Once we headed into the desert the Shia would be reluctant to follow us into what was Sunni-dominated territory.

We carved a route into the western suburbs through slums edged by sprawling cemeteries, collapsing tenements, affluent suburbs of flat-roofed villas built around mosques and ragged parks where the homeless slept and children never played. On my direction, Sammy changed course often, guiding the three-rig packet into passageways where sheets were strung between buildings for shade and unassuming displays of dish-dashes and *djellabas* dripped on the windscreen where they had been hung out to dry.

Every street is a souk pin-cushioned with umbrellas advertising Coke and Marlboro, our consumerist dream drifting into Baghdad. Almost everyone is in business, poor families often with such modest displays you wonder why they bother – six eggs, a handful of tomatoes, a cabbage, batteries in packs with Chinese lettering, sandals with pointed toes, live chickens and dead chickens. Men were mending shoes, sharpening knives, working on treadmill sewing machines, beating pots and pans. Women float by like black-sailed ships, like shadows of each other.

Men were driving to work, to meetings, to prayers. The muezzin were chanting again, words like small birds taking to the air. Insects pattered on the glass. The general was gazing out of the window with a fixed expression. He had known these streets for eighty years and seemed to be memorizing each one as we passed. He was going into exile. He knew that once we got out, if we got out, he would never see the city of his birth again.

The Tigris divides Baghdad like an orange, with sections fanning out east and west. The original city founded by the Abbasids in the eighth century was circular with high walls and a moat. Inside the walls they built magnificent mosques and the caliph's palace with its celebrated green dome topped by mounted horsemen, a vision that moved poets to verse in ancient times.

An old friend of mine at Oxford once described Baghdad as the most beautiful city in the world. In medieval times, maybe. There are no stone quarries on the fertile plain where they raised Baghdad. The city was constructed from sun-dried bricks vulnerable to fires, floods and invasion. All that remains of the Abbasids are a few unexceptional ruins and an abundance of florid similes of Baghdad as heaven on earth, the mother of the world, the mistress of nations, dome of Islam, the city of peace.

Wishful thinking.

It was more like Stalingrad. The only time Krista had ever shown any discomfort in front of me was when watching some documentary about Iraq. The camera crew were in Baghdad and she noted out loud that every building seemed to be covered in bullet holes. I searched quickly for a witty reply that would explain this away, but in vain, and the next few minutes had been spent in an awkward silence.

I glanced at the time and shook my wrist to make sure my watch wasn't broken. No, the seconds were clicking away like heartbeats and I thought how time and age are relative, that who we are and what we do is ill served when we measure time by the shifting hands of the clock.

It had just gone eight. It was still morning. The last hour had seemed like twelve hours, like twelve months, like a lifetime. Forty minutes on the train and I get only a little way through reading a book. Ten minutes pounding my shoulder with the recoil from a rifle and time stretches, reforms, rewinds the strands of your DNA. The firefight with the Mahdi had seemed like an eternity. I only appreciated how short-lived it had been once it was over. More than a hundred people had died in the suicide bomb and shoot-out that day. It would make three paragraphs on the wire services and flash around the world. Lives part-lived, snuffed out in a second. Scenes were flashing out of sequence through my head. I had to blink several times to get rid of them and focus.

Eight o'clock. We had eleven hours of light. We had to keep moving.

While I was directing Sammy, I pulled up my shirt to see where the ricochet had hit me. The skin was puckered closed, with little bleeding. On prodding, I could feel the lump of the round deeper inside than I liked. I liberally disinfected my thin-nosed Leatherman pliers with iodine, then probed into the wound site. I managed to get a grip on a corner and pulled out the bullet in a slow steady movement that brought sweat to my brow.

The round had struck under my SAPI plate – which was high in order to protect my heart and lungs – flattened almost to the same shape as a beer-bottle top, and dug itself deeply into my abdominal muscles. A minor if messy wound and I sighed with relief. I had delayed inspecting the damage in case I discovered something I didn't want to.

I splashed on a little more iodine, then strapped on the smallest field dressing I could find in the trauma pack provided thoughtfully by the Green Berets. There was also a bottle of Augmentin and I slugged back a couple of prophylactic antibiotics to prevent any nasty infection that might preclude me from attending Sunday dinner. Job done.

Just in time, too.

'Roadblock,' Sammy said.

The general came to life. 'Go right,' he instructed.

Sammy immediately took his advice and we bounced over a cobbled street candy-striped with skeins of wool spread out and dyed dark red and blue and green. The road broadened into a plaza with arcaded shops where men worked giant looms below the shade of finished carpets, and I recalled that, in each, the weaver would have concealed an error because only Allah is perfect.

'Left.'

We swerved around a donkey cart hauling burlap sacks, Abdul and Seamus behind us, turning like clockwork, and it occurred to me that even though we were trying to maintain a low profile, we obviously weren't three Iraqi drivers. They would be thumping horns, flashing lights, trying to overtake even on roads barely wide enough to take one vehicle.

'Fuck,' I said as we edged around a corner.

Up ahead, a blue and white Kia with revolving lights occupied the centre of the junction. Two cops were slowing the traffic, eyeballing the drivers and lethargically moving them on.

Baghdad these days was covered in VCPs, both permanent and temporary like this one. I was amazed we had come as far as we had without being forced to stop again.

As we came around the corner, another two police vehicles were parked up. There was also a little cluster of American soldiers and two Humvees. The presence of CF troops should prevent any funny business from the IP. Our CAC cards equated us to US forces and they would support us as such.

'VCP ahead, mixed IP and Coalition Forces,' I sent back over the radio.

'Roger that,' came Seamus's deep voice. They were still around the corner.

Sammy eased up behind a truck piled about 6m high with old car tyres. We were six cars back in the queue and waiting. I thought about calling Cobus to see if the Task Force Fountain team had any influence with the CF units out in the west of the city, but on reflection I thought, probably not. Not without a full colonel to shout down the phone anyway. Instead I took the opportunity to call Davor, the officer in charge of the SF team.

'Hello, mate, it's Ash, you still on the job?'

'Naw, man, we're finished work for the day. We've been up all night – I'm beat and I'm going to hit the sack.'

'Right . . .'

'OK, man, let's have it?'

'Mate, I'm sorry to ask, but if there's anything you can do to help us out of the city I'd really appreciate it.'

'There was an *incident* out on the south gate. I've seen the intel.'

'Ask no questions.'

'I don't intend to.' But he asked, 'Where are you?'

'We're nearly on to the Abu Ghraib highway.' I glanced at my map. 'Coming from the south, northwards up the boundary of security zones 28 and 54.'

'Got it.'

'We'll join the highway about ten klicks west of the Green Zone. The local IP may well try and stop us leaving the city. I know you guys have direct comms lines to different units around the city . . .'

I let my voice trail off. I really had no idea what he could do, or whether this was pushing the limits of favours. If he told me to fuck off, I'd understand.

'Shit, Ash, I'm not sure what I can do, man.'

'No problem, mate. Just thought I'd ask. It's not as if you can just call in an air-strike on any IP seen on the Abu Ghraib highway after all.' I laughed, but I was thinking that actually that would be a fucking fantastic idea.

The line was quiet for a few seconds.

'I don't know if there's anything I can do, buddy,' Davor said again. 'Good luck.'

'Cheers, Davor.'

'Be safe, brother.'

The file had gone through the checkpoint. It was our turn. One of the cops waved the truck in front forward and, as the *jundhi* turned left, the cop's gaze settled on us. I leaned forward past the general and showed my CAC card. He glanced at it indifferently and then looked up at Sammy. He did a double-take and looked at him again, hard.

At that moment a US soldier walked up, a sergeant in desert ACU camouflage, looking alert and professional, as was the Humvee gunner covering him from over the road with a 240 GPMG.

'How are you doing this fine morning, Sergeant?' I grinned in faux *bonhomie*.

'Pretty good, thanks, how are you guys?'

'We're good.' I looked back and waved at the vehicles behind me. 'Three vehicles in my packet, mate. The van and the car behind are with me.'

The sergeant looked back questioningly at the minibus, but then relaxed when he saw the Peugeot bringing up the rear. Les, Seamus and Dai were all obviously Westerners in body armour and shades, all holding their CAC cards up. In the front seat, Les had also turned down his sun visor and in the weak sunlight the bright colours of the A4-sized American flag there were easy to see.

'OK, come on through.' He turned and held up three fingers. 'These three coming through,' he called to the other troops.

'Thanks, stay safe.' I waved.

Behind him, the Iraqi policeman glared daggers at Sammy.

We rolled through and rejoined the traffic. Behind us I could see the IP talking into his walkie-talkie, staring after us. That looked like trouble.

'Sammy, don't head up the highway. They're watching us. Pull right into that street.'

We swung off the road into another street full of shops, and

I got on the radio to tell the rear car we were taking a small detour to confuse the IP.

We were fine for two minutes, then we ran straight into a traffic jam that looked impossible to penetrate. Shit. Blue flashing lights appeared ahead of us. Then more, coming the opposite way. The only thing between us was 50m of Iraqi traffic jam.

'Sammy get this thing turned around now,' I told him.

I leapt out of the back door and got on the radio.

'Guys, we need to clear some traffic fast. IP is up ahead.'

Les and Dai immediately debussed with helmets and rifles. The three of us started trying to force the vehicles to move on to the pavement to clear a path behind us. Seeing that we were not soldiers or police, some drivers merely shouted back and waved their fists.

Seamus put his foot down and the Peugeot zoomed backwards, slamming into the car behind. He went forwards a metre and did it again. The driver got the message. Following Seamus's lead, Sammy got into character as well. The powerful SUV had no difficulty shunting the smaller cars around us and, with Les, Dai and me gesturing with our weapons, we had soon cleared some space to move.

I was checking constantly on the IP up ahead. They were playing the same game. With flashing blue and red lights on the roofs of their Kias and half a dozen IP waving AKs, they were steadily hacking a way through the jam towards us in a slow-motion race to see who could clear a path first.

Les and Dai's huge physical presence and the brutal application of rifle butts to car windows and doors was working a treat. Seamus nudged along a few cars that moved too slowly, but it was clear that we were moving away faster than the IP could move forward. The chaos we were leaving behind us was going to be harder for them to break through.

Suddenly, like rope untangling, we were clear. We mounted up and zoomed off to the sound of a rude cacophony of horns and angry voices. Even pedestrians leaned out on to the street and shouted in Arabic.

Sammy laughed. 'They are saying many bad things about you, Mister James.'

'None of it's true, Sammy.'

'Agh, but perhaps it is.'

He accelerated down a narrow avenue, manoeuvring the vehicle like a MiG-27 through the maze of *jundhis*, kamikazes, donkey carts, bicycles, women rolling butane canisters along the side of the road, all human life going somewhere. The general seemed to be enjoying this last scenic tour around his hometown. I was glad one of us was, because my nerves were getting shredded.

There were a couple of choppers way off, Kiowas probably, but they were too high for me to be sure. Were they following us? Did the Americans have comms with the IP? On the highway we made better time, but we were sitting ducks. In the backstreets we could easily get trapped. There was no clear and easy answer. Just intuition. Just kismet. Just put your foot down.

'Oh, for fuck's sake,' I moaned as more blue and red lights appeared 100m ahead at a traffic circle.

Sammy instantaneously hung a left, the other two vehicles followed, but the IP were soon on our tail, sirens howling like a baying mob. The road was wide enough for two vehicles to pass, but only just.

'I go straight,' said Sammy, and put his foot down.

The general glanced at me with what looked like approval, and I thought what a feisty old bugger he was to remain composed after an IED, the mother of all gunfights and now in a car chase with half of Baghdad's finest hunting us down.

General Mashooen pointed at a tumbledown shop.

'My tailor was here. I would come to see him, then take a taxi to Mutanabi Street to buy my books,' he said, and added reflectively, 'Saddam was an ignorant man, but even he showed respect for books.'

Mutanabi Street had vanished in a pall of smoke and dust on Friday 5 March, shortly before I left Côte d'Ivoire to return to Iraq. I'd read about it on the net. A bomb left in the Shabandr Café had killed thirty-eight people and destroyed a tradition dating back to the tenth-century poet who gave the street its name. For a thousand years Iraqis had wandered among the stalls and iron-shuttered shops, hunting down rare books in every language.

'They say Cairo writes, Beirut publishes and Baghdad reads,' the general said. 'They used to read. Now they learn about life from Al Jazeera.'

'That's incredibly interesting, sir,' I said, then thumbed the radio. 'Can you see them yet, guys?'

'They're 100m behind us, mate,' said Seamus.

The wail of sirens was growing louder. I gestured. Sammy took another left and roared through a fish market where traders were setting up their stands, unloading iced trays of fresh fish from donkey carts and open trucks.

'I can knock over some stalls, Mister James, slow them down.'

'No, we don't want to get a bad name now we're leaving,' I said. 'Anyway, you may block the others.'

Suddenly we slid out into a clear, much wider street and Sammy gunned the engines. For a minute the road was empty and we zoomed ahead, every second a bonus taking us further from the police. Then I heard the roll of thunder as a four-rig patrol of Humvees stampeded towards us like bulls running the *corrida* in Pamplona.

'*Amerikeyeh*,' shouted Sammy in panic, his word both a warning and a curse.

He would have swerved straight off the street, but the curbs were a foot high along this section and there was nothing he could do but cling on to the steering wheel. With their turret rings mounted with .50 cals and Mk19s, if the Humvees took us as a threat, a few unhurried bursts from the gunners and we'd be toast, blackened relics like the railway yards and storage tanks we'd passed along the way, ruins left from the three-week blitz that had levelled half of Baghdad at the start of the war.

The seconds stretched; it was only seconds: our combined speeds had the velocity of a bullet.

'Stop,' I yelled.

Sammy slammed on the brakes, the motion throwing me forward and it felt like a fist had punched me right in the place where the bullet had entered my abdomen. Abdul braked, but half a second too late, the minibus grazing our rear bumper. I frantically dug out my day sack and my fingers were all thumbs as I worked the zip on the side pocket.

I ripped out the Stars and Stripes and threw it forward over Sammy and the general like a Technicolor blanket.

'Hold it up to the windscreen,' I directed.

The seconds did that stretching thing, creeping by. The Humvees roared. Sweat trickled down my back. I may have said a prayer, and let out my breath as the patrol charged by without so much as a glimpse in our direction.

'Thought that was the long goodbye,' I said as Sammy accelerated again.

'They're just racing home for some pizza,' he replied. Sammy had always been fascinated that the CF had taken the time to build a Pizza Hut in the Green Zone immediately after the bombing stopped.

'Make mine a pepperoni . . .' said General Mashooen, and we burst out laughing.

Sammy slowed for a moment, then put his foot down again. He had seen a blue and white police truck on the next street over as we zoomed through a junction. They had turned off their sirens and had been paralleling us on the wide street to our right.

We burst out on to a large square with blocks of concrete barriers set on the broken tarmac. On the far side, behind a row of buildings, was the ramp up on to the highway. The IP emerged on our right. The sirens went on again as they piled towards us past a whitewashed mosque that rose like a giant wedding cake on one side of the square.

Men in white dish-dashes were standing around clicking prayer beads and gossiping. We gave them something to gossip about, crossing the space at 100kph and shooting like an arrow down a narrow passage only wide enough for one vehicle. Pedestrians threw themselves against the side walls, hexing us with curses. There was a café below an arched arcade and, where the zinc tables spilled out into the street, they went flying. When the IP entered the passage, the noise of the sirens magnified between the mud-brick walls.

'Now put your foot down,' I said.

Sammy punched straight out of the alleyway into the stream of traffic going up the highway ramp, driving flat out, switching lanes, blasting his horn. Abdul was a metre from our rear, doing well considering he'd looked terrified when we first set out on the journey, Seamus a metre behind him, Les and Dai with weapons readied and eyes peeled on the cops weaving through the traffic in our wake. We clipped the side of a black Merc, bumped a slow-moving Toyota into the side barrier and Sammy almost lost control, swerving around a *jundhi* driving like a lunatic on the wrong side of the road.

The cop cars were coming but they weren't getting any closer. We surged on to the highway proper and shot past a line of oil tankers. The highway turned in a long curve and I felt a snatch of relief when I caught sight of the cluster of blocky CF vehicles in the distance, marking the checkpoint.

The traffic slowed as vehicles joined from another ramp. More cops were coming up from the side as well. Stuck in the traffic

I could only watch helplessly as our pursuers overtook the same line of oil tankers. The cops were going to catch up with us before we got to the checkpoint. I prepared myself to order Sammy to ram the vehicles in front out of the way, wondering if the CF would see us as a VBIED threat piling towards them and open fire.

We were almost there when a thunderous clatter ripped the sky apart and I thought another suicide bomber had let rip. But there was no dust, no aftershock. I ducked involuntarily. The sound was coming from above. I leaned sideways to look up and couldn't believe my eyes. Two Kiowas close enough to touch swooped down and I realised that, with the swarm of police cars chasing us, it was our three cars that looked like the enemy. I sat there blankly, waiting for the inevitable machine-gun fire.

CHAPTER 23

*C*HRIST ON A *crutch!* My breath caught in my throat. I couldn't swallow. I knew these birds of prey. The Kiowa Warrior is a single-engine scouting chopper equipped with Hellfire missiles, Hydra 70 rockets and machine-guns. I remember a pilot telling me that they were so loaded up with weapons that they were difficult as hell to land if you got into engine trouble.

Now, all those guns and rockets seemed to be pointed at us. Did they think we were insurgents? It was more than possible that the IP had called in to the Americans that they were in pursuit of AIF enemy forces, in which case we were up shit creek.

I waited for the spray of incoming from the .50 cal and heard nothing but the roaring engines ratcheting up the volume to a deafening pitch and slowly fading away again as the flyboys skimmed inches above the roof of the SUV. What the fuck are they waiting for? We kept going. They may have been trying to warn us off approaching the VCP, but to stop and wait for the IP to catch us was a death sentence for Sammy and his family.

In our Spartan days, we kept a low profile, waited our turn in backed-up traffic and mocked the contractors who barged in overt convoys to the front of the line, flashing their CPA passes. The faults we see in others we always end up duplicating. Still, it was an emergency. No time for discretion now. Only a blind and deaf man could have failed to notice our manic procession with half the Baghdad police force in pursuit.

'Slow down, but keep going towards the checkpoint,' I told Sammy.

I held the Stars and Stripes out the window and let it stream behind us as we overtook the line of cars waiting to reach the barrier.

As the Kiowas turned for a second buzz, we continued closing down the space to the checkpoint, not knowing what to expect when we got there. I had hardly believed we were going to get this far, and now the gate was in sight I hated to think that success would be snatched away from us.

The Kiowas almost broke my eardrums, swooping down once again. I was certain we were in for it this time and was astonished to see in the side mirror that the cops were more startled by the helicopters than we were. They had given up the chase and were driving off like an unsettled swarm of flies in all directions. I realized that the attack angle of the Kiowas had been aimed behind us at our pursuers. I looked back to see Dai holding a huge flapping Union Jack out of the back window of the Peugeot. Good man.

My back was drenched. I was panting.

We'd reached the gate.

A couple of American troopers were holding back the traffic at the front of the line to let us through. One was black, the other white, both big guys, rifles pointed down. I caught a flash of sergeant stripes. Sammy stopped in the shade of a metal awning and the white guy waved away my pass as I tried to show it to him. He leaned in the window.

'You Ash?'

I goggled at him. 'I am,' I admitted.

'Got a message for you. Guy named Rick in some Special Forces team said to say if you got this far: Thanks, bro, you made him a hundred bucks,' he explained. 'Those boys are taking bets on how far you'll get.'

I wondered which of them had bet against us.

'I'll get a lot further if you keep these cops off my tail,' I said.

'They ain't coming through my gate,' he assured me. He pointed, first towards the city, then out into the wilderness. 'Inside it's a fucken' mess. Out there it belongs to the Marines.'

I realized their uniforms were different – desert digicam with plain brown Interceptor body armour.

'Oorah, Sergeant.'

I held my fist out and he tapped it with his.

'Oorah, sir.' He grinned. So did I. *Semper* Fucking *Fi*.

'Thanks, mate,' I said, and – as simple as that – my little convoy slid out of Baghdad into Anbar province.

The Kiowas flew over once more and disappeared through the low-hanging clouds. I wondered if it was Davor's parting gift or a coincidence. I would never know. The Green Berets must have passed the word down the line to the guards on the last checkpoint. It wasn't fate looking out for us. It wasn't Allah. It was fellow soldiers.

Sammy put his foot down and in a few minutes Baghdad vanished in the grey haze behind us as we raced through the nondescript suburbs clinging to the edge of the city.

'Next stop, dinner at the Marriott, boys,' I said over the radio.

'Dinner's on me if we get there,' Les came back.

'Done.'

We headed towards Highway 10 with its roaming gangs of highwaymen, windstorms, sandstorms, freak floods, IEDs, vehicle-borne IEDs, a normal day's driving in Iraq and comparatively less risky than what we'd already been through that day. Once we cleared the small towns on the outskirts of the city, the arid waste stretched in all directions, grey, flat and featureless. The road ahead was virtually empty and vanished into infinity at the horizon.

'Just another 500 klicks, lads,' I said over the net.

'I am ready,' Sammy laughed.

I turned to General Mashooen. 'You all right, sir?'

'Yes, and me, I am ready,' he answered, and we all had a good chuckle.

We had covered the first 15km through the city in what had seemed like a hundred years. Just another 500K – 300 miles – to the Jordanian border. If we averaged 100K an hour, not difficult on the highway, we'd reach the frontier in daylight.

Only one small problem, we had to pass Fallujah, 55km west of Baghdad, and the most dangerous city on earth – not my phrase, by the way, it was coined by the Marines who had daily run the gauntlet of the two main thoroughfares, known as Mobile and Michigan. IED alley for short.

Tribal heads in this part of the world had been firm supporters of Saddam and had backed the al-Qaeda uprising. It all came to a head in 2004 when insurgents famously ambushed and killed four Blackwater PSDs in Fallujah. A mob mutilated the bodies, burned them and strung them from the bridge over the Euphrates. The images and film clips had flashed around the world.

The marine and army assault on Fallujah in November that year ended in arguably the most savage house-to-house combat in the war. The city's infrastructure was shattered, the residents fled and, while the Sunni fighters who had escaped continued their battle against the Coalition, other parts of Iraq prospered with aid money providing roads, water, schools and security.

By 2006, Sunnis were sick of the struggle against the CF and had grown tired of the al-Qaeda foreign fighters with their Wahabist fundamentalism, a cruel and divisive Islam totally alien to the more liberal Sunnis of Iraq. Tribal leaders met in Anbar province and what emerged from the summit was the Awakening Movement, a Sunni self-preservation pact that became known as the Sons of Iraq and spread across the entire country. When they stopped shooting Americans, the Americans gave the Sons of Iraq aid, money and new guns that they turned on their erstwhile fanatical comrades.

The Sons of Iraq may have preferred shooting Shias, but were not averse to slotting foreigners and strangers. They were proud, armed to the teeth and maintained a network of roadblocks around their tribal homelands. I saw the first of these obstacles up ahead. For some reason, we were allowed to pass through without being stopped, although men in turbans denoting their tribe observed us like hawks from the side of the road. Others stood in the backs of open trucks mounted with machine-guns, weapons cocked, their belts of cartridges gleaming in the sunlight.

We passed a cart laden with sacks pulled by a donkey, an old man with bare feet guiding the rig. It was a scene from the Bible, except for the smoke from his cigarette, and it was always hard in a war zone to understand that while we were fighting some battle between opposing forces, right and wrong, Shia and Sunni, the West and Islam, life for most people carried on: they sowed and reaped, they celebrated births and buried their dead. I remembered the wedding party driving in noisy procession through the city the morning I arrived and it was hard to believe it had been only four days earlier.

We passed through a second checkpoint. I could see the outskirts of Fallujah rising in the distance. Awakening-council checkpoints would be all over the place now. If we were entering a trap, there was nothing I could do about it. We couldn't turn back to Baghdad.

We passed the third checkpoint. I heard engines igniting, the muted sound as alarming as RPGs exploding around me. Gearboxes crunched. The engines growled as the motors turned over, then hummed as five pickup trucks filled with militiamen began to tail us. Some of them were in a mixture of pseudo-military uniforms, others in a mishmash of civilian dress. They all appeared relaxed, and were holding their weapons casually, not ready to use.

'They're tailing us, mate. We're keeping an eye on them.' Les's voice came over the net.

Everyone was set. If we had to take them on, we were ready for it. It was suicide, but we were ready.

The first of the five cars accelerated to overtake and drew alongside when it reached the SUV. The front passenger wore a black beard and a white turban that looked freshly washed. He studied Sammy and the general in their red and white headscarfs. He stared at me for several moments, pointed at himself, then pointed at an exit ramp ahead. There was little choice. I gave Sammy the nod and he turned off the highway.

In a few minutes, the way was blocked by a metal barrier. The driver in front flashed his lights. The barrier cranked up to allow us access to the city limits of Fallujah, and I imagined the road to hell would look like this: bleak, dusty, dilapidated, the same style of barrier, but rusted permanently open. The ubiquitous roadside herd of goats munched stolidly on rubbish and old tyres, watching us drive past without interest. The little boy herding them looked out from his *shemagh* and a coat too big for him, shouted some abuse and drew his finger across his throat. The little shit.

The driver ahead led us into the usual chaos of careworn streets that comprises the centre of so many townships in the Middle East. Men sat under arcades, playing dominoes, drinking tea, smoking, always smoking. Women in black stumped by, carrying loads. You imagine towns in the Mesopotamian desert would be colourful, picturesque, romantic. They are not. They are mean, decaying, hostile, and smell of shit and urine, donkey, camel and human.

We followed an avenue dotted with young palms, the fronds still wrapped in plastic, and stopped in an open square outside a mosque that must have been damaged by the Marines in their assault on Fallujah and was still being repaired. The men in turbans jumped from their vehicles and surrounded our little convoy with rifles readied. I imagined I heard the click of safety catches two cars behind me as the Brits slid off the safety on their weapons. I remembered Les once saying that dying was part of living, being taken prisoner for him would be worse than death.

Sammy in his red and white *shemagh* stepped from the SUV, hands held high. One of the gunmen prodded the barrel of his AK into his plump belly. Sammy didn't flinch. He spoke softly, a smile pinned to his heavy lips. Now I could see them close up, the gunman and his comrades looked both fierce and impoverished, ground down like the small town, bleary eyes, scruffy beards, loose clothes, intricate turbans and dirty feet in broken flip-flops.

What I assumed was the commander of these Sons of Iraq materialized from the building beside the mosque. I noticed several official vehicles with Iraqi flags parked up in the shade next to the building. There was a Humvee, obviously ING, with a huge Iraqi flag painted on the gun shield.

The guy approaching was heavily built, with a white smock and loose white pants, a clipped beard threaded with grey, a pockmarked face and intelligent eyes likes chips of flint. He clapped his hands and threw out instructions.

'We must get out,' translated General Mashooen. 'Without rifles.'

'Lads, we have to debus, without rifles,' I said over the net.

'Fuck that,' Les replied immediately.

I noticed the head guy approaching Sammy. He seemed relaxed. They both bowed, shook hands, touched chests.

'They look friendly to me, mate,' I said to Les. 'Let's go along with it.'

I debussed. The other Brits joined me, looking reassuringly unfazed, ignoring the weapons of the Iraqis. We stood either side of the general, who seemed to be inspecting these ex-Saddam loyalists and al-Qaeda militiamen as if they were on parade. They eyed his white moustache and fierce scowl warily.

Abdul slowly unloaded his bus of passengers behind us.

The sharp eyes of the commander passed over our unlikely party, the women with heads covered, the children, Sammy with his plump hands gripping his waist, Abdul, the general, and us, four Brits with our shades and pistols stuffed down our chest rigs.

One of the guards stepped in front of Les, shoving his rifle forward, trying to stare him down. Les just gave him a bland look I recognized as meaning that if he tried anything Les was going to feed him that rifle. The other militiamen shuffled restlessly in the manner of troops eager to brutalize unarmed civilians.

The chief asked Sammy something and Sammy pointed me out.

'He ask me who in charge. I say you,' said Sammy with the demeanour of someone not wanting to look important. Cheers, Sammy.

The big man walked over and stared at me grimly, looking me up and down as if sizing me up for a suit.

I thrust my chin out, shoulders back – keeping a stiff upper lip in front of Johnny foreigner, but inside I had a sudden desire that the ensuing conversation be carried out through intermediaries, or ideally perhaps by telephone from my hotel in Jordan.

'*Ahlen wah sehlen,*' the commander said. Then, 'Please. You are very welcome here,' in a bloody good English accent, and I thought, Jesus, he must have done a BBC Learning English course.

He spoke to his men, who stood down and gave us grins full of bad teeth. Teeth like a recce patrol Dai would have said; all blacked up and well spaced apart. He spoke to Sammy, and we traipsed towards the building beside the mosque. The atmosphere visibly relaxed and I felt my tense shoulders unwinding.

'This better not be a fucking trap,' Les whispered.

'No, they would have shot us in the open.'

'Maybe in there's where they keep the swords so they can cut our heads off.'

'Don't be silly, mate, they'll use a blunt spoon on you.'

We passed through a serene courtyard with a fountain at the centre and entered through a pair of doors into a cool shady hall scattered with cushions and lit by the light falling obliquely through a row of high arched windows. We were invited to sit and dropped down cross-legged in a circle, the women and children to one side, Sammy chatting ten to the dozen with the commander. Turns out that he was an ex-air-force officer like Sammy. Although they had never met before, they had many mutual friends and had both served at the nearby airbase.

Several men brought *chai* in proper tea cups with a plate of sweetmeats. The old comrades asked politely in English about each other's health, about their children, the state of everyone's health, and then switched to their own tongue to get down to the nitty-gritty. I caught enough Arabic words to think they were talking economics. With its wars and currency fluctuations, like the US dollar, gold and precious stones in the Middle East are understood and appreciated by everyone. I wondered how much we would have to pay to get past this.

When Arabs barter, they want to reach a deal where neither party feels they have given away too much. With their short fuses and long memories, Arabs in any negotiation consider future harmony.

I sipped tea, gazed out into the yard with its dappled light, words flowing over me like moody jazz. Arabic spoken well is melodic. The Koran is one long poem. You can lose yourself in its rhythms. I could understand why boys taught in the *madrassas* by chanting the Prophet's words turned into fanatics, all that testosterone, all those virgins. At least the volunteers in the Mahdi Army thought they knew what they were fighting for. I felt for the squaddies sent to Afghanistan. In the War of Terror, it was hard to know exactly which bunch of turbaned tribesmen were allies and which were the enemy. Since 9/11 our grasp on the moral imperative had loosened. If your friends die or you come home with horrific injuries it's important to know why, to maintain your humanity.

I was tired suddenly. The injury was sapping my strength. Snapshots from the firefight were running through my head, a round taking the padding out of my Kevlar vest, another whistling across my helmet. I could see in my mind's eye the Mahdi militiaman creeping into position, the scope on his Dragunov gleaming, the long barrel like a compass needle seeking my life. I'd beaten him to the draw. One blink and it would have been me, not him. Now he was on the battlefield with his brains spilled in the dust and I was drinking tea from Doulton china.

Two green birds hopped across the gravel in the courtyard. The seconds were eating time. The pressure running a mission chips away at your mental reserves like the tide lapping at a sandcastle yet, perversely, I felt myself relaxing. I gazed out at the fountain, the water rainbow-coloured in the glare of the sun, and wondered what I was doing in this God-forsaken town when I could have been sitting in a lawyer's office in London. I'd be looking at the clock there, too, that's the trouble. It's not action that gets at you, it's the waiting, that moment of stasis when everything stops except your emotions. You feel an ache in your right shoulder. A faint migraine that's not exactly there but coming like a plane through clouds.

I could smell the cordite clinging to my clothes. I could taste the death smell of my own breath. The scenes at the checkpoint that morning were vivid in my mind, the suicide girl approaching the doomed Iraqi soldiers, the daylight vanishing in black smoke, the eager expressions of the Mahdi boys racing through the blazing ruins. These pictures stay with you, change you in some way. When it's them or you, you count yourself lucky.

After ten minutes of fast and furious Arabic – it sounded like they were having an argument – Sammy translated, and I was astounded that the Iraqi gossip machine had already got word of our escape from Baghdad. The Sons of Iraq knew the police had been pursuing three cars and you didn't have to be a genius to work out that the people they wanted to 'question' were going to turn out to be Sunnis.

'We are famous, Mister James,' added Sammy.

'Not too famous, I hope. We've still got a long way to go.'

The commander roared and rocked backwards and forwards, his eyes shifting constantly from Sammy to each of the four of us. He kept nodding, scratching his beard.

'Very good,' he said. 'Top notch.'

I glanced at my watch, wondering when might be a polite moment to leave, when my senses took a full-on assault from an aromatic blend of exotic spices. My nose twitched. I heard the juices bubble up in my stomach. Action hollows you out. I was starving. A gaggle of women in *hijabs* appeared with trays of naan bread, hummus, meatballs, falafel, sticky white rice, fresh dates, jugs of cold water.

The chief threw out his two hands. 'You eat,' he said.

That was the order and we obeyed, dipping the naan into the communal bowls, swigging down glasses of mint tea to follow. Dai handed out fags. It was all very jolly, and forty-five minutes passed before I mentioned that we still had a long way to go.

The commander nodded, came to his feet and slipped into leather shoes with the backs pushed down. We shuffled back to the square and he insisted on shaking our hands.

'You are very welcome,' he said. I imagined him summoning up the words from his course. 'A very rum business,' he added bizarrely.

He continued in Arabic and Sammy translated. He had taken the names of the Shia policemen who had killed Sammy's cousin and presumably Aunt Zahrah. That's what they had been discussing. Not a price for crossing their territory. I'd got it all wrong. The raised voices were their anger over the Shia domination of Iraqi security forces, the eternal ethnic struggle that would eventually rip Iraq to pieces – three at least. The commander would do what he could to ensure the 'murderous Shia dogs', as he put it, were 'judged by Allah'. He had become grim again, and looking at that pitiless, pockmarked face, I realized that I would not want to be in the shoes of those Shi'ite policemen.

We saddled up. There was some further discussion with Sammy before the commander swung into the passenger seat of an open Toyota and led the way back through town. We gassed up, courtesy of the Sons of Iraq, and three vehicles escorted us to some point in the desert that must have marked the border of their territory.

They peeled away, honking their goodbyes, and we motored on at a steady 120K through the empty moonscape of the Western Desert.

A convoy of oil tankers appeared in their own private dust storm on the horizon. I was about to tell Sammy to swerve off the highway, but they charged on with a release on their air brakes and a deep-throated tooting of horns. Iraqis are a noisy lot.

I had made this same journey in reverse from Amman to Baghdad with Les when we first came to Iraq with Spartan in 2003. Three and a half years had gone by and it felt as if we had never left, not fully, that when we were chased out by our own guards there was unfinished business, an inevitability that we would return.

I could see for miles across the desert. It was like seeing into the future. The next time I glanced at my watch, we were two hours beyond Fallujah, two hours to the border with Jordan. We overtook a few laden vehicles making the same journey, and it didn't occur to me at the time that the families in the cars coming from the opposite direction were Iraqis who had been turned back, a possibility I couldn't even begin to consider.

Mostly, though, the road was clear: no bad guys, no American patrols, a few local *jundhis* sticking to their own districts, and I wondered if the pockmarked tribal chief had called other cells in the Awakened Movement to ask for our safe passage. Whatever Sammy had told him, it had worked.

I thought back over our flight from Baghdad. It was a miracle that we had got out unscathed. It was a miracle that we had come through the shoot-out first thing that morning with nothing more than me getting a scratch on my tummy. Even the three vehicles were running smoothly, the kilometres cracking away behind us, the journey taking on its own silent momentum. Sammy was full of beans, even breaking into the occasional song, he was so happy. He told me that he had a contact in Amman, a Jordanian, and even knew other Iraqis living there. He was looking forward to joining the diaspora and told me of his plans for the future as we hummed along the highway.

Fucking hell, I thought, we're going to make it.

CHAPTER 24

A S THE SUN weakly heated the day to its warmest point, clouds
began to form in narrow ribbons low in the sky. The road
must have dropped fractionally into some geological defile and,
as we crested the dip, I saw hundreds of cars gathered around the
border checkpoints in what seemed to be a vast scrapyard and
thought for a moment it was a trick of the light.

There was no time to take this in. We had to get off the road.
We could not exit Iraq or enter Jordan with our arsenal of weapons.
I signalled to Sammy and he drove cautiously into the desert,
keeping a close watch for potential IEDs, not that I expected to
find any out here in the middle of nowhere. We stopped at a pile
of rocks that rose a little higher than all the other piles of rocks
and turned off the motor. About 50m away stood a low patch of
scrub. I studied this scene, this speck of life in the dead landscape,
and committed it to memory. Just in case. And also nailed it as a
waypoint into the memory of my GPS.

Everyone stepped out of the vehicles, stretching and scratching.

'Toilet break,' I called out, and Sammy echoed it in Arabic. We
had parked the vehicles all in a line to give us a little privacy. The
women and children all walked around the other side. Qusay
stayed with us.

'We bury our weapons here,' I said to the others.

'Shit,' cursed Les. 'Oh well, knew it was coming. I'll get the shovels.'

We had taken a couple of folding entrenching tools from our pile of gifts from the SF specifically for this purpose. When the families all came back from their loo break, the four of us Brits went around the back to start digging. The Iraqis all settled on to blankets as if for a picnic.

Despite the hard ground, in short order we had a long shallow grave. We wrapped our weapons in black rubber bodybags, also placed in the gift pile as a macabre joke, I assumed, zipped them up and laid them out. All of them had a round chambered and the safety catch on.

Dai looked unhappily at his empty hands.

'This is like going out stark bollock naked,' he said. He turned and glanced across the wasteland. 'If you could find all the guns out here, you could start your own bloody war.'

Sammy handed me a pair of old AKs and finally his gold-plated Tariq.

'You're going to miss this,' I said.

'No, no, no. It belongs here in Iraq. We bury the past, Mister James. Then we live again.'

'You should be a philosopher, mate,' said Seamus.

'This will be my new job in Amman.'

'You'll probably have to work as a waiter, my son,' said Dai, always right on the money.

Sammy's weapons went into another bag and were laid down on top.

We looked down at the pit as if in those body bags were old friends we were leaving behind. Colonel Ibrahim would have known by now where we were heading. It was unlikely that he had agents waiting for us at the border, but we couldn't be sure, and we were now, to quote Dai, stark bollock naked. More likely in the desert, we could fall into the hands of bandits, freelancers unaligned to any ideological group. Four unarmed Brits would make a very nice kidnap prize to sell on to the highest bidder.

We piled dirt back into the pit and kicked the excess spoil around to flatten the place out, before beating our trousers and coats to get rid of the Iraqi dust. I took another reading with my GPS, standing directly on top of the weapons.

It was time for another change around. I wanted to hide my team among the Iraqis. Sammy's family spread out in the cars, Qusay running to grab the wheel of the Peugeot like he was grabbing the best ride at the fairground. I stayed in the SUV with a *shemagh* on, body armour off. Les, Dai and Seamus got into the minivan, hidden behind the kids, also with *shemaghs*. From now on, this short last hop to the border, we would be protected by them.

Ayesha jumped in the back of the SUV with her children, the *abaya* covering her head. Her eyes met mine and she smiled. I had been worried that she might have been the hysterical type, but she had come away from the brutal scenes at the checkpoint without a murmur. I had a tendency to underestimate people and was trying to overcome it. I had done the same on occasions when an untried young soldier came into the platoon and, often as not, he turned out to be one of the best I had. In those last few days, the mask of the obedient Muslim wife had slipped and I had begun to see in Ayesha the firm features of a quietly determined woman. While the men get fat and talk too much, Iraqi women are the force that keeps the country going, like Fara, like the girls I'd seen carrying 10kg gas canisters on their heads and working in the fields in 40°C of heat.

'Last leg,' I said to the group in the bus, as we prepared to drive off.

'*Merci,* James, thank you,' Fara called.

I bowed extravagantly as if I were French and she smiled. It was the first time a smile had come to her lips in days, and I noticed the look of relief on her features. Fara had never believed we could make it out of Baghdad, that after losing her aunt she could save her children. Finally, there was a glimmer of hope.

Sammy fired up the SUV, turned and drove the same way we had come to get back on the road. Almost immediately I could make out the flags above the dust cloud hanging over the border, the Iraqi flags in a line, the Jordanian flags way off in the distance across an area of no man's land.

What I had thought was a mirage when we crested the dip a mile or so back on the highway turned out to be the end of the road in every sense. As we slowed to join the line of vehicles waiting to cross the border, we had to drive between a gypsy camp of family cars, minivans, old trucks, even horse carts that belonged to people turned back by Iraqi immigration.

Those people, like Sammy, had burned their bridges. They had nowhere to go and sat in total shock in their cars. Others wandered blindly along the highway. Women with children clung to piles of bags, weeping, staring into space. One pathetic group sat around a fire, cooking God knows what.

The families without automobiles would have reached the border by taxi and then been turned away for the want of papers, or connections, or funds for baksheesh. Nothing ever works in the way you expect, even giving bribes is complicated, essential in one instance, a grave insult in another, the difference so subtle you have to be an Arab to understand it all.

As we edged towards the border I watched grim Iraqi soldiers searching vehicles, pulling open bags, scattering possessions in the dust. One in every three or four cars was turned away. You could hear even from the distance stunned and horrified people shouting and crying and pleading. I could see the guards pushing them back to their cars with rifles readied.

Some of those people joined the shanty town of gridlocked vehicles and would remain at the border until . . . until what? There was peace, an amnesty, they starved to death? Others drove straight off to take their chances with the terrain and the bandits. They would try to cross illegally into Jordan in the dark, a desperate task without 4x4 vehicles and good navigation gear. The border guards ignored them. If we had to, we could do it. The arms dump and the place to turn off the highway to reach it were engraved in my memory.

A woman wailing and carrying on was working her way down the line of cars, crying out verses from the Koran. She reached the SUV, slapped the side window then held her fingers to her mouth. Sammy gave her our last bottle of water. There was no food. There was nothing we could do. Another woman came and I understood from my limited Arabic that she had no money and no petrol for her car to return to Baghdad. Like Sammy, I gritted my teeth and turned my face away from her. I wasn't a robot and the depth of emotion in her face brought tears of shame to my eyes. There were only so many people I could save. I needed to focus on my people.

It took another two hours to pass through that pitiful line of refugees before we got to the border. The customs men rifled through our luggage. Immigration pored over our papers and a tall, handsome man, a dead ringer for Elvis but with a huge broom of a moustache, stamped our passports.

That was it. It was almost a letdown. I was so tense I thought something inside was about to snap. It was like I'd swum the Channel. I was elated and exhausted. The razor-wired fence in the distance was my white cliffs of Dover. I had expected at least raised eyebrows when they came across eleven Iraqis and four Brits travelling in a group. But it was late afternoon, night would soon be falling, and the officials were coming to the end of their shift. We were in. We'd made it.

Sammy accelerated and led the three wagons across the area of no man's land to Jordan. He stopped at immigration, left the engine running, and gave the officer his best wide-toothed grin as he handed over the eleven passports for his family. I passed Les's and my own through the window. Seamus and Dai stepped out of the following vehicles and did the same.

The official vanished into his hut for what seemed like an hour and then came out with all fifteen passports, which he gave to Sammy. I didn't quite catch what he said, but Sammy and the official were both soon raising their voices and a couple of armed guards emerged from the hut to join in.

Sammy broke off to explain that the official thought the visas in the Iraqi passports were forged. I waved away the notion like it was a bothersome fly but didn't doubt for a moment that the immigration man was right. I thought if I ever got my hands on Sammy's contact at the Jordanian Embassy I'd wring his neck like a chicken.

I stepped out of the car. The family gathered around, Ayesha crying, the children crying. Even my mates looked dumbstruck. We'd been through hell in the last forty-eight hours. We were worn out, knackered, unarmed, I had a hole in my stomach, and this little man clutching our passports had the power to turn us back. Our safety was just yards away over the wire fence and, I must admit, it did go insanely through my mind to mount up and try and burst our way through.

Common sense prevailed. I shut Sammy up, asked him to translate, and told the official that I had been personally with both General Mashooen and his son, Wing Commander Mashooen, to the Jordanian Embassy and had seen with my own eyes the visas being applied. What's more, as a British subject going about my lawful business, I was appalled by this needless bureaucracy.

The officials went into a huddle, then said that, yes, we Brits were free to enter the country. But not the Iraqis.

I had thought, as Sunnis, the Jordanian officials would be impressed by having such distinguished immigrants entering the country. I had been wrong and tried another tack. I asked to see the officer in charge of immigration.

Again they went into another debate before the officer went off with all fifteen passports to make my request known. After a deliberately long wait, and with the sun now low on the horizon and the evening chill coming back, I was led through the complex to an office. I came to attention and introduced myself as Captain James Ashcroft. I would have to do some pretty fancy dancing between the raindrops, no two ways about it, and give the performance of my life.

The man in charge was also a captain and spoke reasonable English. I looked him in the eye as we shook hands. He asked me to sit and I faced him across a narrow desk on which our passports stood to one side in a neat stack. Over the predictable glasses of hot sweet tea brought by an orderly, I learned that he had three sons and a daughter and had spent a year studying in England.

'I wish my Arabic was as good,' I said. 'Your English is perfect.'

'No, no, no,' he said modestly.

He looked duly saddened on my behalf that I merely had two daughters – 'but was trying for a son'. I took a photograph from my wallet, showing Krista with the girls.

'Very beautiful,' he remarked, and I touched my hand to my heart.

He placed his glass back in the saucer. Now he got serious. Was I not a military contractor escorting criminals whom the Iraqi authorities must have deemed enemies of the state? He glanced down at my clothes. I was wearing my fleece, combat pants and desert boots. Not much of a giveaway.

On the contrary, I said, I was a British officer and had come to Iraq on a mission of mercy when my old friend Wing Commander Assam Mashooen found himself unjustly placed on a Shia death list.

'It is a civil war in Iraq,' I added. I knew the captain must be a Sunni and egged the pudding. 'The Shia are killing every important and educated Sunni they can lay their hands on.'

He didn't budge. 'But is it not their war, an affair for Iraqis?'

'You are completely right, Captain, but at Sandhurst I learned to always go back for my friends.'

'Ah, Sandhurst. Very good. The Royal Academy, yes? I like very much the Sandhurst.' His eyes lit up and I didn't bother correcting him. I had my trump card and it was time to play it.

'And I like Jordan very much. Actually,' I continued, 'His Royal Highness Prince Ali was in my year.'

'Prince Ali?' He looked at me puzzled. Then sat bolt upright. 'The Jordan Prince Ali?' He looked at me in disbelief.

'When you train together you are as brothers,' I said. And I reached into the pass-holder around my neck.

I usually carried several things in there; a CAC card, weapons passes, $500, a lock of Krista's hair, my passport when it wasn't sat on some bastard's desk, a Scots library card with which I hoped to confuse potential captors as to my nationality with its blue and white Saltire, and my trump card for if I got into trouble in Jordan: an old photograph, dug out of my shoebox of Sandhurst photos for just these trips in the Middle East.

I showed the captain the photo and his eyes bugged out. A myriad of emotions flashed over his face; the last one, I think, was relief that he had been treating me courteously.

'Very good, Captain Ashcroft. Very good.'

In fact, I didn't know Prince Ali bin al Hussein of Jordan at all, but we had been at Sandhurst more or less at the same time and by chance someone had snapped a photo of a very young James Ashcroft standing next to His Royal Highness. I hadn't technically told any lies, but if the captain stuck out there in charge of this far-flung immigration post wanted to think the prince was my best mate, who was I to meddle in this pleasant fiction.

I was about to say that I'd put in a good word for him next time we met, but that must have been in his mind and I came to my feet instead.

'Thank you for the tea. You have been very kind, Captain,' I said. 'You have important work here. I shouldn't take up any more of your valuable time.'

He, too, came to his feet. He screamed for his orderly and, with a string of shouted Arabic, gave the man the stack of passports. The man stamped and saluted. He gave me a sideways look of horror before disappearing. The visa problem had gone. We shook hands once more and the captain followed me and the orderly back through the complex to the wagons. I stood over the official while he stamped the passports and handed them back to Sammy. The captain very helpfully gathered all his official admin staff together and gave them a right royal bollocking.

Then he turned around and roared an order. Every Jordanian soldier in sight stood to attention.

The captain saluted and shook my hand. 'Welcome to Jordan.'

Seamus grabbed his passport. 'Jesus, what the fuck's going on, Rupert? Did you just give him the blowjob of his life?'

'Fucking fruit,' sniffed Les.

'I thought he'd fucking left us and gone back for that bird,' said Dai.

Sammy stood looking from face to face, wondering why my mates seemed so angry. He still had not learned that that was the way they showed their friendship.

He turned to me. 'What did you say to the officer in charge, Mister James?'

'Ash.'

'Mister Ash.'

'I told him it was Sammy Mashooen out there and he said, "Oh yeah, him, the slow learner".'

He grinned. 'Mister James, you are pulling my leg.'

'Yeah, now shake a leg. Are we going to Amman or what?'

* * *

I was exhausted. I nodded off for a bit of Egyptian PT and woke up on the outskirts of Amman with one of the kids shaking me. We got into the city centre and I thought were hopelessly lost when we turned a corner and there was the Marriott Hotel.

'Dinner at the Marriott, Mister James,' Sammy announced softly. Unbelievable.

We got out, stretched under the starry night sky and ignored the curious looks of the hotel staff. Then there were short awkward conversations as we Brits got out our bags and Sammy and his family prepared to leave. It was an incredible anticlimax. We had just been to hell and back together with these people, and now we were just going to shake their hands and go our separate ways. I didn't know what was appropriate to say on these occasions, if I am honest.

Fara appeared next to Sammy; tears welled up into her eyes. He put his arms around her, something you don't see Arab men do, not in public, not in front of foreigners. She sobbed, long, soft, heartfelt gulps that came from deep down, tears for her aunt, for Iraq, for the future of her children, who came towards their parents, heads lowered, uncertain what they should do but wanting to be there at that moment. I was moved by the affection they had for each other and how that affection had revealed itself in front of us. Then Fara grabbed my head and kissed me on both cheeks. I was just as shocked as Sammy.

'Thank you, James.' And she ran off in embarrassment.

We Brits huddled for a moment, then I turned around and went over to Sammy discreetly.

'Sammy, this is all the cash we have. Cobus gave some as well before we left Baghdad. It's a few grand and should last you a while if you're careful. Keep the bus but you should sell the other vehicles.'

'Thank you.' Sammy was choked up with emotion.

He went around one last time to shake all the Brits' hands, and thanked them all. He lunged at Les and almost got in a kiss on the cheek, but Les's lifetime of boxing reflexes saved him. The two men laughed and shook hands properly.

He hugged me and I hugged him back.

'You sure you're going to be OK? This guy you know in Amman, he can find you somewhere to live?'

Sammy nodded. 'Yes, no problem. I phone to him while you are asleep.'

'It's not going to be easy, mate. Look after yourself.'

'I am ready,' he beamed at me.

AFTERWORD

12 AUGUST 2007

The *Daily Telegraph* reported that up to sixty Iraqi interpreters working for British forces in southern Iraq and Basra may have been murdered by insurgent death squads.

Speaking on condition of anonymity, an interpreter in his early forties said: 'No one here is thinking about our security. The only consideration of the British is how they can use us. The insurgents are not waiting for the British to leave, they are killing us now.'

25 OCTOBER 2008

The *Guardian*: the UN High Commissioner for Refugees (UNHCR) reported that 13,000 Christians in Mosul – half the city's Christian population – had in the space of four weeks been hounded from their homes during a fresh wave of killing and intimidation. Dozens have died and thousands have taken refuge in mountain villages or fled to Syria.

Many of the interpreters killed had been at the hands of Shia extremists. In Mosul the blame lay at the door of Sunnis intent on turning the oil-rich city into a Sunni stronghold backed by al-Qaeda elements.

18 FEBRUARY 2009

The *World Tribune* reported that US security contractors have decided not to cooperate with a request from the Iraqi government for the names of their Iraqi translators.

Industry sources said major contractors have concluded that information on their Iraqi translators could lead to assassination attempts by everybody from al-Qaeda to Shia militias. They said the translators would be accused of collaborating with US military operations in which Iraqi civilians were killed.

'Translators' personal identifiers absolutely will not be turned over,' DynCorp International spokesman Douglas Ebner said.

More than 300 Iraqi interpreters with the US military have been killed since 2003.

Thank you to all who wrote in via my website with positive comments. You clearly enjoyed *Making a Killing* and I hope you enjoyed this second book as much as I enjoyed corresponding with you.

For those of you who sent in negative comments about the wars in Iraq and Afghanistan, I can only repeat that I honestly had nothing to do with the decision to invade either country. Really. I hope this book annoyed you as much as the first one. I especially requested the publishers to put sharp corners on it so that you can shove it up your *doos*.

One of the reasons *Escape* was written was that so many people asked what happened to those characters introduced in *Making a Killing*. I wanted to tell Sammy's story. Although he can by no means be described as 'average', for me he represents the ordinary civilian in that in addition to being my friend, he was also a worried husband and father, trying to do his best for his family in often impossible circumstances.

I have been in many war zones around the world and the media makes much of the politics, the politicians and the soldiers.

Coverage of civilian themes is traditionally limited to the emotionally charged story, usually of some little girl specifically selected by cynical news producers after having been blinded or maimed by US/Israeli/British etc. artillery or air strike. The little girl will raise international outrage, a hundred grand in donations and be flown to London for specialist treatment.

The plight of thousands if not millions of people, the average civilians caught up in events beyond their control, is often sidelined. But in every country the story is often the same. One day, people get up and go to work thinking about what to have for dinner. The next day they may be on the run, wearing the same clothes, their only assets what they'd put into their pockets the day before. They face hardship, deprivation and often torture, rape and death. Many are desperately trying to protect their own families. They hide in the ruins of their homes and neighbourhoods with nowhere else to go, counting the meagre stock of rice, water and grubby dollars that might get them through the next day.

I am always moved by both the determination and despair of these people, and I hope this book gives a little insight into their world.

Iraq is still a dangerous place. General Petraeus's surge worked, but the handover of security to Iraqi forces is turning into entirely predictable chaos and bloodshed. Most police and security positions, even in Sunni areas, are given only to Shi'ites. The hugely successful Sunni Awakening councils are disbanding as the Shia government takes over the task of managing them and, of course, refuses to pay the Sunni apostates, as the Americans were doing. Far better to keep the money and spend it on themselves.

This development has surprised no one. Sunni insurgency groups have enjoyed a 95 per cent increase in recruitment and the bloodshed and violence has spiked as once again Iraqis wage war on each other for power. The only good news in this is that both sides despise al-Qaeda and the remaining foreign *mujahideen* have been forced to withdraw to small areas of influence, including, ironically, Mosul.

On my return to Baghdad I had bumped into a group of ex-Spartan colleagues in the palace chow hall. It had been fantastic to catch up with old friends and hear all their news. Within two months of me leaving Iraq again, word reached me that three were dead and the fourth seriously wounded.

Colonel Mad Dog McQueen was successfully casevaced to Germany and then the US, where he was very shabbily treated in the Walter Reed medical centre in Washington DC. He is still in a terrible state after three long years of operations to repair his shattered body.

Typical of this amazing man he regards himself as lucky, having seen the many other wounded Coalition personnel who have suffered more than him. I did visit and get to see his astonishing gun collection, which would put many museums and the Green Beret armoury to shame. However, he insists that he is 'normal' and not crazy like 'some of those other people' that collect guns. When I visited him, he met me at the airport with one hand, one eye and one ear. He drove me back to his place. I have never been so scared in all my born days.

For his single-handed desert charge against an enemy platoon, whilst already wounded, killing twelve enemy soldiers with literally one hand tied behind his back and rescuing the damsel in distress, Mad Dog was awarded the Bronze Star for Valor and the Purple Heart. I thought he should have got the Medal of Honor. In the book, I actually underplayed his actions that day, including the rescue of a dozen civilian reconstruction contractors from another ambush.

On a trivia note, the photo on the back cover was taken by Mad Dog as he was being casevaced to the Green Zone in a

Blackhawk that happened to be flying past the ambush site. Apparently he saw the view, said 'Neat', sat up, took the photo, tucked his camera away and lay down so the medic could carry on treating him.

Tanya Carillo I presume married her fiancé and lived happily ever after. I hope so. I only knew her briefly but she got under my skin and I remember her fondly.

Ali, the armourer turned black-marketer, disappeared into the chaos of the war and I never found out what became of him, despite several attempts through my remaining network of Iraqi friends still in Baghdad.

Les, Dai and Seamus all returned to the UK and are doing well. Seamus still bodyguards his VIP regularly and Dai returns to Afghan occasionally to top up his tan.

Confused and bewildered by a strange world full of electricity, running water and toilet paper, the Yaapies, including Cobus, have all returned with much relief to the *kraals* and *bomas* of their native land. I can only hope that they find some kind soul who can read these words to them, so that they may hear this story and pass it on to their future generations around the campfires through their strong traditions of oral history, much as I have witnessed on the Discovery Channel. They are an ingenious people and have devised a method of passing quite complex messages by drum, from village to village, far faster than the same message can be carried by a man running.

My last contact with the Green Berets assures me that they are all still well and doing good work in various places. I wish them good luck. I still owe one of them a copy of *Making a Killing* and when I find his address I will send it, I promise. You know who you are!

It is amazing to the soldier on the ground that Donald Rumsfeld still has not been tried and convicted for what they consider to be his terrible crimes against the US armed forces.

Last but not least, Sammy and his family spent two long years as refugees in Jordan. I never took a penny of the royalties sent to me for *Making a Killing*. I just forwarded them on to him and his family, with a little personal top-up now and then, just to keep body and soul together.

Their attempts to request asylum were thwarted constantly by the bewildering early requirement that each Iraqi applicant had to be vouched for by at least a general. Our task-force commander, Mad Dog, was only a colonel.

In the meantime the news reports have been full of the plight of interpreters, attempting to shame, often in vain, the US and UK governments into doing the right thing and sheltering those who risked their lives to help the Coalition Forces.

Finally, in early 2009, Sammy and family were successful in their request for asylum and have now been resettled in the US. Ayesha gave birth to a son in the States. They called him James.

James Ashcroft, July 2009
www.makingakilling.co.uk

INDEX

Now read the book that started it all...

Making A Killing

James Ashcroft's explosive
first mission in Iraq

'The rebel in the centre carried an RPG on his shoulder; it cracked noisily as he released the rocket ... I trained my front sight on the insurgent to the left and squeezed the trigger as he was bringing his weapon to bear. I gave him a triple tap. He definitely went down as I saw the blood spray from one headshot; pure luck, I was trying to put all three in his chest.'

Bored with life on civvy street, James 'Ash' Ashcroft is lured into a $1,000-a-day job as a security contractor in Iraq. It is a place where the rules of war are murky at best, where Coalition Forces struggle to defend their own bases let alone bring peace to the region, and where every insurgent killed spawns a dozen more. A fast-paced, explosive story, putting you into the chaos that is modern Iraq.

'This diary of death and destruction radiates not just personality ... but authenticity'

Andy Martin, *Daily Telegraph*

Order now from www.rbooks.co.uk
£8.99